Sailor's Compass
Collector's Edition © 2024 The PatchWork™

Published by Amazon

Sailor's Compass, along with its accompanying logo and design, are federally registered trademarks of The PatchWork™ Johnstown, Ohio 43031.

No part of this publication may be reproduced, stored in a retrieval system, or transmitted in any form or by any means—electronic, mechanical, photocopying, recording, or otherwise—without prior written permission from The PatchWork™.

"Sailor's Compass" design and graphics are trademarks of The PatchWork™

Editor: Maria Gregory
Cover Design: Team Unstoppable
Cover Photo: Jayson Llait

Printed in United States of America
www.michaelhmoore.life

ers to my next duty sta-
ns in New York. There
world I wanted to go bac-
lled Washington night
ients I knew how to r
system and I spent one
Corpsmen Detailer to see if
e else. That was a fl
how much I pleaded.
efore the end of January
about this time that the
Vietnam was being re
men were going hom
early. Every day it
ing one of my co-
ping that I would b
istmas but no such l
e was scheduled to
t Christmas and wa

Michael H. Moore
―――――――――――――――――――――――――

Sailor's Compass

A Veteran's Memoir of Navigating Life's Seas
Through Culture, Courage and Purpose

The PatchWork™
A Division of Patchworks Ministries, LLC

To my beloved Hideko—your love, strength, and unwavering support have been the foundation of my life's journey. For sixty years, you have been my constant, my compass, and my greatest blessing. This story, and everything I am, is because of you.

Foreword

In a world where so many are adrift, searching for meaning, Michael Moore's Sailor's Compass arrives like a beacon. Just as sailors of old looked to the stars for guidance, Michael invites us to reorient ourselves, to find our true north—not by seeking distant stars, but by diving deep into the wisdom and strength within us.

As a monk, I pray with my community eight times a day, lifting up the Psalms in a rhythm of devotion. Reading Sailor's Compass, I felt that same cadence, an immersion into the joys, hopes, laments, wisdom, gratitude, and praises that fill a life dedicated to God, family, and country. Michael's compass isn't crafted from metal; it's forged through hard-won insights, timeless truths, and an unwavering commitment to self-discovery.

This book isn't merely a guide; it's a companion. Michael doesn't preach from the shore but goes into the deep with us, sharing his experiences with humility and wisdom. He extends a hand to those feeling lost or uncertain, reflecting both vulnerability and strength, encouraging us to embrace our own journeys. As the Apostle Paul says in Hebrews 6:19, "We have this hope as an anchor for the soul, firm and secure." Sailor's Compass embodies that anchor—a steadying presence for life's uncertain waters.

As the son of an Air Force serviceman myself, I hear echoes of my father's story in Michael's reflections. Like Michael, my father embraced a life of faith upon retirement, becoming an Extraordinary Minister of the Holy Eucharist. I now better understand his passion for service as an expression of his faith, which Michael humbly narrates. My mother, too, was a teacher, and I see in Hideko, Michael's wife, the same quiet sacrifices made in love and trust that shaped my own family.

Reading this book is like embarking on a journey of self-discovery and faith, guided by someone who knows the waters well. Michael's stories and insights offer tools for navigating not only our personal seas but also the shared oceans of our communities and families. His is a voice we can trust, especially in an age that often glorifies the artificial and fleeting. He draws us back to what is real, lasting, and true.

As you turn these pages, may you let Michael's words guide you, trusting that you too have a compass—one that, with time and patience, will lead you to safe harbors. In a world as tumultuous as the ocean, let Sailor's Compass be the steady force reminding you of God's unfailing presence and the strength within each of us.

As the Jesuit Teilhard de Chardin said, "We live in a milieu divin," a divine milieu in which everything is touched by God. He is the very air we breathe. To recognize this presence is a source of peace, a grace that grounds us daily.

All through his life, Michael feels the guiding hand of God, and he is sensitive and open to that presence. When you finally set this book down, you'll find yourself more in love with life as it unfolds moment by moment, more attuned to God's sustaining hand.

May this book bless you as it has blessed me, and may Michael's story inspire you to explore your own passion for life and love. May it lead you, as it has led so many others, to waters calm and clear.

That in all things, God may be glorified. (1 Peter 4:11)

Fr. Gerard Jonas, OCSO
Mepkin Abbey Monastery
Moncks Corder, SC

From the moment I first heard Michael—known to most of us simply as "Mike"—share his experiences, I knew his story was something special. It's not just a recounting of military service but a deeply human journey shaped by commitment, compassion, and cultural discovery.

Mike has always been a quiet, humble man, never one to boast about his accomplishments. So, when he attended the Heart of Remembrance retreat at Mepkin Abbey in South Carolina, I was both surprised and amazed as his life story unfolded so compellingly. His gentle nature had kept much hidden, but in that setting, the depth of his journey became clear. From his Navy years to the countless ways he's served others, Mike's story is a testament to a life lived with purpose.

In this memoir, you'll not only learn about the challenges Mike faced in the military but also the lifelong lessons that have guided him. He navigates life with a compass of compassion, loyalty, and an unwavering commitment to doing what's right—whether in foreign lands, in his marriage to Hideko, or in quiet moments of reflection.

What makes Sailor's Compass unique is Mike's humility. He doesn't rely on grand tales of heroism, though there are moments of courage. Instead, he shares simple, profound lessons from everyday acts of kindness and love, painting a vivid picture of a life lived in service—not just to a uniform, but to the people and values that define his compass.

As I worked with Mike on this memoir, I was continually inspired by his wisdom and grace. His story offers lessons on how to stay true to our own compasses, no matter how unpredictable life's seas may be.

May Sailor's Compass guide you as it has guided me. Mike's story is more than a memoir; it's a reminder that, even in life's most challenging moments, we can find our way through humility, resilience, and an unwavering sense of purpose. I hope that, as you read these pages, you feel the strength of his journey, the depth of his wisdom, and the gentle yet powerful light that he has offered to so many.

With gratitude and admiration,

Maria Gregory
Author of "The Lion You Don't See"

Introduction

Life, like the sea, is a vast and unpredictable journey. It is filled with moments of calm, punctuated by storms that test our resilience, and guided by unseen currents that shape who we become. In this memoir, Sailor's Compass, I invite you aboard to sail with me through the waters of a life defined by service, culture, and unwavering commitment.

This book is not just a recount of my time as a veteran, though my years in the Navy form its backbone. It is a reflection on how the principles learned in service—discipline, courage, and a deep respect for others—have shaped the person I am today. My experiences range from harrowing moments on the battlefield to quieter lessons learned through cross-cultural encounters, compassionate service, and the bonds of family and friendship that have anchored me through it all.

For over sixty years, my life has been intertwined with that of my wife, Hideko. Together, we have navigated the challenges of cultural differences and personal growth, drawing strength from our shared journey. Her unwavering support and partnership have been my true north, guiding me through both calm and tumultuous waters.

In these pages, you'll find stories of hope, hardship, and humor—moments that have made me reflect on what it means to serve, not only as a soldier but as a husband, a father, and a friend. You'll read about the lessons learned in foreign lands, the compassion forged through connection, and the compass that has always pointed me toward a life of meaning and purpose.

As you read Sailor's Compass, I hope you find that it is not just a story of one man's journey but a testament to the idea that, in the face of uncertainty, we can all find our bearings through commitment to something greater than ourselves. Whether you're a veteran, a spouse, or simply someone seeking direction in life, this memoir is for anyone who has ever navigated their own seas and come out stronger for it.

Welcome aboard. May this story help guide you on your own voyage.

Table of Contents

Dedication 5
Foreword 7
Introduction 13

Part 1 23
    Roots of a Small-Town Life 24
    Love, Life, and Unexpected Turns 25
    A Town Where Everyone Knows Your Name 26
    The Victorian House and Its Warm Embrace 27
    The November Ritual Butchering for Winter 28
    Saturday Mornings and Sweet Escapes 29
    The Saturday Bath and More Than We Bargained For 30
    The Ration Book and a Boy's Quiet Pride 31
    Lessons from Uncle Elmer and Daddy's Absence 32
    The Great Train Adventure to Oklahoma 33
    Life in Frederick—Dust, Showers, and Childhood Discoveries 34
    A Drive Back to Ohio Leaving the War Behind 35
    A New Home and Sunday School Adventures 36

Part 2 39
    School Days, Bullies, and Life Lessons 40
    A Family Grows—Terry's Arrival and a New Refrigerator 42
    Brothers, Bricks, and Grandma's Unyielding Love 43
    Freedom on Wheels—The Roller Skate Days 44
    Circleville Hamburgers and Summer Nights 45
    Six Weeks in Lancaster—Aunt Dode's Gentle Care 46
    Settling Into Lancaster—New Neighbors, New Life 47
    Big Brother's Role—Vicki's Arrival 48
    A Mother's Fury—The Day I Ran for My Life 49

Silent Fathers and Threats of Reform 51
  A Growing Family and a New Home 52
  Half-Days and New Responsibilities 53
  The Kisors—A Catholic Family Next Door 54
  Learning the Value of a Dollar 55
  The Road to Independence—Earning My Driver's License 57
  Welcoming Pamela and the Arrival of Twins 58

Part 3 61
  Finding Faith—A Journey with the Kisors 62
  Becoming Catholic—A Step of Independence 63
  Dreams of Medicine and Enlisting in the Navy 64
  The Strain of Family Tensions 65
  Active Duty and a New Chapter in Life 66
  Mastering the Nursery—Navy Life in Beaufort 67
  Broken Engagement—A Change of Plans 69
  A Scholarship Lost—The Unopened Letter 70
  The Road Trip of a Lifetime—Seattle and the World's Fair 71
  From Adventure to Employment Finding My Place in Seattle 73
  Back on the Road—Returning to Lancaster 74
  New Beginnings in Alabama and a Path Back to the Navy 75
  Waiting in San Francisco—A Lesson in Patience 77
  Exploring Saigon and an Unexpected Haircut 79
  Learning the Ropes: My First Sutures 81

Part 4 83
  Cross-Trained and Growing—Finding My Way in X-ray 84
  A Chaperoned Courtship—Friendship with Fely 85
  Tokyo R&R and the Name That Stayed with Me: Chiemi's Story 86
  A Meal to Remember—The Popcorn Popper and Nuoc Mam 88
  Goodbye Saigon—Heading Home Before the Coup 89

Boot Camp to Battlefield—Becoming a Combat Medic 91
From Saigon to Okinawa—A New Adventure Unfolds 92
Escape from the Battlefield—Life at Camp Kue 93
Into the Unknown—The Gulf of Tonkin and the Call Back to War ... 95
A Night to Remember—Fate Intervenes on Halloween 97
Love and Ambition—Navigating Hideko's Dreams 99
A Rain-Soaked Realization—The Proposal 100
A Christmas Eve Promise—"Yes, I Will Marry You" 101
Racing Against Time—The Paperwork Chase 102
A Call to the Front Row—Faith, Guidance, and a
    Birthdate Mystery 104
From Rust to Romance—A New Car and a New Beginning 106
The Race to the Altar—A Wedding Day Full of Surprises 109

Part 5 111
From Wedding Cake to Farewell Tears—A New Chapter Begin 113
A Flight of Firsts—Homecoming and New Beginnings 115
A Long Journey Home—From Fallbrook to Fatherhood 117
Heartbeats and Hope—The Arrival of Patrick Edward 118
A Whirlwind Wedding—From Vietnam to Vows 121
Learning, Labor, and New Beginnings 123
From Crib on the Roof to Far Rockaway: Our New York Welcome .. 126
Turning Tears into Hope: A Fresh Start in Long Island 129
Unexpected Blessings and Shifting Roles: A New Year in New York . 131
New Beginnings: Welcoming Chiemi and Building Our Future 133
From New York to Ohio: A Home Before Vietnam 135
A New Home and New Beginnings: Prepping for Vietnam and
    Life on the Home Front 137
Farewell Hugs and New Frontiers: Off to Vietnam 139
From New York to the Boondocks: Navigating a
    New Role in Vietnam 141

Under Fire and on Duty: Life Beside Marble Mountain 143

Night Shifts and Narrow Escapes: Life at the 95th Evac 145

Countdown to Freedom: Final Days at Saint Albans 147

Unwelcome Home: The Final Flight from Vietnam 149

Homecoming Reflections: A Year Lost, A Life Rebuilt 151

Part 6 153

From Battlefields to Birth: A Test of Faith 155

Rest, Reunion, and Unspoken Tensions 157

From Navy Blues to Civilian Shoes: A New Chapter Begins 159

A Family Effort: New Beginnings in the Civilian World 161

Building Porches, Battling Beliefs: A Test of Faith and Friendship . . 163

From City Streets to Country Dreams: A New Home and
    a New Challenge 165

Charting a New Course: Reenlisting Without Faith 167

From Farm Fields to Island Life: A Family's Leap to Hawaii 169

New Beginnings: Life on the Peninsula and School Days 171

Seasons of Change: Family Visits and Fresh Starts 173

Transitions and Travels: From Marines to Family Adventures 175

Pie Fights and Life Lessons: Navigating
    Promotions and Parenthood 177

Desert Drives and Cat Claws: The Journey Back to Ohio 179

From Okinawa to Oakland: A Year of Duty and a Birthday Treat . . . 181

Leading the Class: From Study Sessions to a New Life in Virginia . . . 183

Adapting to Change: Settling Into Life and
    Supporting Hideko's New Path 185

Conflict in Beirut: A Sudden Return to the Frontlines 187

Amidst Ruins: Navigating a War Zone in Beirut 189

From the Frontlines to Family: A Christmas Reunion 191

Facing the Shadows: A Journey to Healing and Letting Go 193

Taking Charge: From Self-Evaluation to Senior Chief 195

Uncovering the Truth: A Doctor's Confession 197

Navigating Turbulent Waters: Command, Crisis,
        and Unexpected Solutions 200
Across the Seas: Beer, Castles, and a Court Martial 203
Hurricanes, War Games, and the Road to Retirement 206
Closing One Door, Opening Another: From Service to Home 209

Part 7 213
From Hammer to Health: A New Path Unfolds 215
Expanding Horizons in Public Health 217
Cleaning Up and Moving Forward 218
From Farm to Garden: Crafting Our Retirement Sanctuary 221
Searching for Purpose in the Quiet of Retirement 223
A Return to Faith: Finding My Way Back 224
Embracing a New Mission: A Journey of Faith and Service 228
Full Circle: Finding Faith, Home, and Purpose 230

Part 8 233
- The Grace of Age: A Life Well Lived: Reflections at Eighty-Four . . . 234
- The Strength of Loyalty: Enduring Bonds:
        Fifty Years of Friendship 237
- Lessons in Leadership: The Journey from
        Command to Compassion 240
- Lost in Translation: Discovering Respect
        Through Language and Culture 246
- Matters of the Heart: Trust, Health, and the Lessons Learned 249
- From Struggles to Blessings: Wisdom Gained Over Time 251
- Guided by Duty: From Corpsman Dreams to Leadership Lessons . 254
- Family Ties, Navy Bonds: A Journey Across Oceans and Decades . 259

- From Corpsman to Commander:
    Navigating Challenges and Cultures 263
- Lessons from a Navy Life: Turning Doubt into Drive 266
- Conclusion: Why This Story Needed to Be Told 270

Treasured Letters 272

Part 1

Roots of a Small-Town Life

I was born in Circleville, Ohio, on March 20, 1940, to Lolabell Hampp Moore and Harold Moore. We lived with my mother's brother, Elmer Hampp, in Stoutsville, Ohio, a small town about eight miles east of Circleville. It was a place where everyone knew everyone—simple, quiet, and tightly knit, much like the family life I was born into. Elmer's wife, Virgil, had passed away in February 1939, just days after giving birth to their son, Ned.

At the time, my mom was only 18 years old, just out of school, and so she moved in with Elmer to help care for Ned and Elmer's young daughter, Eileen. Mom had always been someone with a big heart and a strong sense of responsibility, even at such a young age.

Love, Life, and Unexpected Turns

Life had its way of moving fast in those days. My mom met my dad, Harold, who hailed from Tarlton, another small town not far from Stoutsville. They started dating, and before long, life threw them a curveball. Mom got pregnant, and they were married on September 30, 1939, in Greenup, Kentucky. Mom always liked to recount the story of their wedding day with a laugh—how Dad took himself to a restaurant to eat alone and after they got home, she roasted a hotdog on the stove. She always said it with a bit of humor, but I could tell it bothered her a little, a reminder that life wasn't always as romantic as she'd hoped. After the wedding, they stayed with Elmer since Mom quickly had her hands full with two babies. Karl David, my brother, came along in December 1941, and though his birth name was Karl David, Uncle Elmer—always the jokester—dubbed him "Tator." The name stuck, and for the rest of his life, most everyone called him Tator, except Daddy, who insisted on calling him by his full name, Karl David.

A Town Where Everyone Knows Your Name

Stoutsville was a small, sleepy town with a population of about 200. Life there was simple and predictable. Doors were never locked, and when you visited someone, you didn't bother knocking—you just walked in and called out their name. The town had its share of humble amenities: two grocery stores, a post office, a hatchery, a feed mill, two gas stations, a barber shop, and a cobbler. It also had three churches and an International Harvester farm equipment dealer, where my Grandpa Hampp worked.

The Victorian House and Its Warm Embrace

We lived in Elmer's house, a big old Victorian that stood out for one particular luxury—indoor plumbing. That was a rarity in Stoutsville. The house was heated by a coal stove in what today would be called the family room. In winter, to save on heat, we closed off the other rooms, draped them in sheets, and lived mostly in that one room. It felt both comforting and a little lonely, the way the rest of the house was shut down like a sleeping giant. Raising our own meat was a way of life.

The November Ritual Butchering for Winter

Every November, we would butcher two pigs under Grandpa's supervision. It was a family affair. Grandpa would smoke the meat, and we stored it in the cold, unused rooms at the front of the house. By late February or early March, the meat would start to go rancid, but we still ate it. It's funny looking back now, but back then, you did what you had to. I remember the joy we found in the smallest things.

Saturday Mornings and Sweet Escapes

Saturday mornings, we boys—Ned, Tator, and I—would perch atop Elmer's roll-top desk to listen to the Buster Brown radio show. It was an adventure serial, and we were glued to it every week. Right across the alley from Elmer's house was Walt Meesie's gas station, a small building with two hand-crank gas pumps. Sometimes, Walt would let us boys turn the crank, and that was a thrill. But the best part was his shelf of penny candy. We'd stare at it wide-eyed, hoping Mom would give us a penny to splurge. When she did, we stood on the toolbox to pick out our treasure. Those moments felt like magic.

The Saturday Bath and More Than We Bargained For

Saturday was also bath night, a less glamorous part of life. The water always seemed just shy of boiling. Tator and I would be in the tub together, both of us crying from the heat, taking what felt like forever to sit down in the water. And if that wasn't enough, the bath was often preceded by an enema—so we were clean inside and out. Looking back, I can smile at it now, but at the time, it was no laughing matter!

The Ration Book and a Boy's Quiet Pride

During WWII, when supplies were scarce, Mom would send me to the store with the ration book and a note listing what we needed. I was always the one to go, even though Ned was older. I never minded, though; I liked the responsibility. No money changed hands—everyone in town trusted each other, and accounts were settled at the end of the week. In those moments, I sensed a quiet pride building within me, knowing Mom trusted me to take care of these things. She gave me responsibilities that she didn't give to the other two boys. I was the one who helped dry the dishes or worked with the wringer washing machine.

I still remember the day I got my hand caught in the wringer. It was a sunny day, and we had wheeled the washing machine outside. I was curious—too curious—and stuck my hand in the wringer. I screamed like I'd never screamed before. Mom came running, freed my hand, wrapped it up, and walked me up to the country doctor. I still bear a star-shaped scar on my right palm to this day, a reminder of my stubborn curiosity.

Lessons from Uncle Elmer and Daddy's Absence

For the first six years of my life, the two main men around were Uncle Elmer and Daddy. Elmer worked days driving a gasoline truck, and Daddy worked shifts at Anchor Hocking Glass. Because of their schedules, I mostly saw Elmer, while Daddy was either working or sleeping. Mom took on the brunt of disciplining us boys, and there was always a paddle hanging on the wall, a quiet reminder to behave. I still remember one time when I got a whipping. I tried to be brave in front of Ned and Tator, saying, "It didn't hurt," but Mom overheard and made sure the second round left a mark. I never said that again.

The Great Train Adventure to Oklahoma

In early 1945, Daddy was drafted into the Army Air Force and stationed at a base in Frederick, Oklahoma. That spring, Mom sold our car and bought train tickets from Columbus to Oklahoma. It was a big adventure for us boys. Tator had to wear a harness and leash to keep him from wandering off, but the soldiers on the train were kind and helped Mom with us. They let us boys explore the train, took us to see the back so we could watch the countryside, and even made sure we had something to eat. It was a journey I'll never forget, filled with the excitement of travel and the warmth of strangers who took us under their wing.

Life in Frederick—Dust, Showers, and Childhood Discoveries

Frederick, Oklahoma, where we lived during 1945, was a dry, dusty place. The military housing was simple—a collection of one-room houses arranged in a big square, with a communal bathhouse in the center. There were separate facilities for men and women. Saturday night was bath night, and sometimes we showered with Dad, other times with Mom. I remember feeling confused the first time I saw the difference between men and women's bodies. Until then, I hadn't known there was such a distinct difference. It was a strange realization for a boy my age.

A Drive Back to Ohio Leaving the War Behind

We only lived in Frederick for a few months before the war ended. Afterward, we made our way back to Ohio, riding with another soldier who was heading to Pennsylvania. That drive felt like leaving behind a chapter of uncertainty and stepping into something new.

A New Home and Sunday School Adventures

In early 1946, my parents bought a house in Stoutsville, right next to a campground. Like most houses in town, it didn't have indoor plumbing, which didn't seem strange at the time, but looking back, it was rough living compared to modern standards. The house was just a block from a small brick country church. One Sunday, Mom dressed Tator and me in our best clothes and took us to church for Sunday School. That was a rare treat, especially since the Sunday School room had a sandbox-like table with little wooden cars. Mom didn't go again after that, but she sent us two boys faithfully every Sunday.

In 1946, I started first grade. The school was on the other side of town, about 1/4 mile away. If our house had been on the other side of the campground, I could have taken the school bus, but as it was, I walked. It wasn't an issue, except for one memorable day when I had to go to the bathroom really bad. I didn't make it home in time and ended up messing my pants. When I told Mom, she didn't scold me but said firmly, "Well, get them off. You're going to wash them out yourself." So, I did—scrubbing my soiled pants in a bucket on the back porch. Of course, Mom told everyone about it in the days that followed, laughing at how she'd handled the situation. It's funny now, but it was embarrassing at the time.

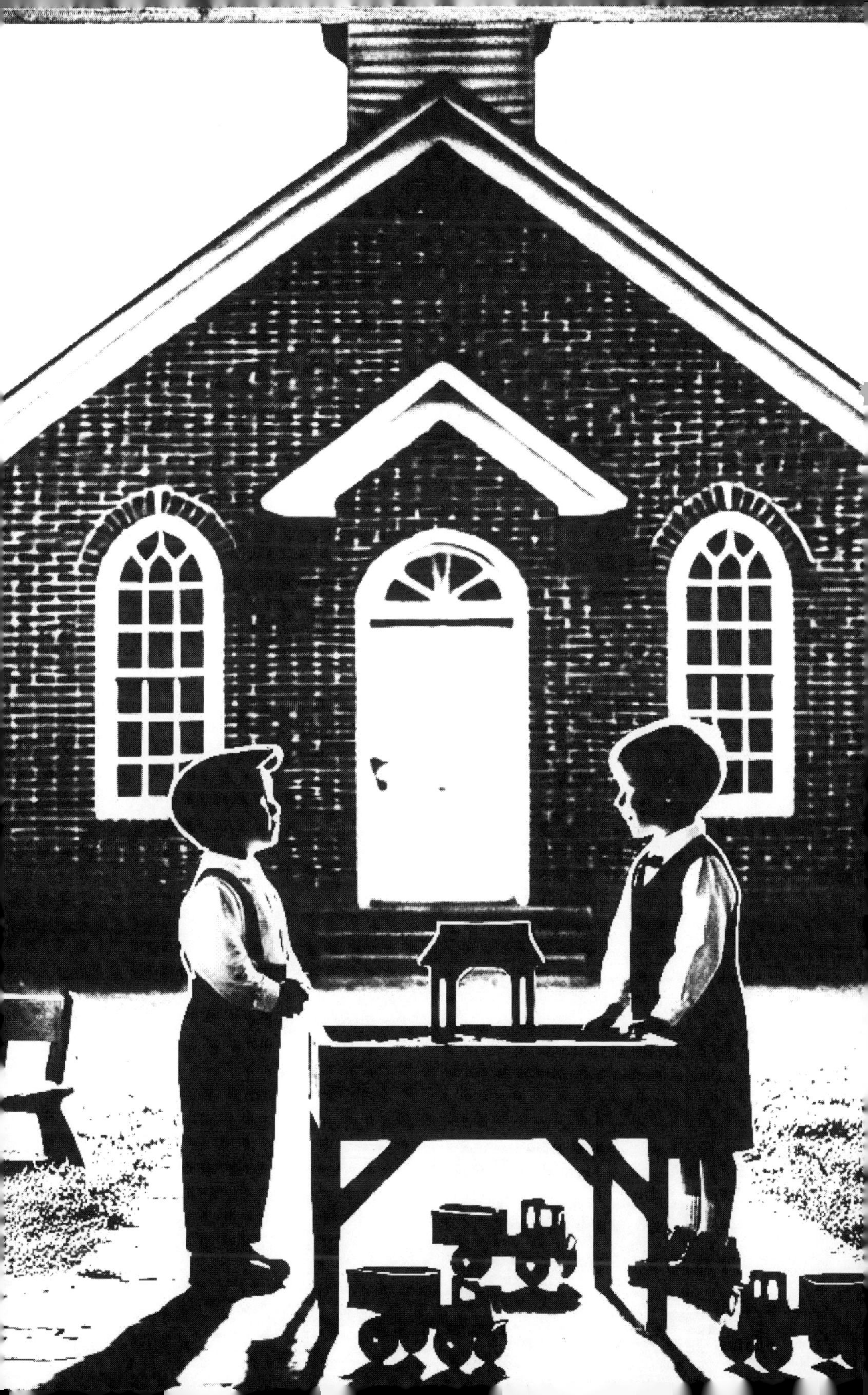

Part 2

School Days, Bullies, and Life Lessons

School wasn't always smooth. There was a boy named Freddy Greeno, a year older than me, who had to repeat the first grade. Freddy was bigger than me and made it a habit of picking on me during recess and on my way home. I was scared of him, not knowing how to handle bullies yet. One day, he took my hat and teased me while I cried. Something snapped inside me, and I tackled him to the ground. I sat on top of him and beat him as hard as I could, both of us crying—me from frustration and fear, him from the shock of being fought back. My uncle Jack, who was a sophomore in high school, came by and pulled me off Freddy. That was the last time anyone picked on me. I had told my teacher about Freddy's bullying, but she had said it was something I needed to handle myself. I guess she was right.

No one officially enrolled me in school back then. It was just something you did.

Ned, who had been in first grade the year before, showed me where my classroom was. My parents didn't attend school functions, but I do remember Mom coming to one Christmas program. I was part of a group singing "Away in a Manger" while we placed fake candles on a Christmas tree. Mom was there, quietly proud, even though she didn't show it with big gestures.

On my first day of school, Mom had told me, "If you get a whipping at school, you'll get one when you get home." I talked a lot in class and often found myself standing in the corner as punishment. But one day, the teacher had enough. She dragged me out of my seat, gave me a good whipping, and made me stand in the corner again. I never said a word about it at home—too scared of getting another whipping from Mom. That was the only time I was ever punished in school.

Many years later, when I was in my early 60s, I mentioned the incident to one of my brothers. Mom overheard and said, "I told you if you got a whipping at school, you'd get another at home. I guess you're big enough now to outrun me!" She still had that sharp wit.

A Family Grows—Terry's Arrival and a New Refrigerator

September 30, 1946, was a big day for our family. Not only was my brother Terry born, but we also got a refrigerator—a big one, too. We needed it to store the baby's milk, and I was taught how to hold, feed, and burp Terry. That early training came in handy as the years passed, because my parents would go on to have four more children before I left home at age 20.

Brothers, Bricks, and Grandma's Unyielding Love

Tator and I continued attending Sunday School well into 1947. We still fought a lot, though—brothers will be brothers. Once, Tator hit me in the head with a brick, and I ran crying to Grandma Hampp. She took a look at my head and said, "Well, he probably didn't mean it!" That was all the comfort I got. I had expected Tator to get a whipping, but no such luck. Instead, she shrugged it off like it was nothing.

One of my favorite childhood memories was the day my parents bought me a pair of Champion roller skates. I loved those skates and spent hours skating up and down the sidewalk in front of our house. Sometimes, I was even allowed to skate across the street and on the sidewalk leading to the church. It felt like freedom—wind in my hair, wheels beneath my feet.

Freedom on Wheels—The Roller Skate Days

A couple of times a month, if Dad wasn't working, we'd drive to Tarlton to visit Grandma Moore. Just before we arrived, Mom would say, "Honey, give them their orders!" That meant we were to sit quietly on the bottom step of Grandma's staircase until she invited one of us to sit on her lap in the rocking chair. On holidays, when cousins were there, we were allowed to go outside and play, but most of the time, we sat and waited patiently.

Circleville Hamburgers and Summer Nights

On certain summer evenings, when Dad was off work on a Friday or Saturday, our family would take a drive to Circleville. Sometimes, we'd park along the street while Dad headed inside the VFW or American Legion to play cards or shoot pool. Mom would roll down the windows, exchanging greetings with passersby, her voice floating out into the warm night air. As the hours went by, she'd eventually send us boys in to fetch Dad, but we always knew it would be at least another half-hour before he'd actually come out. It was the same routine when we lived in Frederick, only there, we'd walk into town. Dad would disappear into a saloon while Mom window-shopped with us boys in tow, patiently waiting.

On nights when Dad opted for a trip to the Hamburger inn instead, the scene changed just a little. While he sat at the counter inside, enjoying a quick meal, we waited in the car--Mom, Tator, and me -- our stomachs growling with anticipation. Once he'd finished, he'd bring out hamburgers for all of us, the brown paper bag filling the car with the tempting scent of grilled meat and onions. But no matter how hungry we were, there was a rule: we couldn't open the bag until we were on the road, heading toward Grandma Moore's house.

Six Weeks in Lancaster— Aunt Dode's Gentle Care

In the late summer of 1947, Mom packed a suitcase for me and told me I was going to stay with my dad's sister, Aunt Dode, in Lancaster. Our family had sold the house in Stoutsville and was in the process of buying a new one in Lancaster. Aunt Dode and Uncle Carl had two children: Wanda, who was a year older than me, and Gary, who was four years older.

I ended up staying with them for six weeks. I loved Aunt Dode— she was such a gentle soul, never a harsh word for anyone. Being there with Wanda felt like having an older sister to look up to. She helped me enroll in second grade and introduced me to her friends. I missed home, but being with Aunt Dode and Wanda made the separation easier.

Settling Into Lancaster—
New Neighbors, New Life

When my parents bought the house in Lancaster, it was five blocks from school, and Anchor Hocking Glass, where Dad worked, was right across the street from the school. Our new neighbors were a man with four daughters and one son, all in high school. They were Catholic, and though I didn't understand what that meant at the time, I noticed how happy they seemed, even though they had recently lost their mother. Mom helped them with sewing and other things, and the girls babysat for us on Saturday nights when my parents went out.

Big Brother's Role— Vicki's Arrival

On March 21, 1949, my sister Vicki was born.

With her arrival, I spent even more time learning how to care for a baby—bathing her, changing diapers, feeding her. The neighbor girls helped out until they moved away a year later. By then, I was over ten years old and trusted enough to babysit my younger siblings while my parents went out. I must have done a decent job since we never had any emergencies.

A Mother's Fury—The Day I Ran for My Life

It was late summer, and Tator and I were on the porch, fighting as usual. Mom heard us through the screen door and hollered, "Get in here!" Tator went inside first, and what happened next still sends a chill down my spine. She grabbed a club and started hitting him all over his body. He was crying, hands flailing, while she screamed at him to put his hands down. I stood there watching, frozen in place, looking through the screen door, feeling helpless.

When she was done with Tator, she looked right at me and said, "Your turn. Get in here!" I was paralyzed for a moment, fear coursing through me. Then instinct took over. I shook my head "no" and bolted off the porch, running barefoot through the backyard and out into the alley. The alley behind our house was gravel, and beyond that were endless cornfields. We always went barefoot in the summer, but in that moment, I was so scared that I didn't feel a single stone under my feet.

I turned the corner and looked back, only to see Mom getting into the car. She was coming after me! Panic set in. I darted into the cornfield and squatted down, heart pounding, trying to catch my breath as she drove by. I didn't know what to do next. I couldn't go home—that much I knew. The only place I could think of was Uncle Floyd and Aunt Bernell's house, just a block away. I stayed there for about an hour, trying to calm down. Aunt Bernell finally told me I needed to go home and face the music. Reluctantly, I went back, and to my surprise, Aunt Dode was there. Mom didn't want to embarrass herself in front of Aunt Dode, so instead of the punishment I had been dreading, she told me I needed a whipping for running from her. She had me bend over the kitchen table and gave me a few swats with the paddle. I cried—not because it hurt, but because I wanted her to think she was being effective.

About 65 years later, I asked Aunt Dode if she remembered that day. Not only did she remember, but she told me something that made my blood run cold. She said Mom had told her, "When I get a hold of him, I'm going to kill him." According to Aunt Dode, Mom was so furious that day, she might have beaten me to death. To save me, Aunt Dode asked if she could come home with her to visit for a while. That was the only thing that kept Mom from unleashing her full wrath.

Silent Fathers and Threats of Reform

When Dad got home that evening, his car was already there, but he never said a word about what had happened. He often threatened to "kick our asses" when we did something wrong, but the actual punishment was always left to Mom. Both my parents frequently threatened to send us to the Boys Industrial School (BIS), a reform school south of Lancaster, which is now a state prison. It's funny how life turns out, because now I go there once a month with my parish priest to do the Mass readings for the prisoners.

A Growing Family and a New Home

In 1953, Mom was pregnant again, and my parents were looking for a bigger house. Us three boys were sharing a bedroom with Uncle Jack, who had graduated high school and was now working in Lancaster. Vicki, who was four years old, still slept in a crib in my parents' bedroom. Mom once told me that one night while she and Dad were making love, Vicki woke up and asked what they were doing. I imagine that might have been what prompted them to find a bigger house. They eventually found a newly built four-bedroom house on the south side of town.

Half-Days and New Responsibilities

Moving to the new house in October 1953 felt like stepping up socially. It was in a nicer neighborhood compared to the working-class west side where we had lived before. There were only three houses on our street; the rest was surrounded by cornfields and woods. Unfortunately, the new school was overcrowded, so Tator and I only attended half-days, from noon to five p.m. That arrangement worked out great for Mom because it meant I could help more around the house. I was now big enough to carry the laundry basket up from the basement and hang the clothes on the line in the backyard. Tator and I would argue over who got to mow the front yard and who had to mow the back.

The Kisors—A Catholic Family Next Door

Jack finally had his own room, and us three boys shared a bedroom, while Vicki had a room to herself. For the first time in her married life, Mom didn't have to share her bedroom with a kid. The new neighbors on one side had a son Terry's age, and the Kisors on the other side had 2 daughters and a son, all a little younger than me. They were Catholic, though at the time, I didn't fully understand what that meant, except that they seemed happy.

Learning the Value of a Dollar

By the time I got to high school, I found a job cleaning windows twice a week at a shoe store in downtown Lancaster. I earned a dollar each time, which seemed like a fortune to me. We had always come home for lunch during school, but now the high school was too far away. Dad gave me 25 cents to buy lunch, but when I got to the cafeteria, I found out lunch actually cost 30 cents. When I told Dad, he said, "Tell them it's not worth 30 cents. Twenty-five is enough," and he never gave me more. If he wasn't home when I was getting ready for school, I'd make myself a peanut butter and jelly sandwich or fry an egg to take for lunch so I could pocket the 25 cents.

In the fall of my freshman year, I got a job delivering one of the Columbus evening papers. If all the subscribers paid me, I earned about six dollars a week, in addition to the two dollars I made cleaning windows. The paper ran a contest for the carriers that fall: if we could get a certain number of new customers, we would win free train tickets and admission to the Ohio State vs. Michigan football game in Ann Arbor. I managed to win, and my manager dropped me off at Union Station in Columbus. Off I went, at 15 years old, to see OSU win. I even bought an OSU pennant, which hung proudly on the wall in our bedroom.

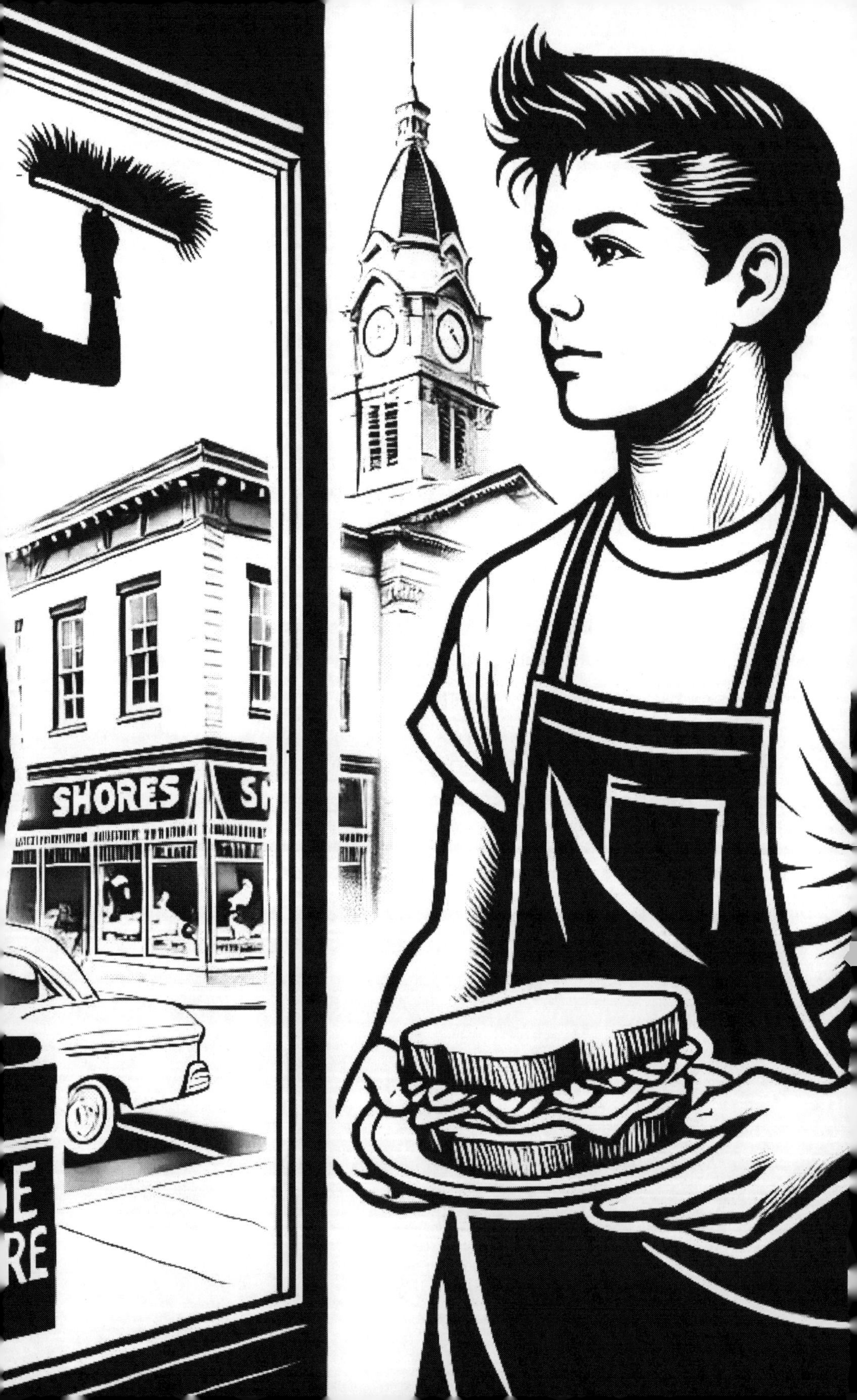
SHORES

The Road to Independence— Earning My Driver's License

I continued working both jobs—the window cleaning and paper route—until the summer between my sophomore and junior years in high school. Then, I started a new job as a janitor and general all-around helper at one of the local department stores. It was during this time that I finally asked Daddy if I could get my driver's license. His response was quick and blunt: "What are you going to drive?" I suggested I could use the family car sometimes, but his answer was firm, "You're not driving my car. When you buy your own car and pay for your insurance, then you can get your license." It wasn't until the start of my senior year that I finally saved enough money to buy a used car, and with that, I was able to get my driver's license at long last. It felt like a huge milestone—both freedom and responsibility rolled into one.

Welcoming Pamela and the Arrival of Twins

My younger sister Pamela was born on January 5, 1954. Grandma Hampp came to stay with us for a few days to help take care of the newborn. At the time, I was still attending school half-days, so I got a refresher course in caring for a baby—changing diapers, feeding, and burping, just like I had done with Vicki. This routine lasted until February 17, 1957, when Mom gave birth to my twin brothers, Timothy and Thomas. Even though I was a junior in high school, working two hours after school and all day on Saturdays, I was still expected to pitch in around the house.

Daddy worked hard, making the money to pay the mortgage, bills, and groceries, while Tator and I were expected to take care of ourselves—and we did. After the twins were born, Daddy bought a clothes dryer, which made life easier, especially with all the diapers to wash. But Mom still used the old wringer washer, and I can still hear her cussing when the clothes got wrapped around the wringer. Only occasionally would she get someone else to help with the laundry.

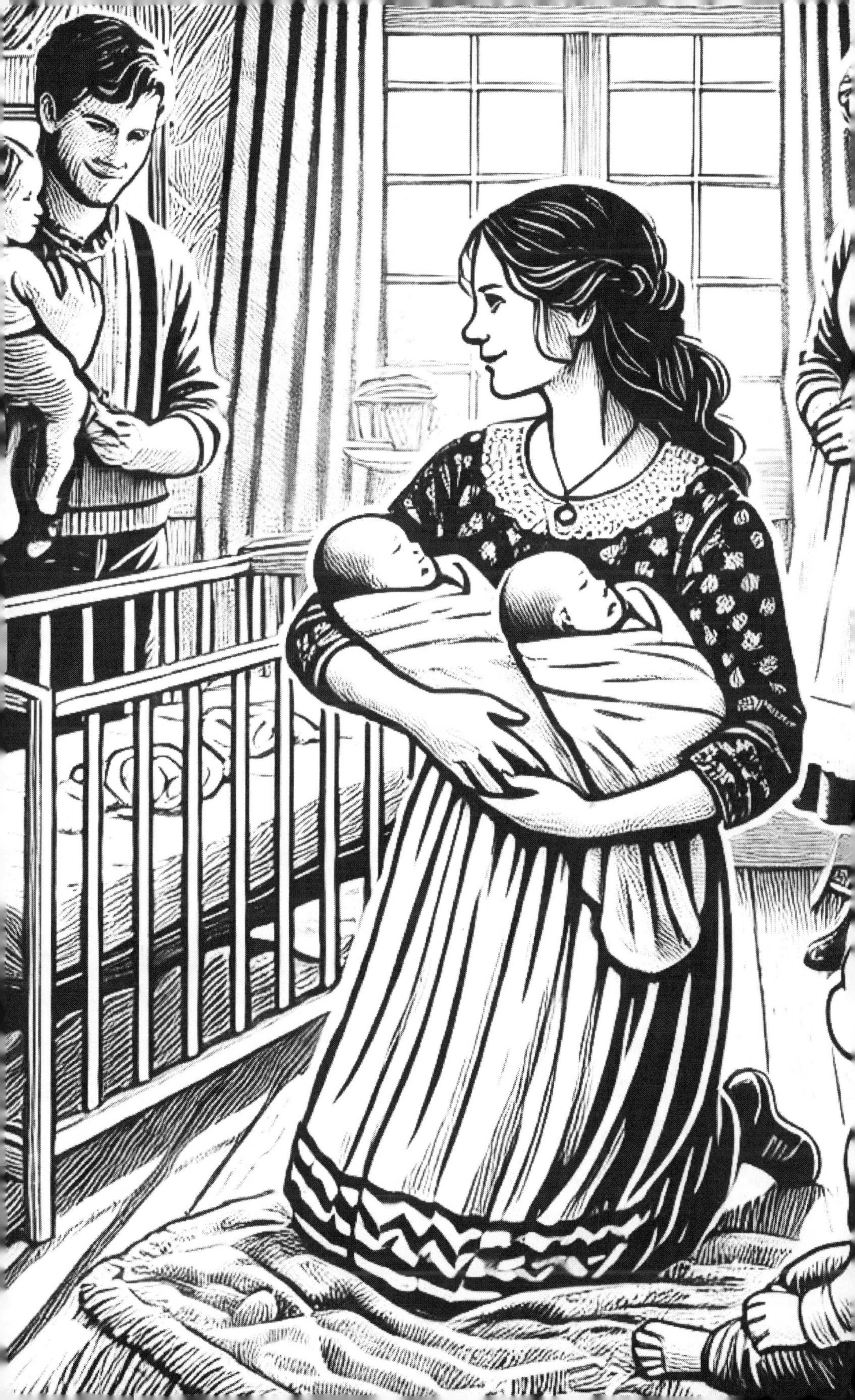

Part 3

Finding Faith—A Journey with the Kisors

Next door, at the Kisors' house, Mrs. Kisor would often invite me in for a snack when I came to collect for the paper. Toward the end of my paper route days, I got curious and asked her about Catholics. She invited me to Mass with their family the next day. I asked Mom if I could go, and she didn't have a problem with it. Their son Raymond, Jr. served as an altar boy, and I was fascinated by the ritual of the Mass. I asked to go again, and the Kisors were always happy to bring me along.

Page | 62

Becoming Catholic—A Step of Independence

In the late summer of 1956, I went to see Father Patrick Byrne, the young and newest priest at Saint Mary of the Assumption. He invited me to attend a class for inquirers—it wasn't called RCIA back then, just a small gathering of people interested in the faith. The Kisors made sure I got to every class. Then, in the spring of 1957, I was baptized as a Catholic. Raymond, Sr. and his wife Wanda Kisor were my sponsors. None of my family attended, and I remember feeling a little sad about that, but also proud of the step I was taking for myself.

Dreams of Medicine and Enlisting in the Navy

Since 8th grade, it had always been my dream to become a doctor, though I knew my parents couldn't afford to send me to college. Still, I held on to that hope. There was a boy in school, a year older than me, who was a Corpsman in the Navy Reserves. Knowing my interest in medicine, he suggested I join the Naval Reserve with the intent of becoming a Corpsman. Mom signed the papers giving her permission since I was only 17, and I enlisted in May 1957. By June, I was off to Boot Camp at Great Lakes Naval Training Center, north of Chicago. After that, I went to weekly Reserve meetings in Columbus until I was called to active duty in July 1960.

The Strain of Family Tensions

After I graduated high school, I enrolled at Ohio University Lancaster, which had just opened a branch campus. All the classes were in the evening, so I could continue working full-time and still live at home. I hadn't saved enough to cover the full tuition, so Mom cashed in one of her insurance policies and gave me $250 to make up the difference. That gesture of love and sacrifice didn't sit well with Daddy, though. He was angry that Mom had given me the money, claiming it was his money since he had paid the premiums. He called me a "damned Catholic" and a "mackerel snapper." He hated Catholics, despite having several Catholic friends from work. I remember him saying he should have kicked me out of the house when I joined the Catholic Church. We didn't speak much after that. Even though I continued to live at home, I worked full-time and went to school at night, so our paths rarely crossed.

Active Duty and a New Chapter in Life

For the next three semesters, I worked hard enough to pay my own tuition. Around this time, I started dating a girl who worked at the same department store. We didn't go out often because I was either working or at school. She wasn't Catholic, but that didn't matter to me. We eventually got engaged a week before I was called to active duty in the Navy. Tator had graduated high school and gone on active duty a month before me, and we were both sent to Hospital Corps School at Great Lakes, Illinois. After we completed training, Tator was sent to Naval Air Station Lakehurst in New Jersey, and I was stationed at Naval Hospital Beaufort in South Carolina. I arrived there two weeks before Christmas 1960.

Mastering the Nursery—Navy Life in Beaufort

My first assignment at the Naval Hospital Beaufort was in the newborn nursery. The Navy nurses were amazed at how easily I handled the newborns, but thanks to Mom, it was all second nature to me. Changing diapers, feeding, burping—I'd been doing it since I was a kid. I was quickly promoted to senior corpsman of the nursery, which meant I worked more day shifts and fewer evenings or nights. However, between my work in the hospital and corps school, I was still on duty every other weekend. I tried to attend Mass when I could, though it wasn't often. The hospital didn't have a Catholic chaplain, but one came from the nearby Marine Corps base every Sunday to say Mass in the hospital auditorium. On my weekends off, sometimes I went to Mass, and other times I just slept in.

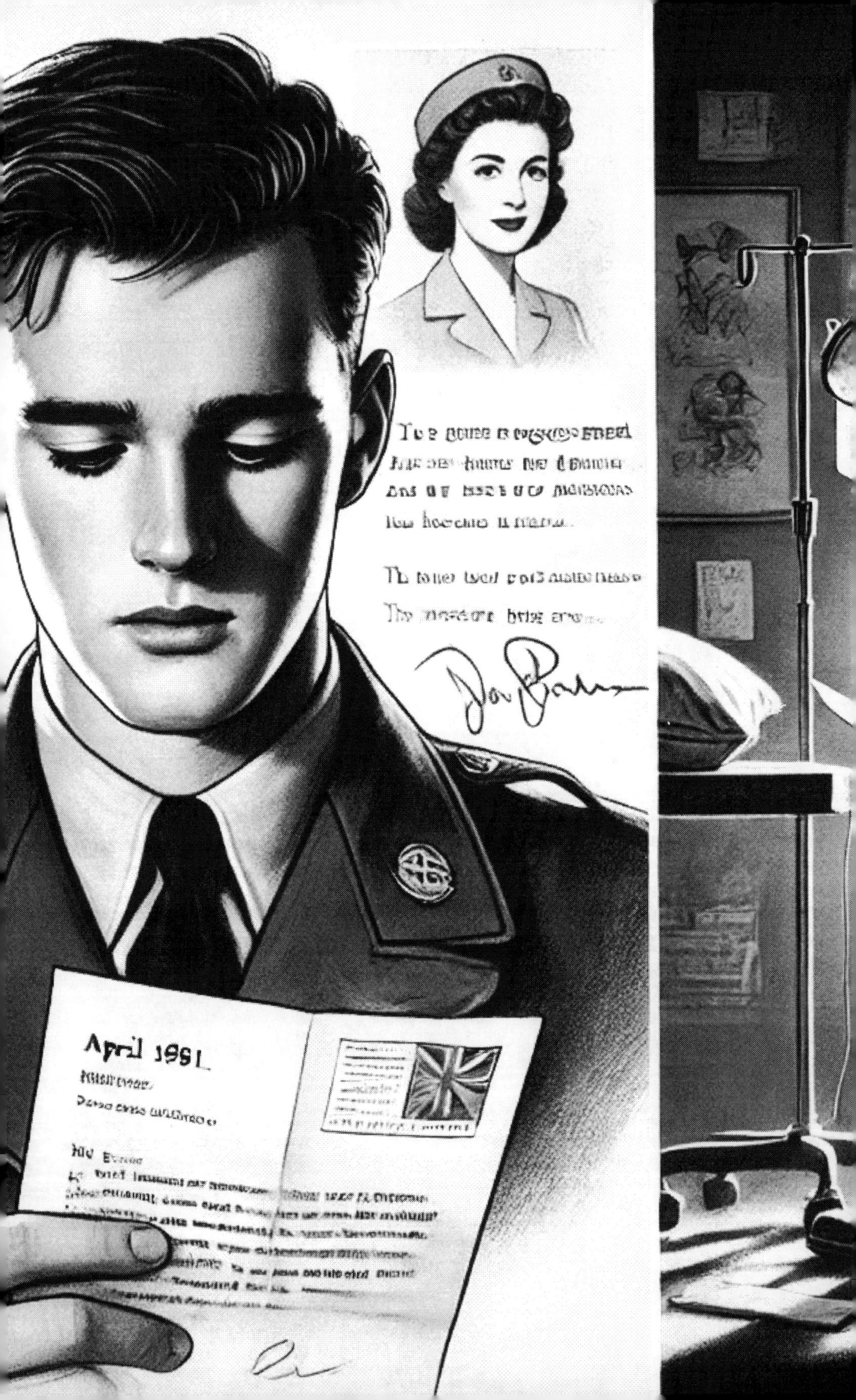
April

Broken Engagement— A Change of Plans

In April 1961, I got ten days of leave to go home and visit my family and my fiancée. Since I had worked for Christmas 1960, I was told I would get leave for Christmas 1961, so we made plans to get married during that holiday. With my leadership skills recognized, I was made senior corpsman of the medical ward, and I was even awarded Outstanding Corpsman for a bimonthly period. I was told there would soon be an opening in surgery for a corpsman to train as a surgical technician, and I applied. It seemed like I was the one who would be selected, but that also meant I'd be the lowest-ranked corpsman in surgery and likely wouldn't get leave at Christmas.

In June 1961, I wrote to my fiancée, explaining the situation and proposing an alternative. I told her I could get leave over Labor Day and suggested renting an apartment in Beaufort. I would come home by bus, and then she, her mother, and her sister could ride back with me in my car. We could get married in Beaufort instead. A couple of weeks later, I received a letter from her, saying it wasn't enough time for her to prepare. Besides, she said, she wasn't willing to live with me while I was still in the Navy. She wanted to stay close to her family. I was frustrated, and all the guys I worked with told me to "dump that woman." I wasn't sure if I wanted to make the Navy my career, but I knew that a wife's place was with her husband. So, I wrote back and told her that our engagement was off and that I wouldn't marry her. She never told her family we were no longer a couple. As it turned out, I didn't get the surgical technician position, so I was able to come home for Christmas after all. However, I was made senior corpsman of the surgical ward, and that's where I stayed until I left Beaufort.

A Scholarship Lost—The Unopened Letter

In February 1962, I went to Savannah State College to take a scholarship exam for nursing school. In April, I was notified that I had been awarded a full-tuition scholarship to Bellevue Hospital School of Nursing in New York City, with classes starting in August 1962. I was released from active duty on July 25, 1962, and took a Greyhound Bus back to Ohio. The day after I got home, Mom handed me a letter that had been sent in late June. It was from Bellevue Hospital, informing me that their classes were full for 1962, and I would have to wait until 1963 to start. The letter also mentioned that the scholarship could be transferred to Harlem Valley State Hospital in upstate New York, but I needed to notify them immediately. I called the hospital, but it was too late—the scholarship had been given to someone else.

I sat there, devastated. Mom always opened and read any mail that came to the house, no matter who it was addressed to, but this letter she hadn't opened. I couldn't help but cry—an opportunity slipped through my fingers because of one unopened letter.

The Road Trip of a Lifetime— Seattle and the World's Fair

Around that time, a fellow corpsman and friend, Myron, who had been discharged at the end of June, had asked me several times to join him on a road trip to the World's Fair in Seattle. Each time I said no, explaining that I was starting school in August. But after I quit crying, I started thinking. With five younger siblings at home, I knew it was time for me to leave. I called Myron at his mother's house in Birmingham, Alabama, and asked if he was still planning to go to Seattle. When he said yes, I told him I was coming. The next day, I took the bus to Birmingham.

It took a couple of days for Myron to get everything ready, but soon we were off, driving across the southern border of the U.S., stopping frequently and camping in state parks or roadside rest areas. Visiting National Parks along the way was a real treat. One particular memory stands out: our visit to the Grand Canyon. We arrived in the afternoon and settled into our campsite. At the ranger station, we asked about hiking down into the canyon, and the ranger pointed to a halfway distance, telling us it would be a good day's hike. The next morning, we started early, and by 9 a.m., we had already reached the halfway point. Feeling confident, we decided to continue all the way down to the Colorado River.

We made it to the river in less than two hours, but we had long since finished the water in our canteens. We refilled them with river water—since that was all there was—and decided to soak our aching feet in the river. I took off my loafers and wasn't surprised to see my white socks were bloody. My feet hurt, but after soaking, we started the long trek back up. It was then that we realized why the ranger had only suggested going halfway.

The hike back up was brutal. We didn't make it back to our campsite until well after 8 p.m., completely exhausted. We agreed that there was no way we wanted to sleep on the ground that night, so we packed up and headed for the nearest motel with a pool and a restaurant since we hadn't eaten all day.

From Adventure to Employment Finding My Place in Seattle

The next day, we continued on to California via Route 66. Our next stops were Yosemite National Park, a drive through the Redwoods, and Giant Sequoia National Park. From there, we visited San Francisco and crossed the Golden Gate Bridge. We drove up the west coast on Highway 101 until we reached Seattle. There, we rented a small room with two beds in a rooming house, paying for two weeks.

The next day, we headed to the World's Fair. There were long lines for every attraction, but we could at least say we had been there. After that, we toured Seattle, took a ferry to Bremerton, visited the Olympia Brewery, and even got a free beer.

Realizing we couldn't stay in Seattle without finding jobs, we visited an employment agency. Since I had experience working on a surgical ward, I was sent to The University of Washington for an interview in their surgical research department. I was hired two days later to help prep animals for surgery. Myron drove me to work while he continued looking for a job. I called Mom to tell her to sell my car and send me the money so I could find an apartment.

Back on the Road—Returning to Lancaster

A week passed, and Myron still hadn't found work. One day, he told me he was planning to leave. I called Mom again to ask if the car had been sold, but she said, "I was going to put an ad in the paper tomorrow." I realized I couldn't stay in Seattle without my car or the money from its sale. We talked it over for a couple of hours, and then I called Mom back to tell her not to sell the car after all. We were coming home.

Early the next morning, we hit the road, driving back along the northernmost east-west highway. We made a stop at Glacier National Park and enjoyed the breathtaking views. I got to see parts of the United States I had never even thought about. We drove through Washington, Montana, and into North Dakota, where Myron's car broke down. Luckily, we were near a small town, and it happened during the day. We hiked into town and found a repair shop. The owner towed the car and made the necessary repairs, but we were now much poorer and had to ration our remaining money carefully.

With what little we had left, we couldn't afford toll roads or food, so we drove straight through until we reached Lancaster a day and a half later. We arrived home exhausted and hungry, with only a quarter tank of gas and 41 cents between the two of us.

New Beginnings in Alabama and a Path Back to the Navy

Three days after getting back to Lancaster, Myron sold his car, and I withdrew the remaining money from my savings account. We packed up my car and headed to Alabama, arriving the Sunday before Labor Day. Once there, I helped Myron paint his mother's house and make much-needed repairs. His mother, a widow, was grateful for the help. We did such a good job that his best friend asked us to paint his house too. By the time we finished, I knew I needed to find a way to support myself, so off I went to the Navy Recruiting Office.

I decided to reenlist for six years but had to wait two weeks for my new orders to arrive. During this time, from July 25 to the end of September, I didn't think about church, Mass, or anything related to my faith. I never attended Mass or even considered it. It was as though that part of my life had drifted into the background.

At the end of September, my orders came through. I went back to Lancaster to collect my uniforms, drop off my car, and apply for a passport. I stayed just long enough—about four days—to visit my grandparents and see a few relatives. Then, I took the bus back to Alabama to say goodbye to friends one last time. From Birmingham, I flew to San Diego to attend survivor school at Naval Base Coronado—the same place where Navy SEALs are trained.

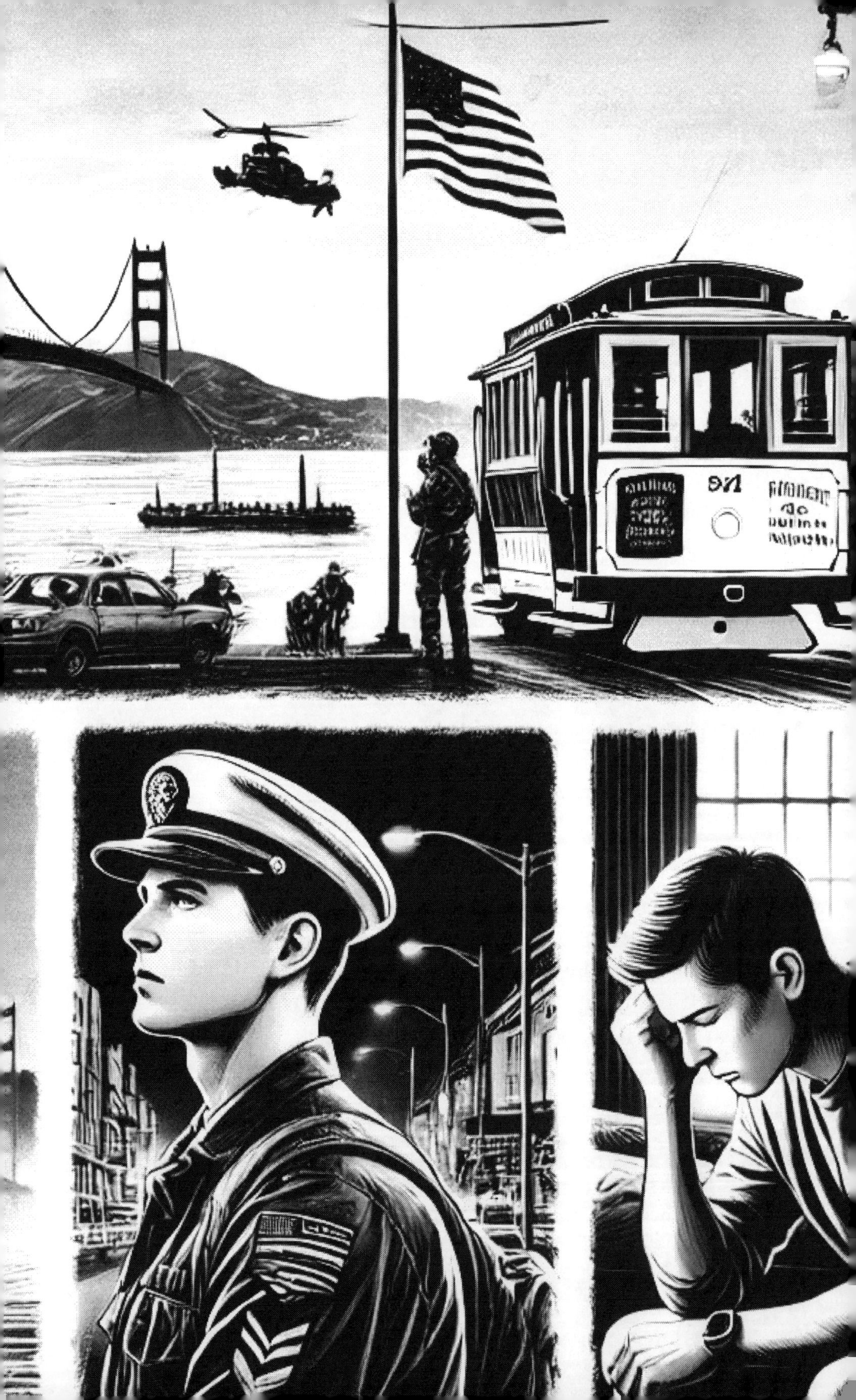

Waiting in San Francisco— A Lesson in Patience

After two intense weeks in San Diego, I headed to San Francisco to pick up my official passport and prepare for my flight to my next duty station in Saigon, Vietnam. But there was a snag. By early November, my passport still hadn't arrived. I was billeted at the Treasure Island Naval Base, and every afternoon, I was told to call the personnel office to see if my passport had come in. There were three other shipmates also waiting for their passports, so we spent our days as tourists, riding the cable cars, exploring Fisherman's Wharf, Chinatown, and visiting all the popular sights of San Francisco.

At that time, Tony Bennett's song "I Left My Heart in San Francisco" was playing everywhere, and it took on a special meaning as we stood at the Enlisted Club on Treasure Island, looking out over the bay at the city's lights. I could see why people fell in love with San Francisco.

One by one, my shipmates received their passports and flights, until I was the only one left waiting. Finally, everything came together, and on December 14, I left Travis AFB for a flight to Honolulu. There was a four-hour stopover, and it just so happened that my mom's brother was stationed in Hawaii with his family. I made a quick phone call, and they came to the airport to see me during the layover.

From Honolulu, we flew to Wake Island, then Guam, and finally to Clark Air Force Base in the Philippines before arriving in Saigon on December 17. Upon arrival, a bus took us to the transient hotel. A man boarded the bus to explain where we were and what we needed to do, but I was so exhausted that I didn't hear a word. Once in my room, I put my bags down and just stood there, completely disoriented. I didn't know where I was or what I was supposed to do next.

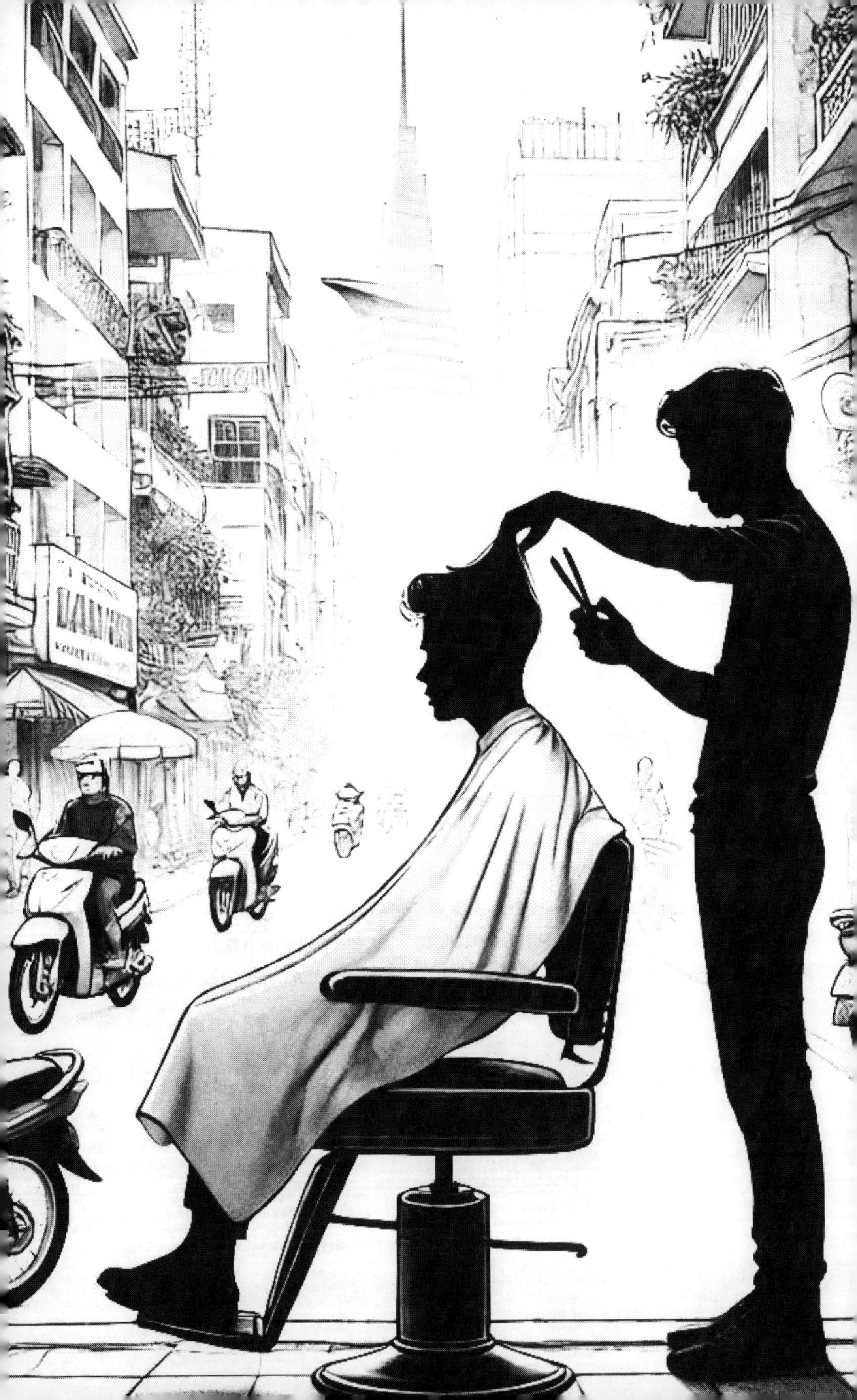

Exploring Saigon and an Unexpected Haircut

After a while, I went down to the reception desk to get some clarity. Since I didn't have anything scheduled for the rest of the day, I decided to go out and explore. I kept it simple—just a walk around the block so I wouldn't get lost. The walk went well, so I expanded my route to two blocks, then three. On each walk, I passed a barber shop, and since I needed a haircut, I went back to the hotel to exchange some dollars for Vietnamese piastres. Then I returned to the barber shop. The haircut itself was fine, but afterward, the barber dipped a comb into a jar of white cream, something that looked like Wildroot Cream Oil. He combed it through my hair again and again until my entire head was white. I finally had to ask him to stop, and he ended up washing it out. I still have no idea what it was!

The next day, with my fresh haircut, I reported in and was assigned to the American Dispensary Saigon. It was a joint operation with one doctor and nurse from the State Department, one doctor from the Navy, and one from the Army. There were also two Army nurses, three nurses from Thailand, and one nurse from the Philippines. The medical staff included six Navy corpsmen, two Army medics, and one Air Force medic.

The dispensary itself was housed in a building that had once been the residence of a French government official before World War II. It even had a swimming pool and servants' quarters out back. Being the new guy, I was assigned to sick call, so I had to learn quickly. For an EKG, you observed one, then did one under supervision, and then you were on your own. The same went for suturing. I watched other corpsmen suture a few times before it was my turn.

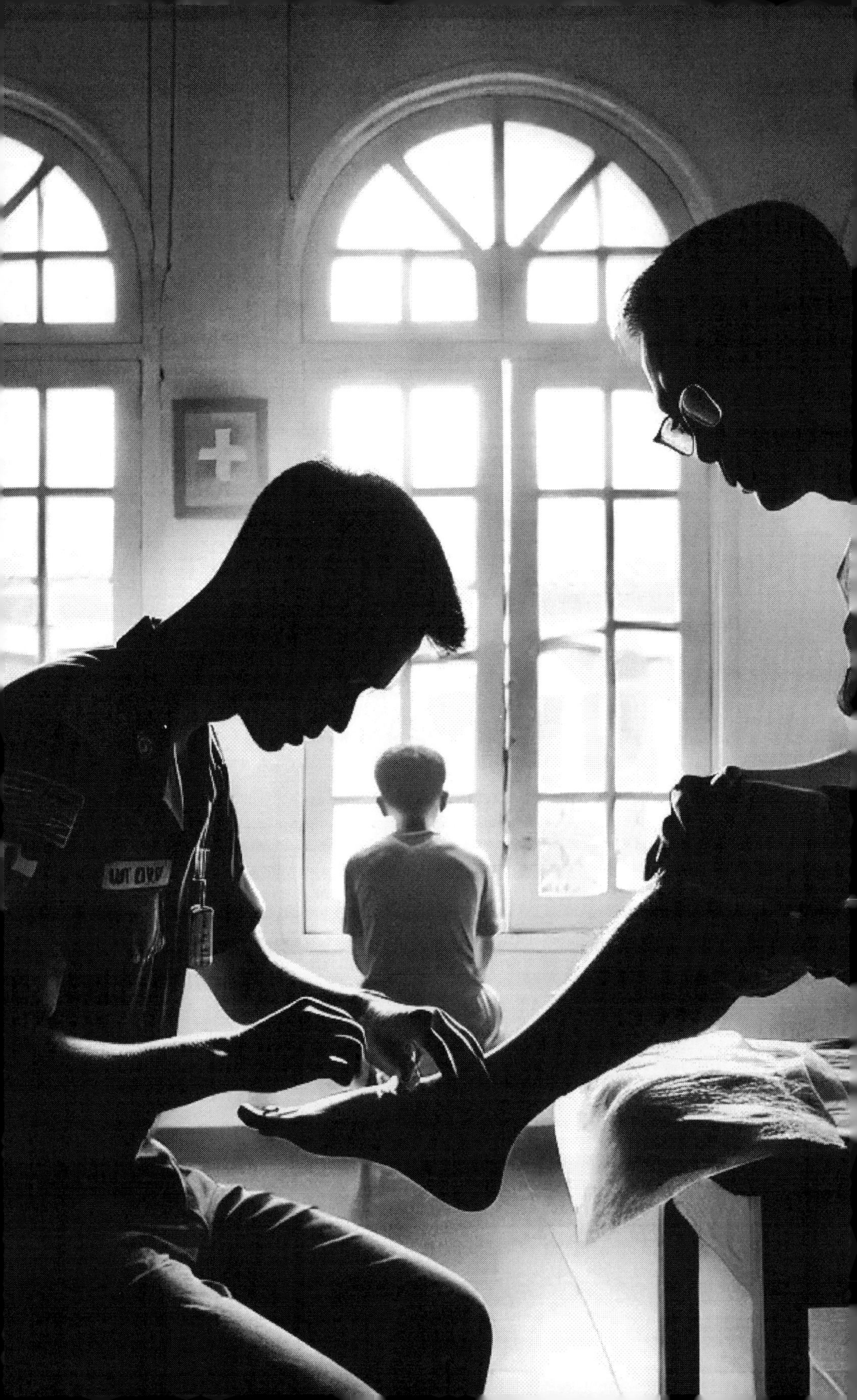

Learning the Ropes: My First Sutures

My first patient was a Vietnamese worker with a nasty cut above his ankle. A band-aid probably would have sufficed, but one of the other corpsmen insisted it was time for me to try my hand at suturing. It took me over an hour, but I managed to place two perfectly neat sutures. The wound healed nicely, and when I saw him a week later, I felt a quiet sense of accomplishment.

The more I practiced, the more proficient I became. On duty, we were the only medical personnel in the building except for one nurse upstairs who cared for the inpatients. One Sunday, the Australian Ambassador came in with his injured thirteen-year-old son. The boy had a deep gash on his forehead, just above his eyebrow. I cleansed and numbed the wound before carefully closing it with nine sutures. A few weeks later, the dispensary's commanding officer received a letter from the Ambassador, praising the care his son received and expressing gratitude for the professional job I had done. It was a proud moment for me.

Part 4

Cross-Trained and Growing— Finding My Way in X-ray

All of the corpsmen were cross-trained in multiple roles, and in my last few months there, I began working in X-ray. It was a fast-paced environment, and we all had to be flexible, but those experiences helped me grow as both a corpsman and a person. The younger corpsmen got to know the civilian nurses quite well, and occasionally, we were invited to their homes for meals. I learned to eat just about anything, and honestly, most of it was better than Mom's home cooking.

A Chaperoned Courtship—Friendship with Fely

One of the Filipina nurses knew I was Catholic and invited me over to her house to meet the Secretary of the Philippine Ambassador, which led to another dinner. Fely, the secretary, was the same age as me and had four brothers who had all graduated from the University of Washington. She was the youngest and was born in Manila while her brothers had been born in Seattle. We had a wonderful meal, and afterward, I was invited to attend Mass with her the next Sunday.

When I went to pick her up in a taxi that Sunday, I was surprised to find another older woman accompanying us. It turned out we always had a chaperone—whether it was the nurse from the dispensary or someone from the embassy, we were never alone. Still, we managed to have fun despite the watchful eyes.

Tokyo R&R and the Name That Stayed with Me: Chiemi's Story

After four months in Saigon, I was able to go on R&R (Rest & Recuperation) to Bangkok for three days. The Thai nurses I worked with gave me wrapped gifts to deliver to their families and even gave me the phone number of one nurse's fiancé. He picked me up at the hotel and took me to meet her parents. They lived in a gated compound with a guard at the entrance and a large circular driveway with a fountain in the middle. The compound was surrounded by five very large houses. My driver spoke English, and the family treated me like I was a long-lost son. During my time there, someone from the family showed me around every day. It was an experience I will never forget.

Four months later, I took a day R&R to Tokyo. I traveled with an Army Sergeant who had been stationed there before his assignment in Saigon, which was great because he knew his way around the train system and the must-see sights. While in Tokyo, I bought a record by the popular Japanese singer Eri Chiemi. I liked it so much that I decided if I ever had a daughter, I would name her Chiemi. And later, I did.

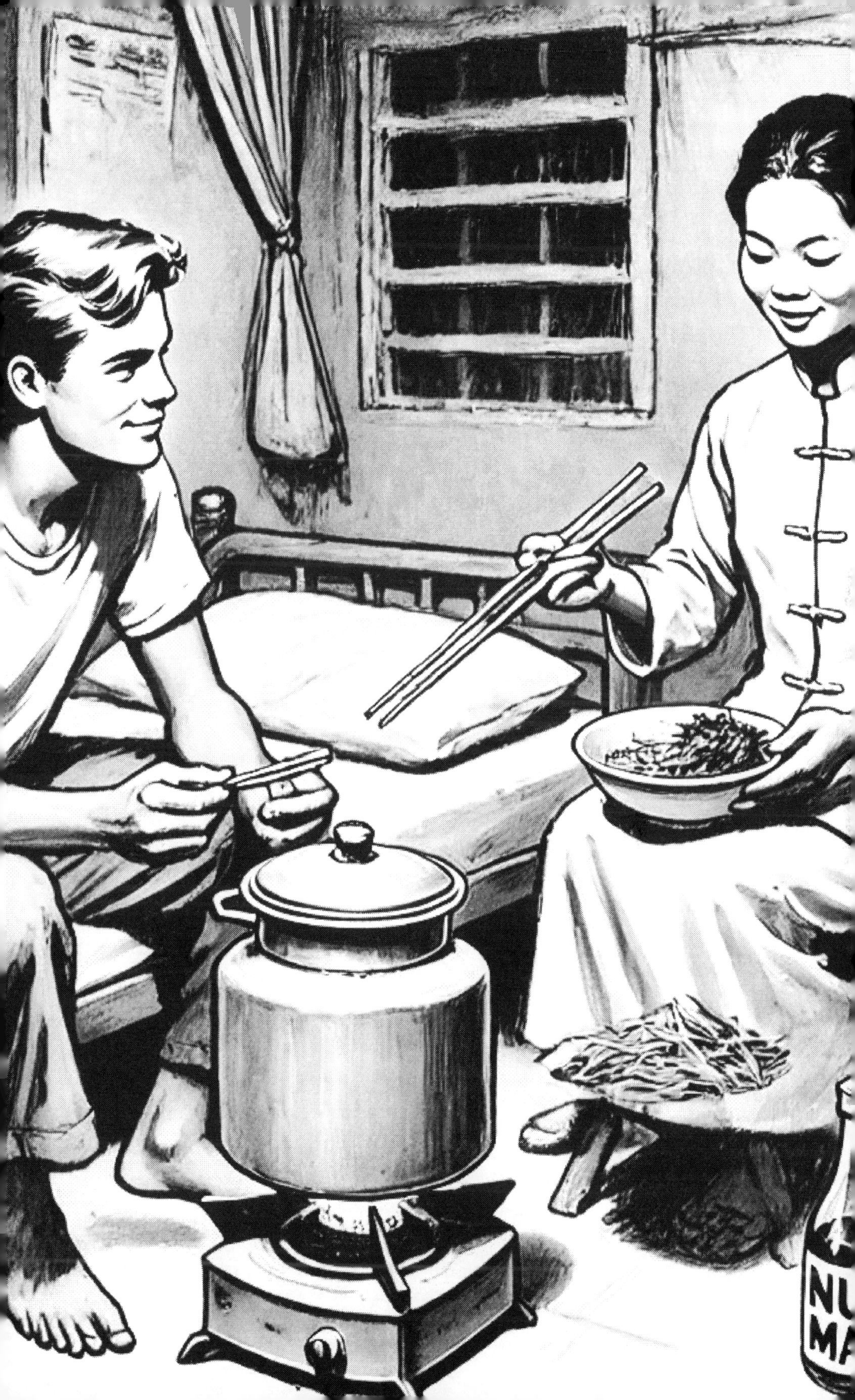

A Meal to Remember—
The Popcorn Popper and Nuoc Mam

Back in Saigon, with only four months left on my tour, my mother sent me an electric popcorn popper. I tried it once, but it was more hassle than I was willing to deal with. However, the maid who cleaned my room and did my laundry used it nearly every day to cook rice to take home. She lived in a slum behind the hotel, and once in a while, I would buy her small gifts like soap, candy, or cigarettes. She would often ask me to come to her house for a meal, and I always refused—until one day, I gave in.

The next day, with her freshly cooked rice in tow, we made our way to her dwelling behind the hotel. The path was narrow and littered with trash, leading to a building with four rooms—two upstairs and two downstairs, with a different family in each. There were no stairs to reach the upper floor, so I had to climb a ladder to get to her room. She must have been to the market earlier because she had a variety of vegetables and even a small watermelon. I could tell she was going out of her way to impress me.

She pulled her cooking utensils from under the bed, brushing off the roaches and bugs, while I sat on the bed watching her chop vegetables. She lit her one-burner gasoline-powered camping stove and began cooking, adding nuoc mam (a Vietnamese fish sauce) to the mix. When the meal was ready, she handed me a bowl filled with vegetables and a pair of chopsticks. By this time, I had become pretty proficient with chopsticks. In fact, I used to dump a bottle of aspirin onto my desk and pick up the pills with chopsticks just for practice.

She added more nuoc mam to my bowl, and I took a bite. I swallowed, and it came back up. I swallowed again and finally kept it down. When the vegetables were finished, she cut the watermelon, covered it in more nuoc mam, and handed me a piece. I quickly finished, thanked her, and made my exit. I was sure I'd end up with diarrhea or some other exotic disease, but luckily, I didn't.

Goodbye Saigon—Heading Home Before the Coup

Not long after, I moved to a different hotel and left the popcorn popper with her. In November 1963, a coup d'état took place, and all military personnel were confined to their hotels for a few days. Afterward, life resumed as if nothing had happened. Shortly after, I received my orders to report to Field Medical Service School at Camp Pendleton in January 1964.

I left Saigon a week before Christmas and headed back home to Ohio. It felt good to be back in Lancaster, even if it was only for a few weeks. My friends in Birmingham wanted me to visit, but I never made it down there.

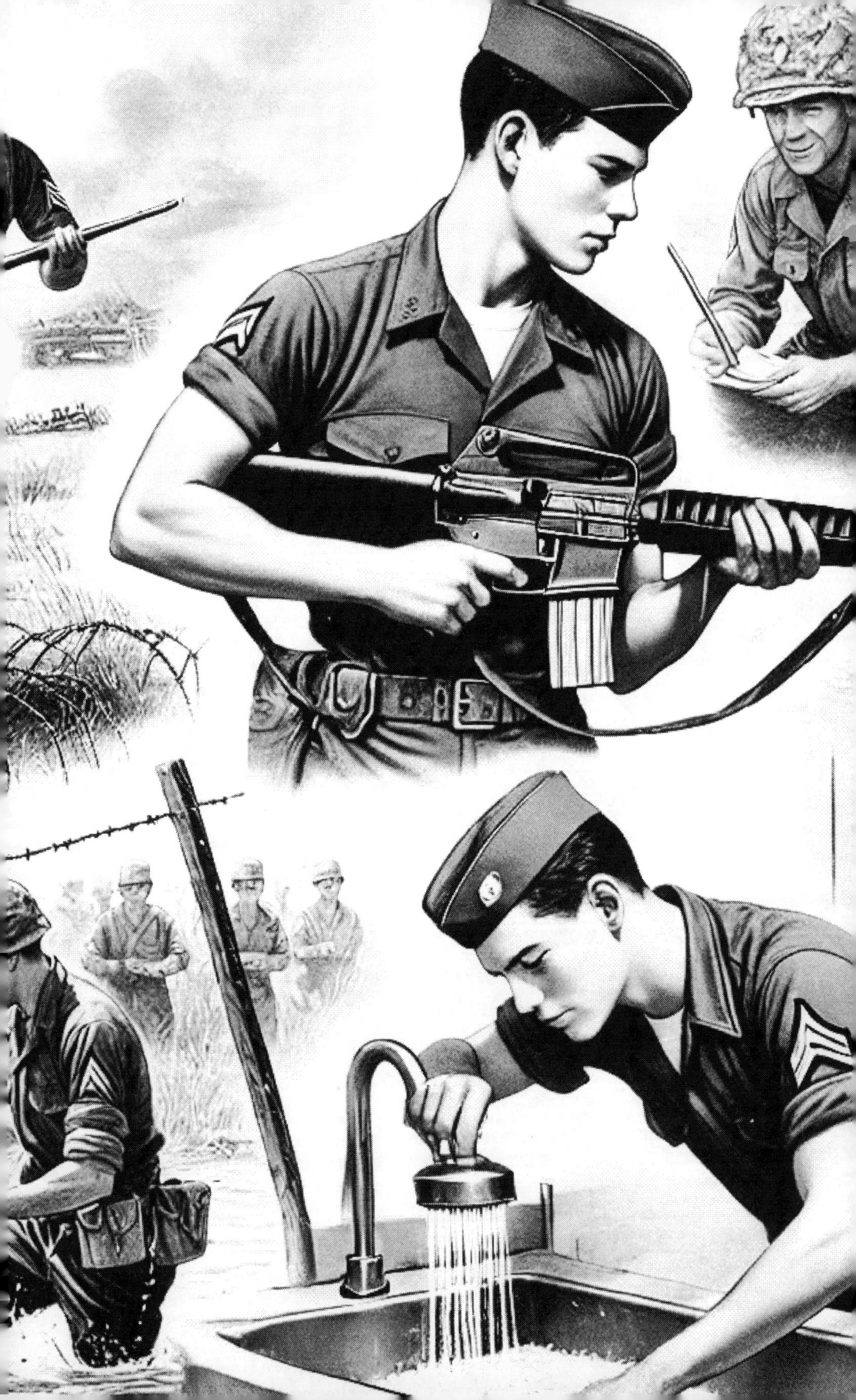

Boot Camp to Battlefield—Becoming a Combat Medic

By that time, Dad had sold my '57 Chevy and bought himself a new car. That was fine by me—I didn't need a car at that point anyway. In January, I left for Southern California and reported to Camp Pendleton to begin training as a combat medic. The classroom sessions covered treating various combat wounds, while the field training involved learning how to fire a rifle and a .45 caliber pistol (the weapon corpsmen were expected to carry). But most of our training consisted of PT (physical training) to keep up with the Marines. Toward the end of my training, we had live-fire exercises and spent time crawling through the mud under barbed wire. We'd been in the field since early morning and didn't finish until late afternoon. Once we returned, we were told to rack our rifles behind the barracks to clean them after lunch. I had a different idea. Instead of cleaning my rifle later, I took it apart and washed it thoroughly with water and Tide in the mop sink. Once finished, I placed it in the rack and pretended it still needed to be cleaned.

After lunch, the staff sergeant had us take our rifles apart and begin cleaning. I went through the motions and was the first to finish. When I presented the rifle for inspection, the staff sergeant said, "Damn, Doc, that looks good. Good job." I managed to get away with it—at least until the end of my training when I had to turn the rifle back into the armory.

At the butt end of the rifle stock was a metal plate held in place by a small screw, and under the plate were all the implements needed to clean the rifle. When the armorer opened it up, everything was rusted. He asked me about the terrible condition of the cleaning tools, and I replied, "I don't know. That's just the way they are." Somehow, I got a free pass on that one!

From Saigon to Okinawa— A New Adventure Unfolds

After finishing my training, I was assigned to a military transport ship that would take me to my next duty station in Okinawa. We had a two-day stopover at Pearl Harbor, Hawaii, so I called my uncle, and he came to the pier to pick me up. It was great to see them again. I offered to treat them to dinner, and we went to a Chinese restaurant. They couldn't believe how adventurous my palate had become—nothing like the food Mom cooked at home. Later, my two older cousins took me out on the town. I stayed with them that night, and the next morning, my uncle dropped me off at the ship.

I arrived in Okinawa in late April and was assigned to the 2nd Battalion, 12th Marines, an artillery unit stationed at Camp Sukiran, which was almost in the middle of the island. I became the senior corpsman at sick call, and my experience in Saigon came in handy. Every couple of weeks, the Marines held live-fire exercises, and a corpsman had to go along to provide medical support in case of injuries. We were also responsible for handing out cotton balls for hearing protection when the big guns fired. The protection was minimal at best, and I'm sure most of us, like me, ended up with hearing problems later in life.

Escape from the Battlefield—Life at Camp Kue

After a couple of months, some friends who worked at the Division Surgeon's office asked if I wanted to transfer to the admissions office at Camp Kue, an Army hospital just up the road. I jumped at the opportunity—no more big guns or time in the field! My new job involved tracking Marines who were admitted to the hospital, ensuring their units knew where they were.

The best part was that I had every night and weekend off—more than I could ask for. Life was good, so good that I decided to buy a car—a 1950 Ford two-door coupe. It cost me sixty dollars. The car ran great, had new tires, but was rusted all over, and every window except the windshield was cracked. Still, it got me where I needed to go. With the car, I could explore Okinawa with friends on weekends. Then, in August 1964, the Gulf of Tonkin Incident happened, and everything changed. I was reassigned from the Army hospital to the 3rd Battalion, 9th Marines, for deployment to Vietnam. The fear of returning to war was palpable, but I accepted my orders.

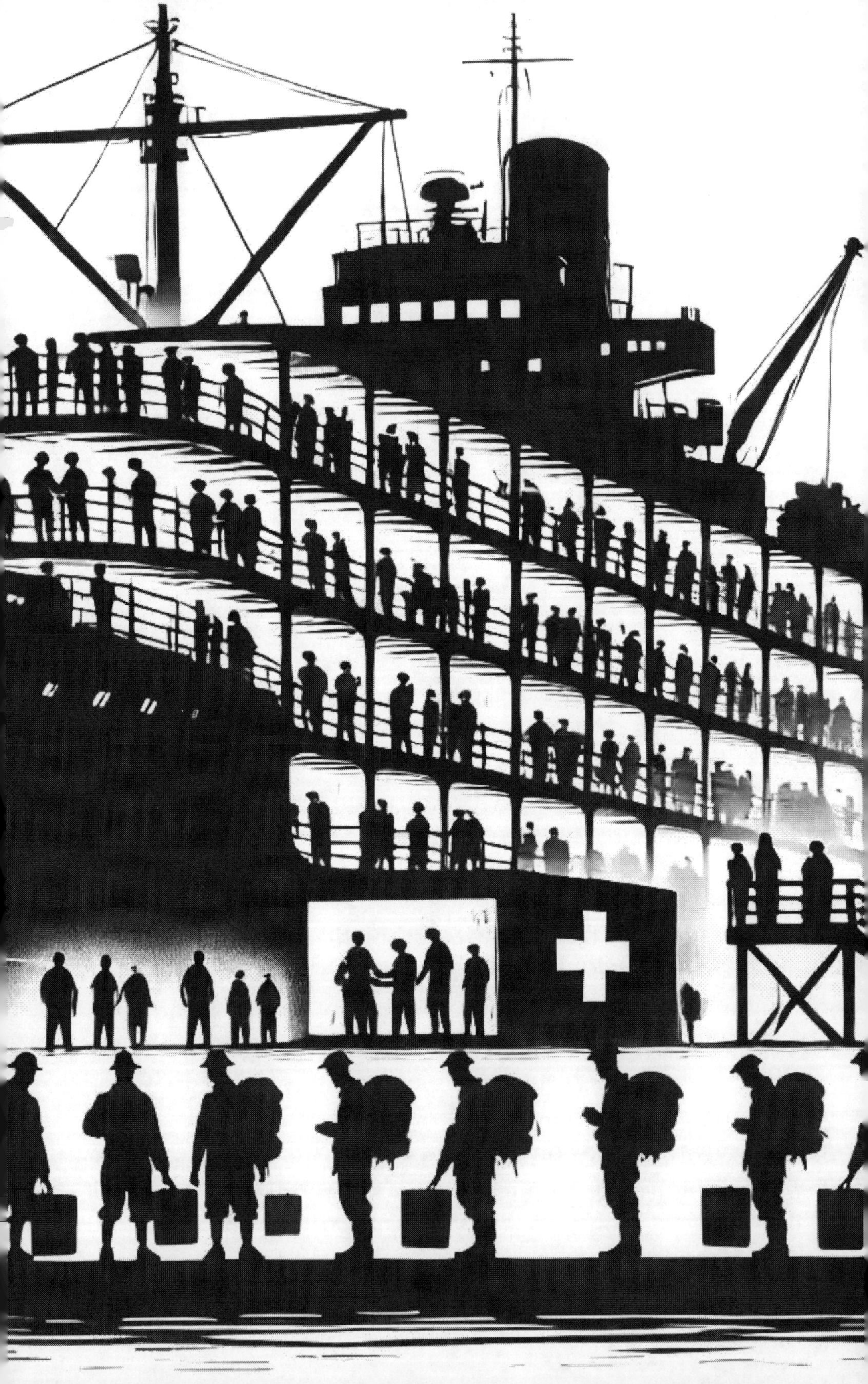

Into the Unknown—The Gulf of Tonkin and the Call Back to War

We sat on the pier for nearly 16 hours, waiting to board an old World War II troop transport ship, the USS Renville. The berthing area was four decks down, extremely crowded, with metal-framed bunks and stretched canvas. The biggest shock was the ventilation—or lack of it. Only one small pipe brought outside air into the compartment, and the air quickly became stifling.

On the second day at sea, the evaporators, which convert seawater into fresh water, broke down. The ship's engineers worked hard to repair them, but in the end, they could only produce enough fresh water for the ship's boilers, the galley, and the medical spaces. There was no fresh water for laundry or showers.

I went to the sick bay to see if they needed help with sick call for the Marines and was surprised that none of the other corpsmen had volunteered. It turned out to be a cool place to work, both literally and figuratively. I even got to sleep on the floor in the X-ray darkroom, which was a welcome escape from the heat below deck. While we were underway, the ship's doctor had to perform an appendectomy, and I served as the scrub nurse.

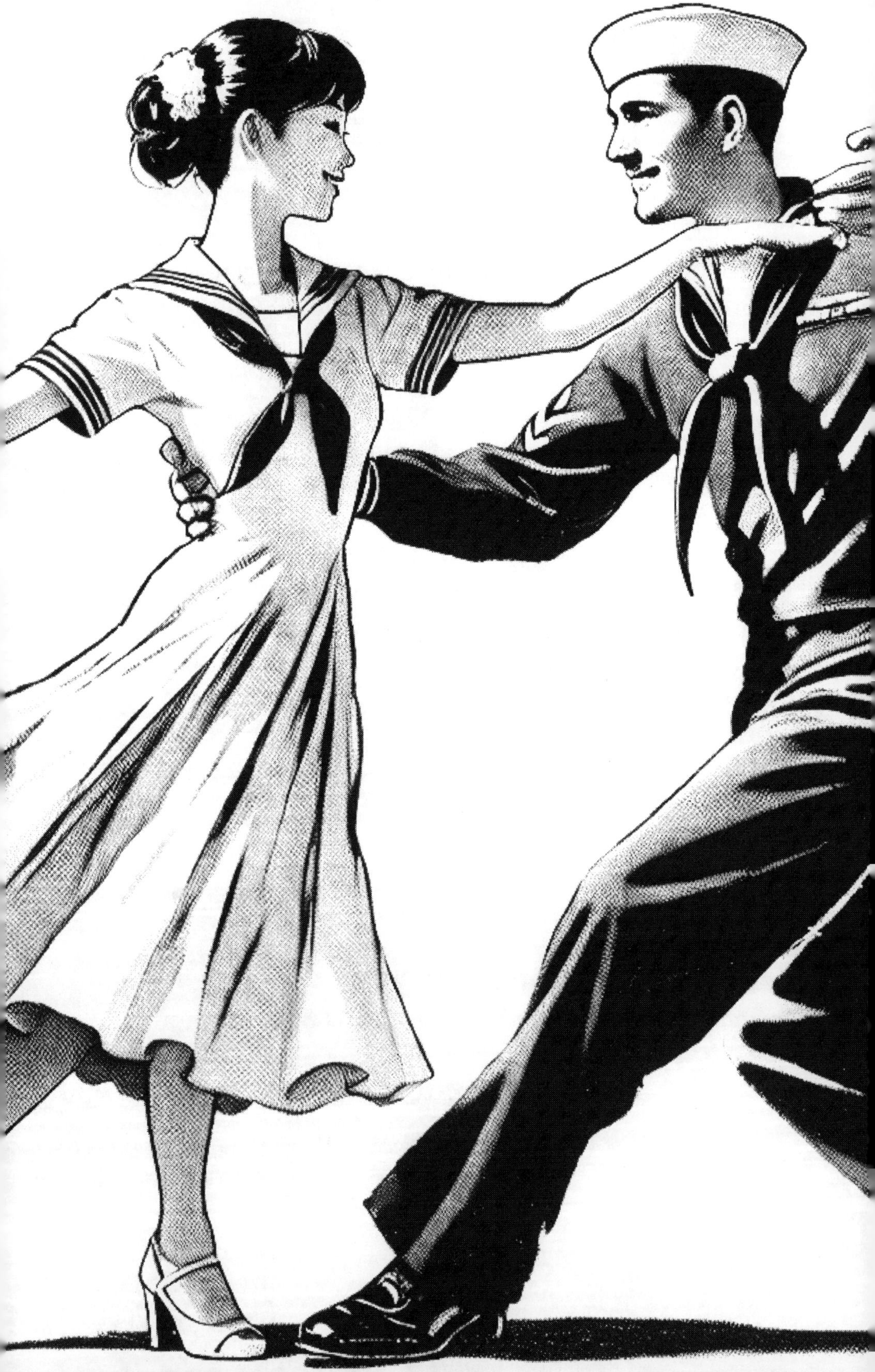

A Night to Remember—Fate Intervenes on Halloween

We spent 67 days cruising up and down the coast of Vietnam, providing medical support to the Marines on board. When we finally returned to Okinawa, the Battalion Medical Officer was so impressed with my work that he requested my assignment be made permanent. A quick phone call to my friends in the Division Surgeon's office, and I was on my way back to the admissions office at the Army hospital.

There was another Navy corpsman who worked in the EKG lab at the hospital. He was married with three children back in the States. He had been asking out an Okinawan coworker, but she kept saying no—until finally, she agreed, on one condition: it had to be a double date. The corpsman asked me to be his wingman, but I initially said no. I had just returned to the hospital and wasn't ready to start dating anyone. But he kept asking, and eventually, I gave in and agreed to go.

We planned to take the girls to a Mexican restaurant for dinner and then go dancing at the Noncommissioned Officers (NCO) Club on base. Everything was set—we were supposed to meet the girls at a specific bus stop at 6:30 on Halloween. My friend and I arrived well before 6:30 and waited. The bus came, but the girls didn't get off. We shrugged it off since the buses ran every ten minutes, so we waited for the next one at 6:40. Again, no sign of them. The same thing happened with the 6:50 bus. I told my friend that if they didn't arrive on the 7:00 bus, I was going to grab a taxi and head back to base.

The 7:00 bus arrived, but still no girls. I said goodbye to my friend, stepped to the curb, and flagged down a taxi. Just as I was about to get in, Katsu Higa and Hideko Matayoshi stepped out of the taxi, and we all had a good laugh about the timing. That was the first time I met Hideko.

We got into the taxi together and headed off to the restaurant. During dinner, I spent time getting to know both of them. Katsu, or Katy, had worked in the Army Hospital's EKG Lab for several years, and Hideko worked as a nurse's aide on the medical unit. What intrigued me about Hideko was that she had been awarded a four-year full-tuition nursing scholarship to the University of Hawaii by the U.S. Army. Currently, she was taking English classes at the University of Okinawa.

After dinner, we went to the NCO Club, where there was live music and dancing. I was a bit clumsy on the dance floor, but Hideko was a natural. She led me with such grace that I couldn't help but compliment her. It was a wonderful evening, but as all good things must come to an end, we put the girls in a taxi and headed back to the barracks.

About a week later, one of the Okinawan girls who worked in the emergency room stopped by the admission office to ask how my date had gone. I didn't even know anyone else knew about it! I told her it was fun, but I hadn't planned to ask Hideko out again. She smiled and said, "I think she'd go out again if you asked her."

Love and Ambition—Navigating Hideko's Dreams

The next day, I went up to Hideko's floor at the hospital to see her and ask her out. She told me she had an English class right after work, so I offered to take her to class. That became our routine—me driving her to class, and later, helping her review her homework before she turned it in. We also managed to squeeze in a few more nights at the NCO Club or catch a movie on base, but we saw each other almost every day.

As we spent more time together, I noticed how anxious Hideko was about school. She was the first person from her village to receive a scholarship for high school and the first to get a scholarship to attend university in the U.S. I could sense the pressure she felt not to fail. In mid-December, I asked her if she would still receive the scholarship if she were married. She explained that the scholarship was only for unmarried students, and recipients were required to return to Okinawa and work in their chosen field for four years after graduation.

A Rain-Soaked Realization—The Proposal

By this time, I had grown to love her deeply. She was smart, kind, and always put others before herself. I found myself needing time to think, so I went for a long walk around the barracks one evening. It started to rain, but I kept walking, lost in thought. I realized how much Hideko meant to me and how serious our relationship had become.

The next night, after a late evening together, I took her home. As we stood outside, I said, "Instead of going to school, let's get married." She didn't say anything right away. She just looked at me for a long moment, and finally said, "I'll have to think about it." After that, neither of us mentioned marriage again for a while.

A Christmas Eve Promise—
"Yes, I Will Marry You"

Then, on Christmas Eve, we went to Midnight Mass at Stillwell Field House, a large hangar building on base. We went with Katy and another friend, and after Mass, we all went back to Katy's house. Under the Christmas tree, there was a small wrapped box with my name on it. I was curious and a little nervous as I unwrapped the box. Inside was a handwritten note from Hideko. It read, "You are my needle, I am your thread. I will follow you wherever you go and love you forever." At the bottom of the note, in simple words, it said, "Yes, I will marry you."

Racing Against Time— The Paperwork Chase

We needed to start the paperwork to get permission for our marriage. This involved gathering six copies of my birth certificate and six copies of Hideko's family register. She also had to undergo a background check to ensure she wasn't a Communist, which was standard procedure at the time. The paperwork typically took about six months, and since I was scheduled to transfer back to the States in May—just five months away—it seemed like we were up against the clock. The long waiting period was designed to discourage military personnel from marrying locals. Fortunately, I had friends in the Division Surgeon's Office, and together, we managed to accomplish the impossible—finishing all the paperwork in just two and a half months.

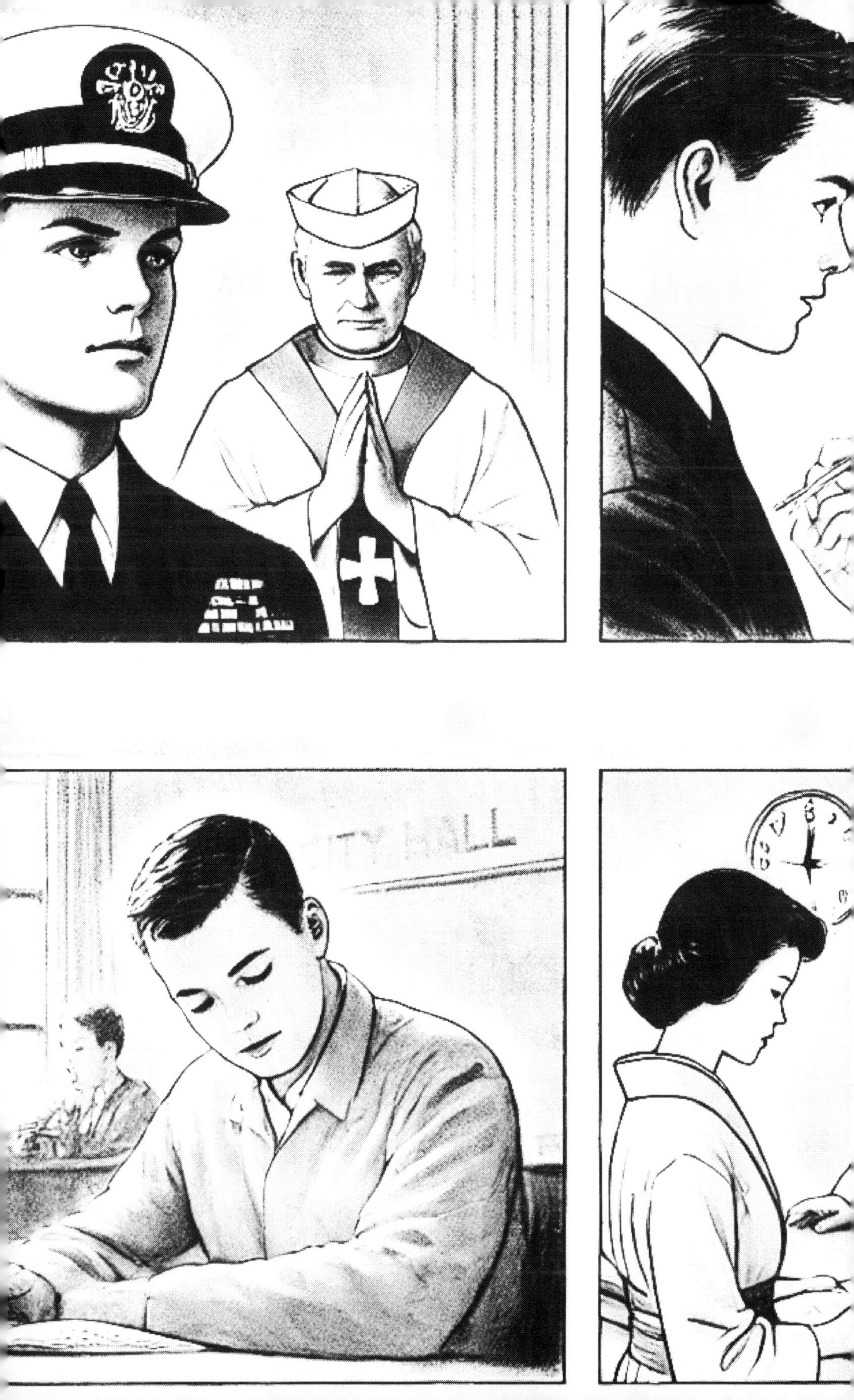
CITY HALL

A Call to the Front Row—Faith, Guidance, and a Birthdate Mystery

One of the required steps was an interview with a chaplain. In my case, it was the Catholic chaplain, who remarked that he hadn't seen me at Sunday Masses. I had to admit I hadn't been going to Mass regularly. I explained that Hideko wanted to be married in the church, and the chaplain gave me the name of a local missionary priest, Father Dominic, whom she could contact for guidance.

Before I left the chaplain's office, he said, "I'll see you in the front row on Sundays from now on," and he was right. That following Sunday, I was in the front row at Mass. Hideko reached out to Father Dominic, a Franciscan missionary, and began meeting with him twice a week. She wasn't planning to convert to Catholicism but wanted to understand the church's teachings on marriage.

It was during this time that Hideko discovered an interesting detail about her birth. When she retrieved her family register, she noticed that her birth date was listed as December 10, 1939. Her grandmother had always told her she was born on the last day of the year. When Hideko pointed this out to the clerk at city hall, the clerk explained that changing the record would require a lot of money and time. Hideko decided to leave it as it was.

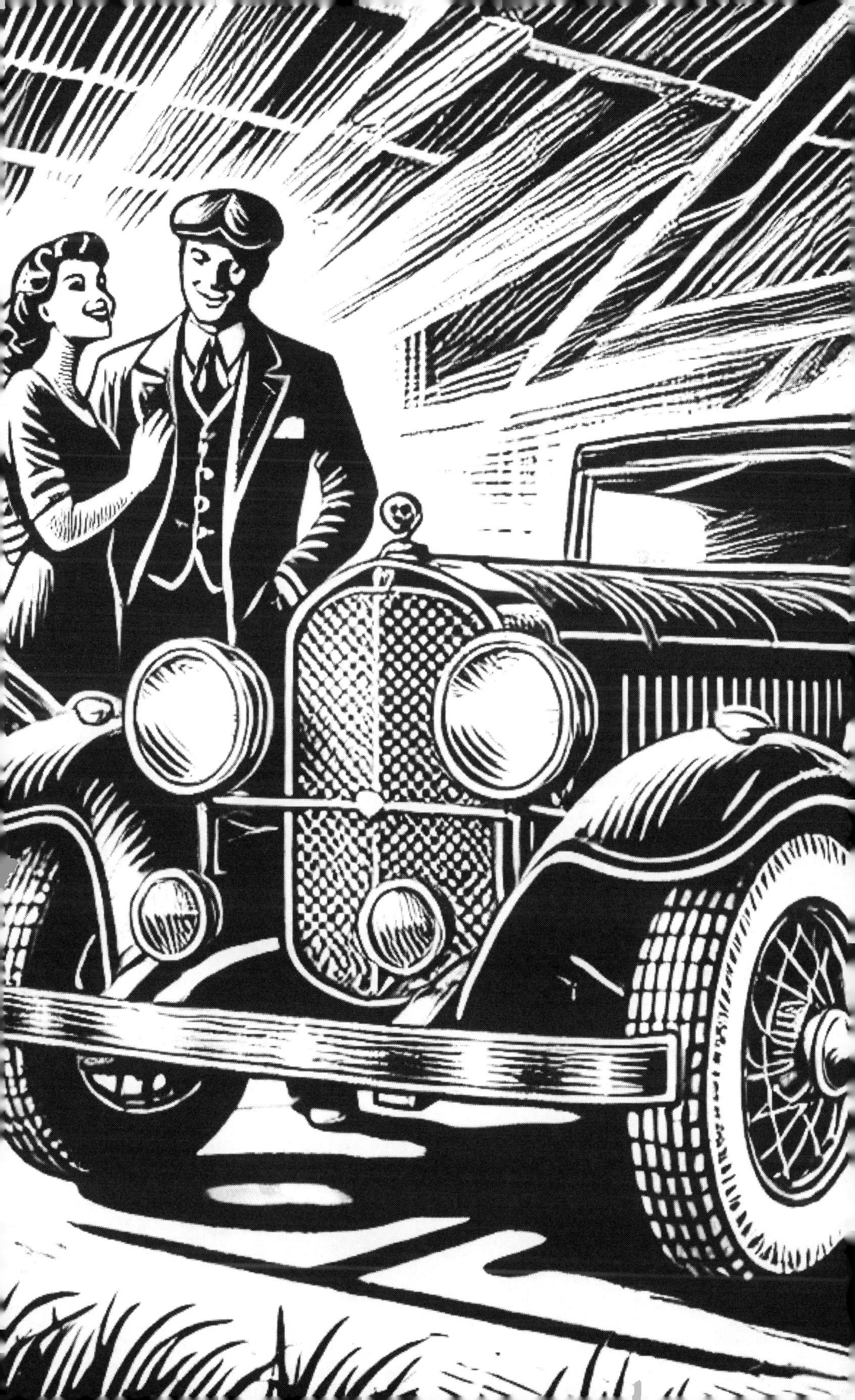

From Rust to Romance—
A New Car and a New Beginning

While we were working on our marriage paperwork, my car's license tags needed to be renewed, but first, it had to pass a safety inspection. Given the cracked windows and its general state of disrepair, I knew it would never pass, so I asked Hideko to accompany me to a junkyard to see about getting some replacement parts. The junkyard owner took one look at my car and asked if I was her boyfriend. Hideko quickly replied, "No, I'm just here to help translate." He told me he had a 1949 Ford with a good body and no cracked windows, but the engine was shot. He offered to transfer the engine and tires from my car into the '49 Ford for sixty dollars. Two days later, I picked up the newly assembled car. It wasn't perfect—it had patches of bodywork that needed painting—but it ran well.

I enlisted the help of a friend from the Division Surgeon's Office to help me paint the car. He brought over a gallon each of Navy gray and Air Force blue paint, along with two brushes. We spent a Saturday painting the car from top to bottom, fueled by a case of beer. We mixed the two colors in a large bucket, and while the paint job wasn't great up close (you could see every brush stroke), it looked decent from a distance. Best of all, it passed inspection, and I was able to renew the tags.

By mid-March, everything was falling into place. We told Father Dominic, and he scheduled a blessing of our marriage for 6:30 pm on March 18, 1965. Before that, we needed to complete the civil ceremony. On the morning of March 16, we went to city hall with our paperwork and were issued a marriage license.

There was no ceremony, but we were now legally married.

Next, we headed to the American Consulate, where the consul verified our marriage license to make it legal in the United States. Again, there was no ceremony, but the consul did shake our hands and say, "Congratulations." It was now lunchtime, and on the way back to the hospital, we stopped at a hotel for a quiet wedding lunch—just the two of us. Hideko had to work, so after lunch, we went home so she could change into her uniform. We had rented half of a small house the week before and had bought a few essentials—an electric hot plate, an electric skillet, a rice cooker, a futon, and some eating utensils. The house had cold running water in the kitchen but an outdoor toilet, similar to my childhood home in Stoutsville. After Hideko finished work, I picked her up and took her to Katy's house for the night, while I returned to the barracks. March 17 was her last day at work, and I was off the rest of the week, including Thursday and Friday.

BEAUTY SHOP

The Race to the Altar—A Wedding Day Full of Surprises

Finally, Wedding Day arrived—March 18. Our marriage was to be blessed at 6:30 pm at the church. Hideko went to the beauty shop at noon while I returned to the barracks to shower and get into my suit. My best man, Richard Mallea from the Division Surgeon's Office, and another friend, Jim Justice, were in charge of bringing Katy to meet us at the house at 6:00 pm. I had also gone to a restaurant near the church earlier in the day to arrange a modest dinner after the wedding. There were only going to be four of us at the dinner, but I wanted to make it special. At 6:00 pm, Richard, Jim, and Katy arrived at our house—but Hideko wasn't there yet. I told them to wait while I went to the beauty shop to check on her. On my way, I saw her in a taxi headed toward the house. I quickly made a U-turn and headed back home. She still needed to get into her wedding dress, and it was already 6:15!

Richard and I left for the church, while Jim and Katy stayed behind to help Hideko get ready. As I pulled into the church parking lot, I saw Father Dominic walking from the rectory to the chapel. He asked if we had already gone inside and were waiting for him, but I explained that Hideko was still getting ready. We were running a little late, but soon enough, she would arrive, and we'd be ready to begin our new life together.

Just then, Jim Justice's car pulled up, and there was Hideko, finally dressed in her wedding outfit. She had gotten dressed in the back seat of the car on her way to the church—something she had never done so fast before, and likely hasn't done that quickly since! She had spent the entire afternoon at her grandmother's house, trying to convince her grandmother and her two aunts to come to the wedding, but unfortunately, they declined.

Part 5

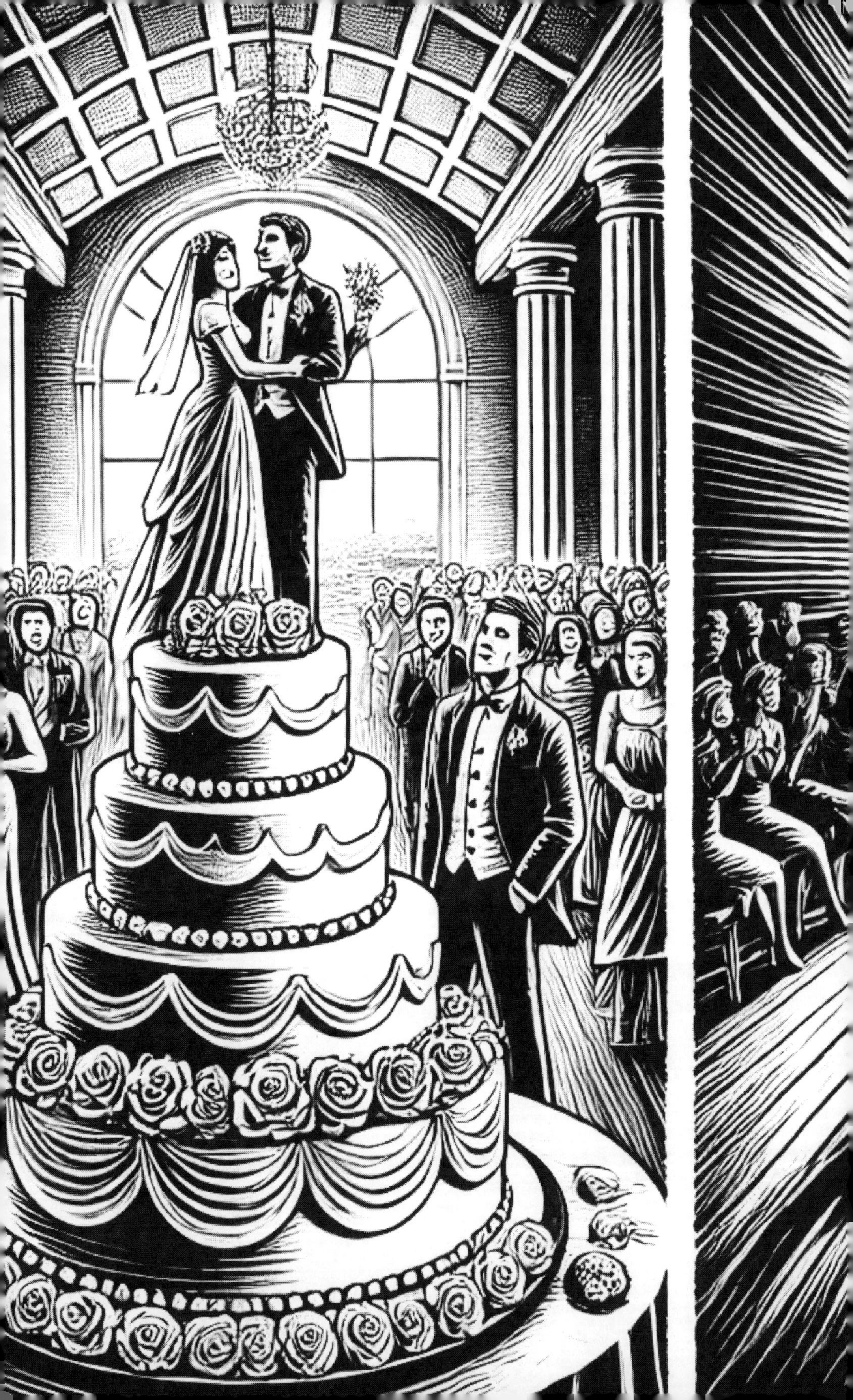

From Wedding Cake to Farewell Tears—A New Chapter Begin

The wedding ceremony went well, and the restaurant reception afterward went above and beyond what I had anticipated. They even had a small wedding cake prepared for us, which was a pleasant surprise.

By late April, Hideko started feeling sick, bothered by certain smells and vomiting frequently. A visit to an Okinawan OB-GYN confirmed what we both suspected: she was pregnant. Around the same time, I received orders to transfer from Okinawa to the 1st Marine Division at Camp Pendleton, California, and we were set to leave Okinawa in mid-May. We had our few possessions boxed up and shipped to Camp Pendleton, and in the days leading up to our departure, we moved into transient quarters.

A couple of days before our flight, we visited Hideko's grandmother and her aunts one last time. It was an emotional reunion for everyone, except for me. I didn't fully understand the tears and thought they were making Hideko cry, which irritated me a bit. But Hideko calmed me down, explaining that they were simply sad to see her leave. Her aunts promised they would come to Kadena Air Base to see us off.

There was only one task left—I needed to sell the car, and I only had one day to do it. The car had served us well, but with most of the Marines already deployed to Vietnam, it was tough to find a buyer. The used car and junk dealers weren't interested and offered as little as $20 or $30, which frustrated me. I was getting desperate, so I returned to a dealer who had offered me $30 previously.

When I walked in, the dealer was negotiating with a Marine Staff Sergeant about a car. The sergeant wanted to spend $60, but the dealer was asking for more. After listening for a while, I saw my chance and offered my car for $60. The sergeant looked out the window, asked how it ran, and suggested we take a ride. We only went a short distance before he said, "Deal." We went to the Army Hospital to have the title transfer witnessed, and just like that, the car was sold. The next day, we were at the departure terminal at Kadena, and as promised, Hideko's aunts came to see us off. They brought along food that Hideko could eat during the flight, knowing she was struggling with both air sickness and morning sickness.

A Flight of Firsts—Homecoming and New Beginnings

Our first stop was Travis Air Force Base in California, and from there, we took a bus to San Francisco Airport. The bus ride was a shock for both of us. On Okinawa, the speed limit was between 25 and 35 mph, but this bus was speeding along at over 60 mph. When we arrived at the airport, we needed to check in for our flight, which required us to go up a level. I grabbed our bags and hopped on the escalator without thinking much of it. When I reached the top, I looked back and saw Hideko still standing at the bottom, staring at the moving stairs. She had never seen an escalator before and wasn't sure how to step on it. I quickly went back down, helped her onto the escalator, and explained how to step off when she reached the top. She handled it beautifully, and before long, we were on our plane heading to Ohio.

When we landed at Columbus Airport, the whole family was there to meet us. The twins, who were now 8 years old, were especially excited because they knew I'd bring them something. After getting settled back in Lancaster, we handed out the gifts we brought from Okinawa. When I handed Mom her gift, I made a little joke, saying, "It's not much, but we'll give you a little more for Christmas." She didn't catch on at first, but when it finally hit her, she screamed with excitement.

We spent the next ten days visiting various relatives and enjoying being back in the States, knowing we had a new adventure ahead of us at Camp Pendleton. The first thing we needed to do was buy a car for our trip to California. While I had been saving money on Okinawa to buy a Datsun (now Nissan) sports car, we now needed something more practical—a family car. We settled on a Chevrolet four-door sedan.

Then, we set off for California via Route 40 to St. Louis, and from there, we continued on the famous Route 66. Traveling that same road brought back memories of my trip on this route three years earlier. It was a mix of nostalgia and excitement, as now I was traveling with Hideko and preparing for a new chapter of life.

A Long Journey Home—From Fallbrook to Fatherhood

We arrived in Fallbrook the day after Memorial Day and found a one-bedroom furnished apartment that we could rent on a weekly basis. Fallbrook was just outside the Naval Weapons Station, near Camp Pendleton. When I checked in at Camp Pendleton, I was assigned to the most remote unit on base—a 90-minute drive from where we were living. At the first chance I got, I started searching for an apartment in San Clemente, a small town just north of the base, to cut down on the commute. I ended up finding a place there and continued working in sick call, honing my skills in diagnosing and treating sick Marines. While living in San Clemente, we bought some used furniture, which we stored for future use.

Then, in early September, my unit was sent to Vietnam, and I was transferred to another unit located in the central part of Camp Pendleton—which, unfortunately, meant yet another long drive. To solve the commuting issue, I applied for and was granted base housing: a two-bedroom unit on the second floor. That used furniture we had bought came in handy, and we only needed to buy a crib and a chest of drawers for the baby, who was due in December.

Heartbeats and Hope—
The Arrival of Patrick Edward

In early December, during one of Hideko's prenatal checkups, the doctor had difficulty distinguishing the fetal heartbeat. A fetal EKG was done, and it was determined that the baby's heartbeat had slowed and was syncing with Hideko's. Because of this, she had to return to the clinic every day for an EKG until the baby's birth. Then, at 2:30 in the morning on December 16, Hideko woke me up to tell me she was having labor pains. I was relieved that we lived on base, just 10 minutes from the hospital. After she was admitted, I was told to go home and that they would call me once the baby was born—there wasn't much space in the waiting room for expectant fathers. It was still early in the morning, so I went home, got ready for work, and spent the entire day waiting for a phone call that never came.

On my way home from work, I stopped by the hospital to check on Hideko. She was still only having occasional contractions, but the hospital staff wanted to keep her due to the baby's slow heartbeat. I was allowed to see her for 10 minutes, and then I went home for the night. Finally, after 3 a.m. the following morning, I got the call—I was a father! Hideko had given birth to a 5-pound baby boy after a very difficult delivery that started the previous evening around 6 p.m. The doctor had considered performing a C-section, but the baby had already dropped into the birth canal, making the procedure unnecessary. We had already decided on the name Patrick Edward, in honor of Grandpa Hampp.

Patrick struggled to breathe when he was first delivered and had to stay in an incubator for five days before we could bring him home. Those first few days were tough—he cried a lot, and Hideko tried, unsuccessfully, to breastfeed. Eventually, I went to the store and bought formula and more bottles. Thanks to my previous experience and Navy training in infant care, I was able to step in and help care for Patrick. He thrived, and Hideko and I quickly adapted to parenthood.

By this time, I had received orders to attend a one-year cardiopulmonary school at the Naval Hospital in San Diego, California, starting in April 1966. We had a new chapter ahead of us, but we were ready for the challenges—and joys—that lay ahead.

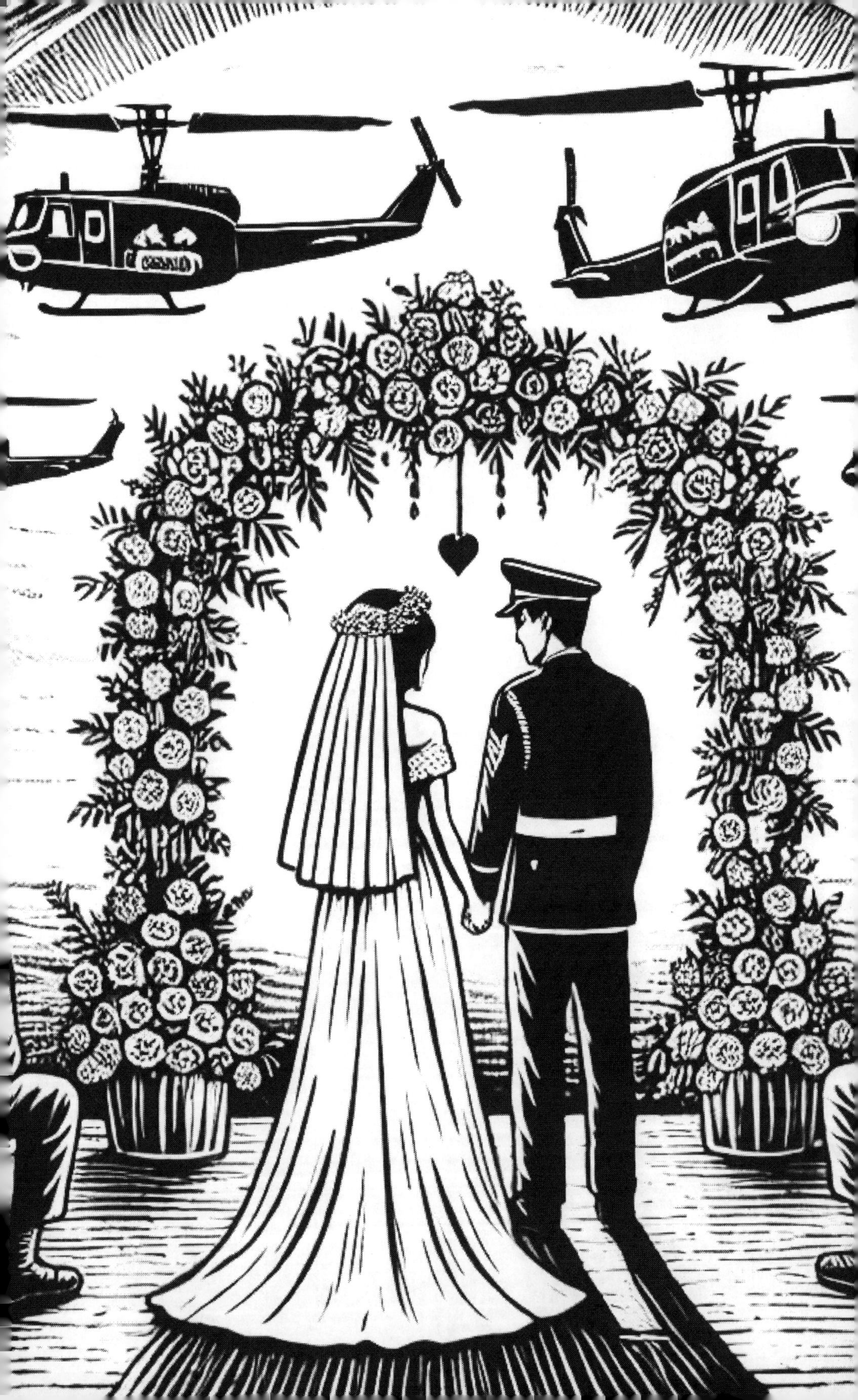

A Whirlwind Wedding—From Vietnam to Vows

My sister's boyfriend, Corporal Herman Tipple (we called him Butch), had just returned from Vietnam and was now stationed at Camp Pendleton, not far from where we lived. We reconnected and invited him over for dinner a few times. Since he didn't have a car, I always picked him up. It was about early March, and we had planned to have him over for dinner one last time before my transfer to San Diego. On the way back to our place, I casually mentioned, "I got a letter from Mom today. Vicki is pregnant."

There was a long silence. Then I asked, "What are you going to do about it?" Butch replied that they wanted to get married. Vicki was only 16 and wouldn't turn 17 until March 21. After thinking it through, I suggested that we drive across the country, spend a few days at home, and then Vicki could come back with us to California where they could get married.

The short time we spent in Ohio was a whirlwind of visiting relatives and showing off our new baby, who was now a healthy 3 months old. The drive back to California felt a lot like our trip 10 months earlier, except this time, the car was stuffed to the brim with gifts for Butch and Vicki. The trunk was full, and I had to buy a roof rack to carry the excess. Vicki barely had any space in the back seat!

We returned to San Diego a few days before I had to report to the hospital, in order to get Butch and Vicki married. Butch had already rented a furnished one-bedroom apartment in Oceanside and had taken a few days off work. The wedding was a small affair, with just Hideko and me in attendance. They were married in early April, and afterward, we wished them well, reminding them that we only lived a few miles away. Vicki would take the bus and visit us a few times, but Butch worked long hours on base, so she spent a lot of time alone.

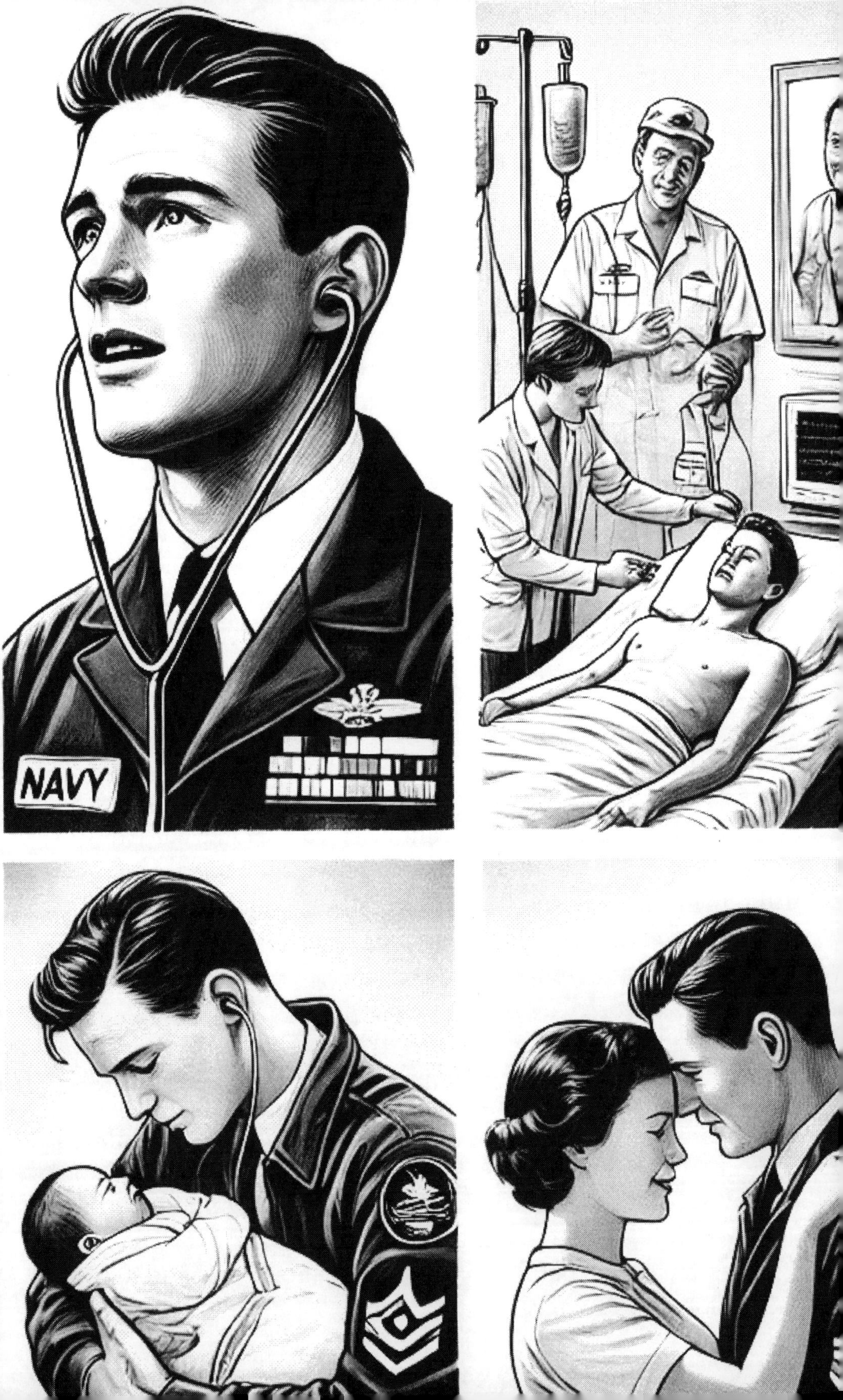
NAVY

Learning, Labor, and New Beginnings

I checked in at the Naval Hospital and began my training as a cardiopulmonary technician. The first four months were intense and strictly classroom-based: anatomy, acid-base chemistry, math, and even learning how to use a slide rule. It all made more sense to me than any previous classes because I could directly see how it applied to the human body. As time passed, we gradually transitioned into more practical work: EKG readings (my experience in Saigon came in handy), pulmonary function studies, drawing arterial blood for gas analysis, and respiratory therapy.

There were four students in the program when we started, so every fourth night I had to stay on board the hospital. One student quit in the fifth month, and another left in the seventh month, which left only two of us. This meant I had to stay on board every other night and every other weekend. It became stressful, and there were days when I felt completely overwhelmed. I remember calling Hideko one night, around the eighth or ninth month, telling her I wanted to quit. I don't remember exactly what she said, but whatever it was, it encouraged me to keep going. I went back to work the next day and pushed through. When I finished the program, I earned one year of college credit from San Diego State.

Meanwhile, Vicki was due in September 1966, and Mom took the train from Columbus to San Diego to stay with us for a few days. Butch and Vicki also came down to visit, and on Saturday, September 17, we all decided to take a trip to Tijuana, Mexico.

We parked on the U.S. side of the border and walked into Tijuana, spending the day sightseeing and exploring. When we returned home that evening, Vicki was feeling tired, so she and Butch went back to Oceanside.

Just a few hours later, Butch called. As soon as they got home, Vicki went into labor, and they barely had enough time to get her to the hospital before she delivered a son, Brian. The next day, I took Mom to Oceanside, and she stayed with Butch and Vicki until she flew back to Ohio two months later.

Before Mom left, Butch was transferred to the northernmost part of Camp Pendleton, the same place I had been when I first arrived in May 1965. They ended up moving to San Clemente, and Mom helped them with the move. Dad also took the train out to visit and meet the baby, but he only stayed for a week.

Upon graduation from cardiopulmonary school, I received orders for my next duty station: St. Albans Naval Hospital in Queens, New York City. We were about to embark on yet another adventure, but this time, it was back to the East Coast.

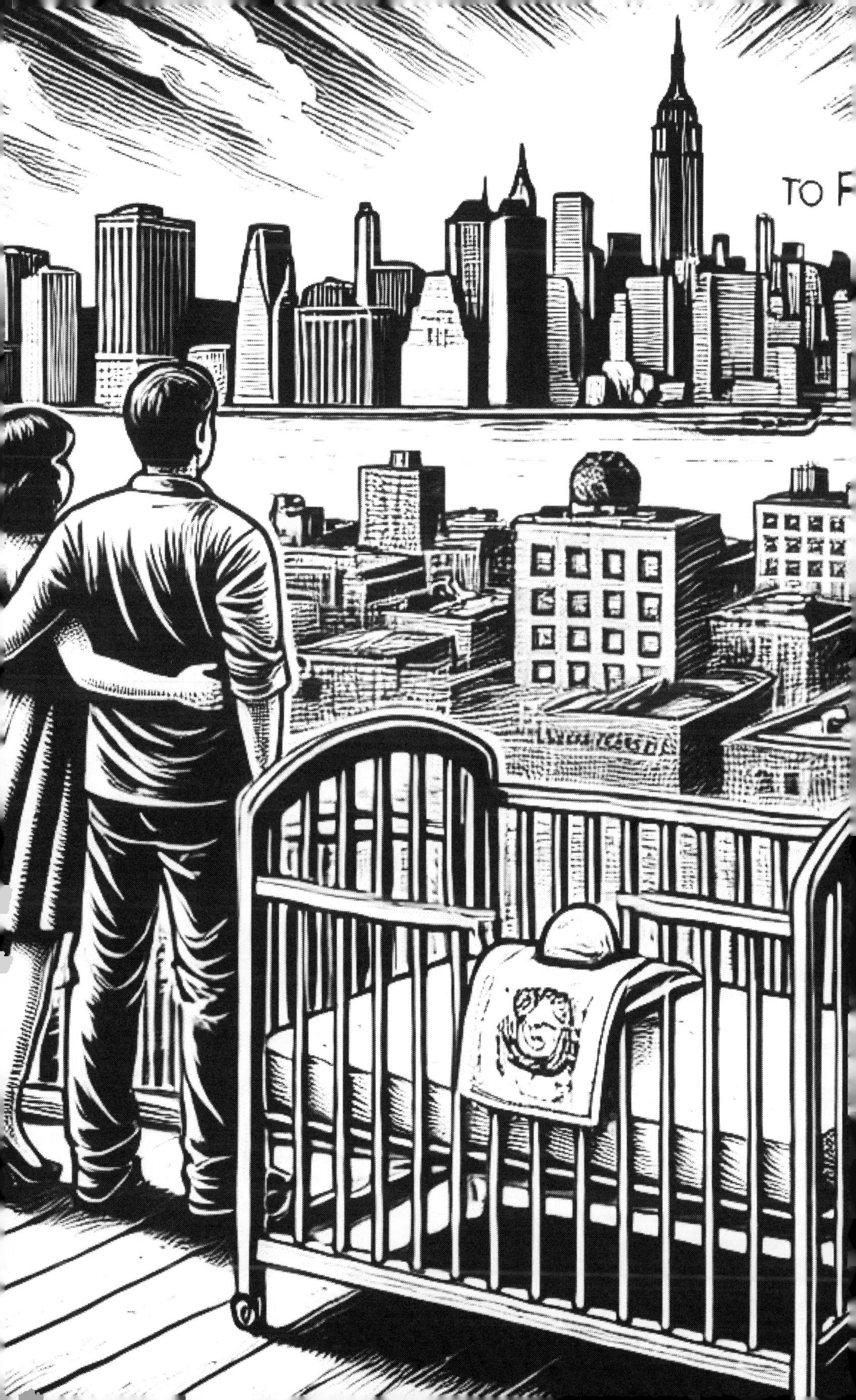
TO

From Crib on the Roof to Far Rockaway: Our New York Welcome

We were off on another cross-country trip, this time with a 16-month-old Patrick. He was such a good traveler, sleeping through most of the journey. By this point, we were done with sightseeing and focused on getting to New York as quickly as possible. I drove about 12 hours a day, with Patrick's crib tied to the roof of the car. Once again, the trunk and back seat were crammed full of our belongings.

We spent just a couple of weeks visiting family in Ohio before heading to New York. I was anxious to get settled in and start the next chapter of our lives. The drive to New York felt like a breeze compared to the long cross-country trips we had taken before. The first night, we stayed in a motel, and the next morning, I went to the St. Albans Naval Hospital—not to check in, but to see if there was any housing available. Unfortunately, there wasn't, so our best bet was to get a newspaper and check the want ads.

We spent the entire day calling and looking at apartments, but there was nothing within our budget. That night, we stayed in a motel near JFK Airport, and I was surprised that the constant traffic noise never let up, not even during the night. The next morning, I told Hideko that if we didn't find something that day, she and Patrick should fly back to Ohio until I could secure suitable housing.

Thankfully, by early afternoon, we found a small two-room furnished apartment in Far Rockaway for $75 a week, paid in advance. The building was an old Victorian house that had been converted into two-room apartments. The kitchen had a two-burner gas range, a small refrigerator, a small sink, and a tiny wooden table with two chairs. A single light bulb hung from the ceiling with a pull chain. It was basic, to say the least.

The bedroom had a full-size bed, which we had to push against the wall to make room for Patrick's crib mattress on the floor next to it. There was a chest of drawers at the foot of the bed, but in order to open the drawers, we had to sit on the bed because there wasn't enough space between the bed and the dresser. The bathroom situation was even more cramped—a small closet had been converted into a half bath with a tiny sink and a toilet. The toilet and sink were so close together that you had to sit on the toilet to use the sink. The full bath was upstairs, shared by all the other tenants in the building. Like the kitchen, the bedroom also had a single light bulb hanging from the ceiling.

We paid for one week and then headed to the grocery store to buy cleaning supplies and some food. When we reached the checkout, after paying, I asked the clerk if someone would bag our groceries. She sarcastically replied, "If you want bags, you'll have to do it yourself—they're your groceries!" All I could say was, "Welcome to New York."

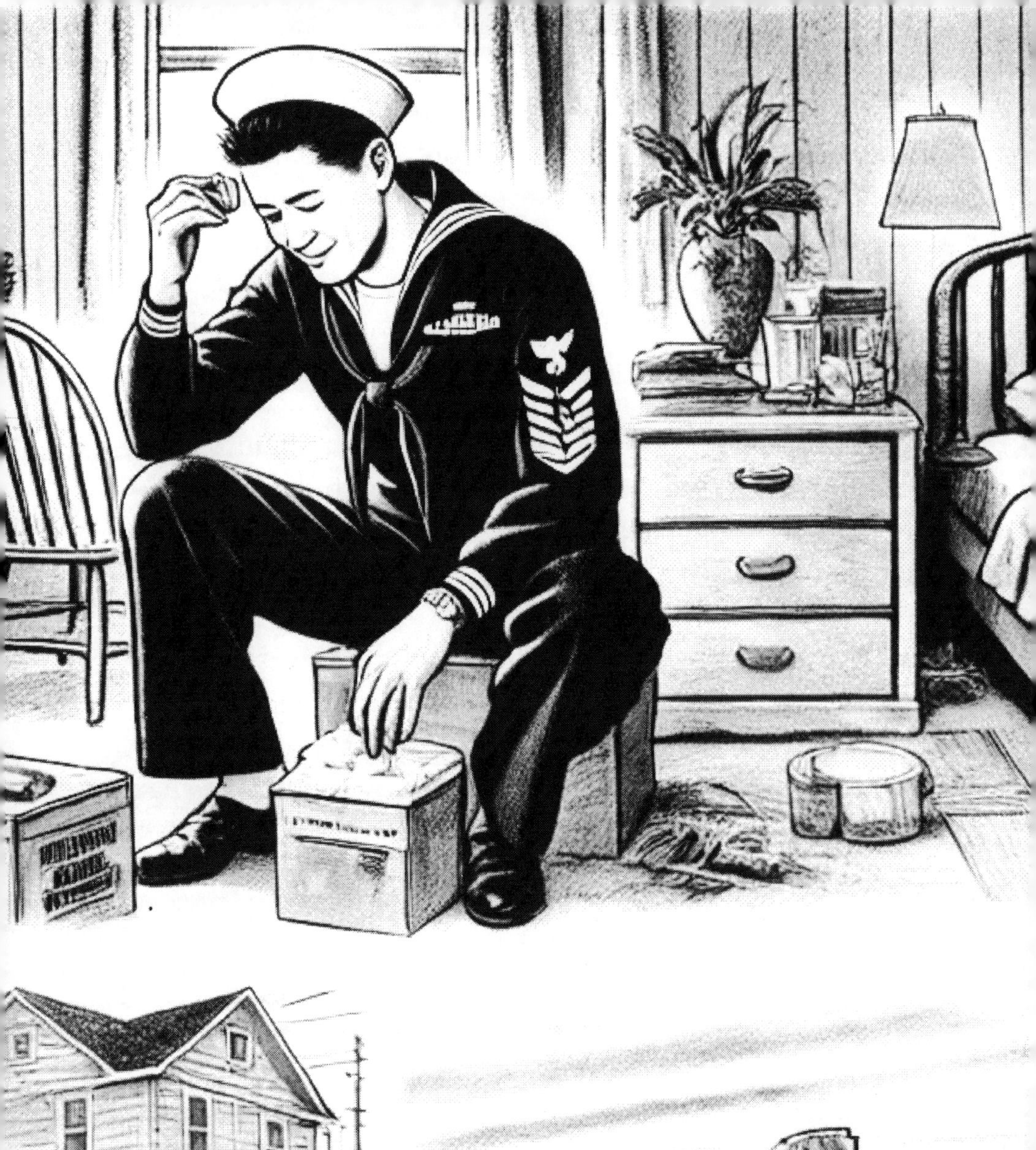
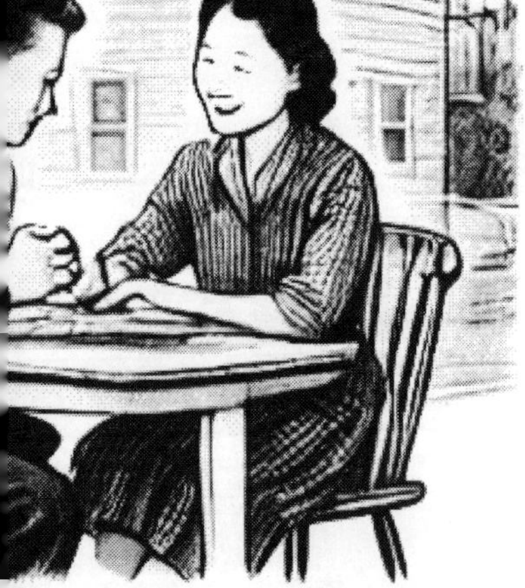
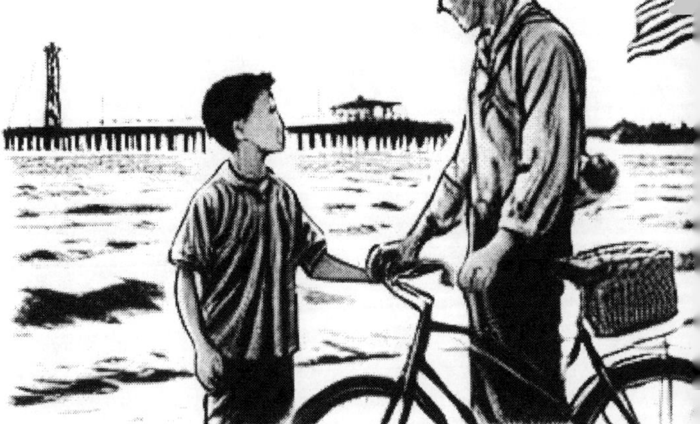

Turning Tears into Hope: A Fresh Start in Long Island

Back at the apartment, Hideko tackled cleaning the bathroom while I took on the kitchen. The first thing I did was seal up all the cracks around the closet door with masking tape. The closet was so full of trash and clutter that I wasn't even going to try to clean it out. By the time we were done cleaning, Hideko made us a simple supper, and it was already bedtime.

That night, I sat on the bed and cried. I apologized to Hideko, feeling so inadequate as a husband and father. The tiny, rundown apartment we had found was not the life I had envisioned for our little family, and I felt like I had let them down. But Hideko, ever patient and kind, reassured me that we would make the best of it. We were together, and that was all that mattered.

The house was only two short blocks from the beach, so the next day, Hideko and Patrick took a walk on the boardwalk while I went to the hospital to report for duty. The first thing I did was put my name on the military housing list and then report to the cardiopulmonary laboratory. There was only one other school-trained technician assigned to the lab, Russ, along with four corpsmen who were being trained on the job. Russ was a native New Yorker, standing about six-foot-six, with a personality to match his height. Although I outranked him, Russ wasn't about to let anyone interfere with how he ran the lab.

Consequently, I spent the first six months of my tour as more of an observer, watching the four trainees.

Early in my second week at the hospital, I received notification that military housing was available in East Meadow, Long Island. The apartment was a 45-minute drive from the hospital, and although our furniture, which we had shipped from San Diego, wouldn't arrive for another week, I jumped at the chance to get Hideko and Patrick out of Far Rockaway. Sleeping on the floor in military housing was still better than the cramped, run-down apartment we had been living in.

Unexpected Blessings and Shifting Roles: A New Year in New York

Hideko, having had such a difficult labor with Patrick's birth, had said she didn't want any more children. Nevertheless, by September 1967, she was pregnant again. When I wasn't on duty, we spent our weekends sightseeing in New York City. Living in military housing was a blessing, as we could always trust a neighbor to babysit, and we took full advantage of every opportunity to explore the city together.

The apartment itself wasn't much. It was built quickly after World War II for military families and was cheaply made, with walls so thin that we could hear our neighbors arguing next door. But Hideko and I were still in the honeymoon phase of our marriage, and we almost never fought—or at least, not in a way our neighbors could hear!

Right after Thanksgiving 1967, I was assigned to night duty at the hospital's front information desk. It wasn't ideal, but I hadn't been doing much in the cardiopulmonary lab anyway. I finished my night duty just before Christmas, and we went to Ohio to spend the holidays with family.

After returning to the lab in the new year, I quickly realized that nothing had changed—I still didn't have much to contribute. Frustrated, I went to the doctor in charge and asked to be transferred to the surgical research lab, where they were doing work similar to the cardiopulmonary lab. Despite my request, I wasn't transferred. Instead, from that point forward, I was put in charge of the cardiopulmonary lab—definitely not what I had in mind.

The next day, Russ was called to the doctor's office and told he was being transferred to surgical research. He wasn't happy about it, especially since he had hoped to stick around long enough to watch me fail. In a last-ditch effort to make things difficult for me, Russ took all the technical manuals for the equipment we used. When I informed the doctor, he didn't want to get involved in a dispute, so he told me to order new ones, which I did. The trainees, however, were thrilled to see Russ go—he had been difficult to work with.

New Beginnings: Welcoming Chiemi and Building Our Future

Finally, I was able to put my training to use. Things went smoother than I anticipated, and morale in the lab improved dramatically. It was about 4:30 in the morning on June 9, 1968, when Hideko woke me, saying she was having labor pains. I quickly got dressed, got Patrick ready, and we rushed to the hospital. What usually took me 45 minutes to drive, I managed to cover in under 30 minutes. Patrick and I sat in the waiting room until about 9:00 a.m., when a nurse came out to tell us that Hideko hadn't progressed much. She offered us the option to go home and wait for a call after the delivery, which we did.

Shortly after 2:00 p.m., I received a call letting me know I had a daughter. I left Patrick with a neighbor and rushed back to the hospital to see Hideko and meet Chiemi. Thankfully, Hideko hadn't experienced any of the complications that had made Patrick's birth so difficult, and both mother and baby were doing well.

Around this time, cardiopulmonary/respiratory therapy technicians were in high demand at civilian hospitals. I managed to secure a part-time job at Booth Memorial Hospital in Queens, working a couple of evenings a week and being on call every other weekend. The pay was good, and we were able to save enough money for a down payment on a house.

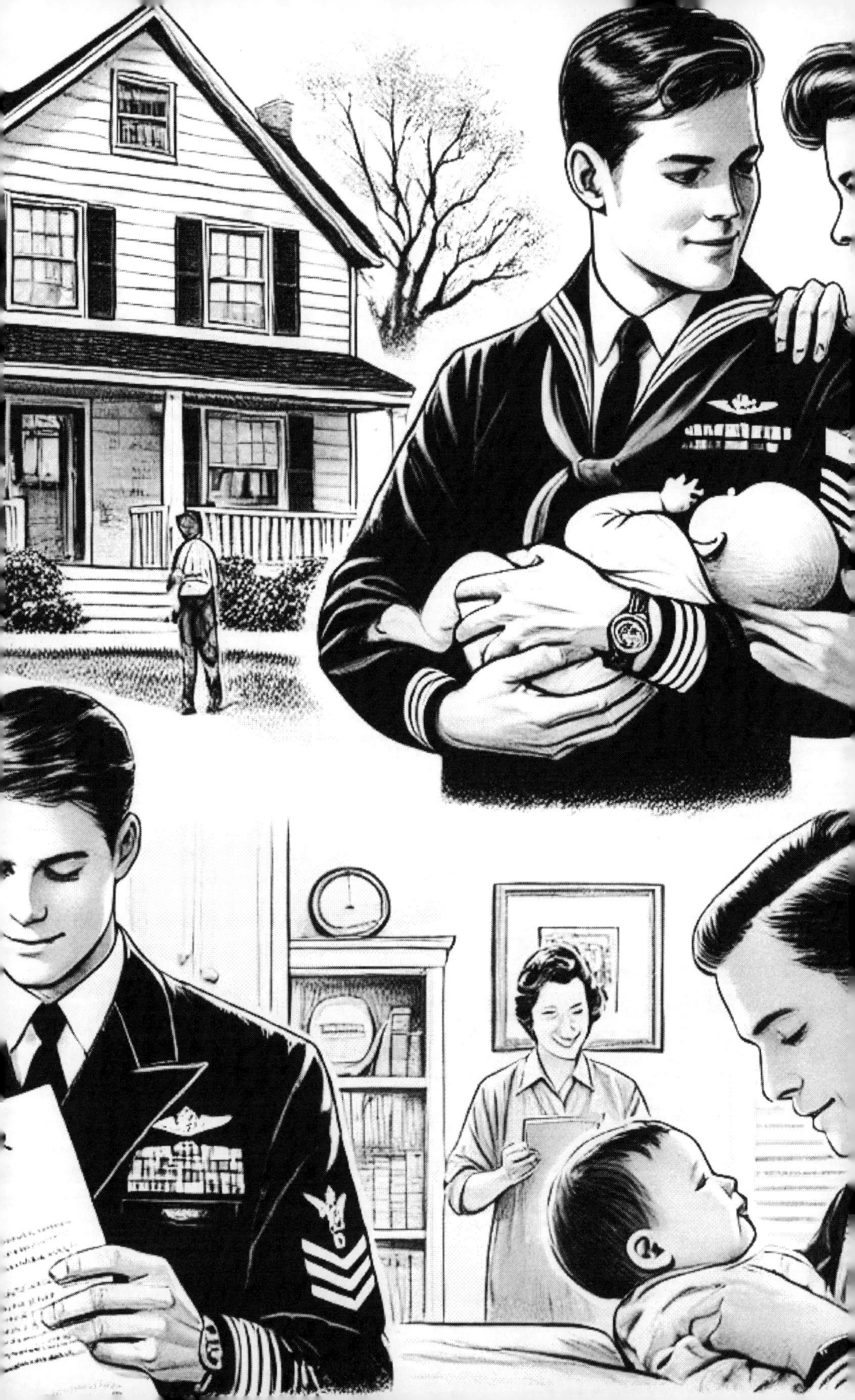

From New York to Ohio: A Home Before Vietnam

In September, I received orders to the 1st Marine Division in Danang, Vietnam, and was to report by the end of December 1968. Knowing we would need more savings before the move, I continued working at Booth Memorial Hospital to build up our funds.

In early November, I called Mom and asked her to set up an appointment with a realtor for Veterans Day weekend so we could look at houses while we were in Ohio. The plan was to drive out on Friday, spend Saturday and Sunday looking at homes, and drive back on Monday. And that's exactly what we did!

We ended up looking at about half a dozen houses on Saturday and made an offer on one that was accepted. The closing was set for the Friday after Thanksgiving. I was transferred from the hospital the day before Thanksgiving, and for once, things seemed to be going smoothly. Hideko was successfully breastfeeding Chiemi, and both children were thriving. I even received a letter of commendation from the Navy Hospital Commanding Officer for my work at the Cardiopulmonary Laboratory.

Though I wasn't looking forward to being separated from my family, I was relieved to be leaving New York. Before we left, our furniture and belongings had been shipped to our new address in Ohio, with a delivery date of December 2. I didn't know what we would have done if the closing hadn't happened on time.

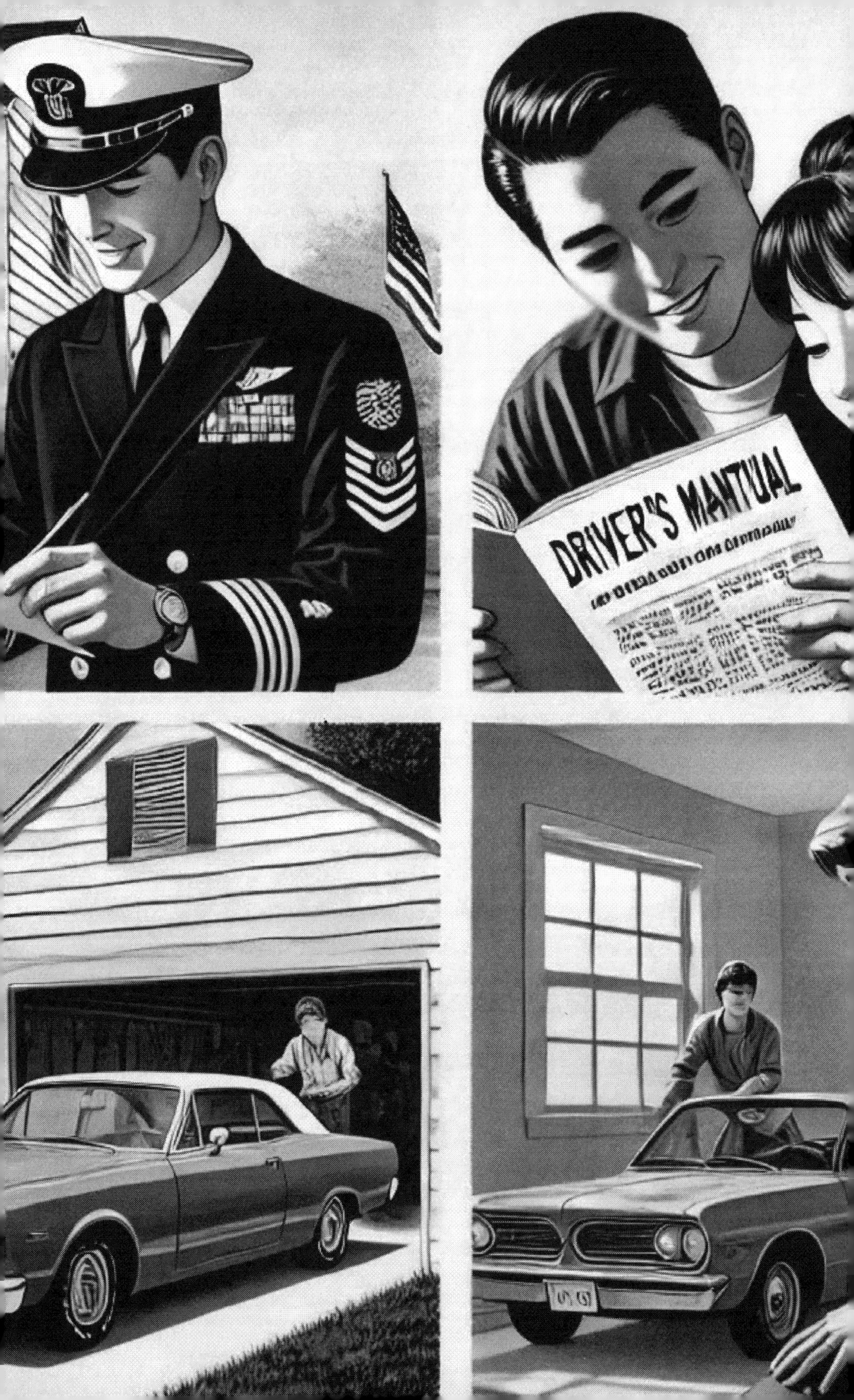
DRIVER'S MANUAL

A New Home and New Beginnings: Prepping for Vietnam and Life on the Home Front

Our new house was fairly new, with three bedrooms, one bath, a separate laundry room, a large living room, and a spacious kitchen/dining area. It even had a one-car garage. It felt like a dream come true for our growing family. Even though the house was in the middle of the block, the bus would stop if you signaled the driver—a blessing, since Hideko didn't have a driver's license yet. I had tried, unsuccessfully, to teach her to drive while we were at Camp Pendleton, but now she could use the bus to take the kids to visit my parents.

Before I left for Vietnam, I took Hideko to the Driver's License Bureau to pick up a copy of the Ohio Rules and Regulations for drivers. She sat down and translated the entire book into Japanese to make it easier for her to study. A few days later, I took her back for her to take the test for her temporary permit, which she passed on her first try.

While we were living in New York, I had been in a car accident, which resulted in us trading in our 1965 Chevy for a 1968 Plymouth Barracuda. It was a two-door, sporty car, but still big enough for our family. Although Hideko couldn't drive yet, I told her to back it out of the garage once a week and let it run for about 15 minutes to keep the battery charged. Before I left, we had arranged for her to start driving lessons in January.

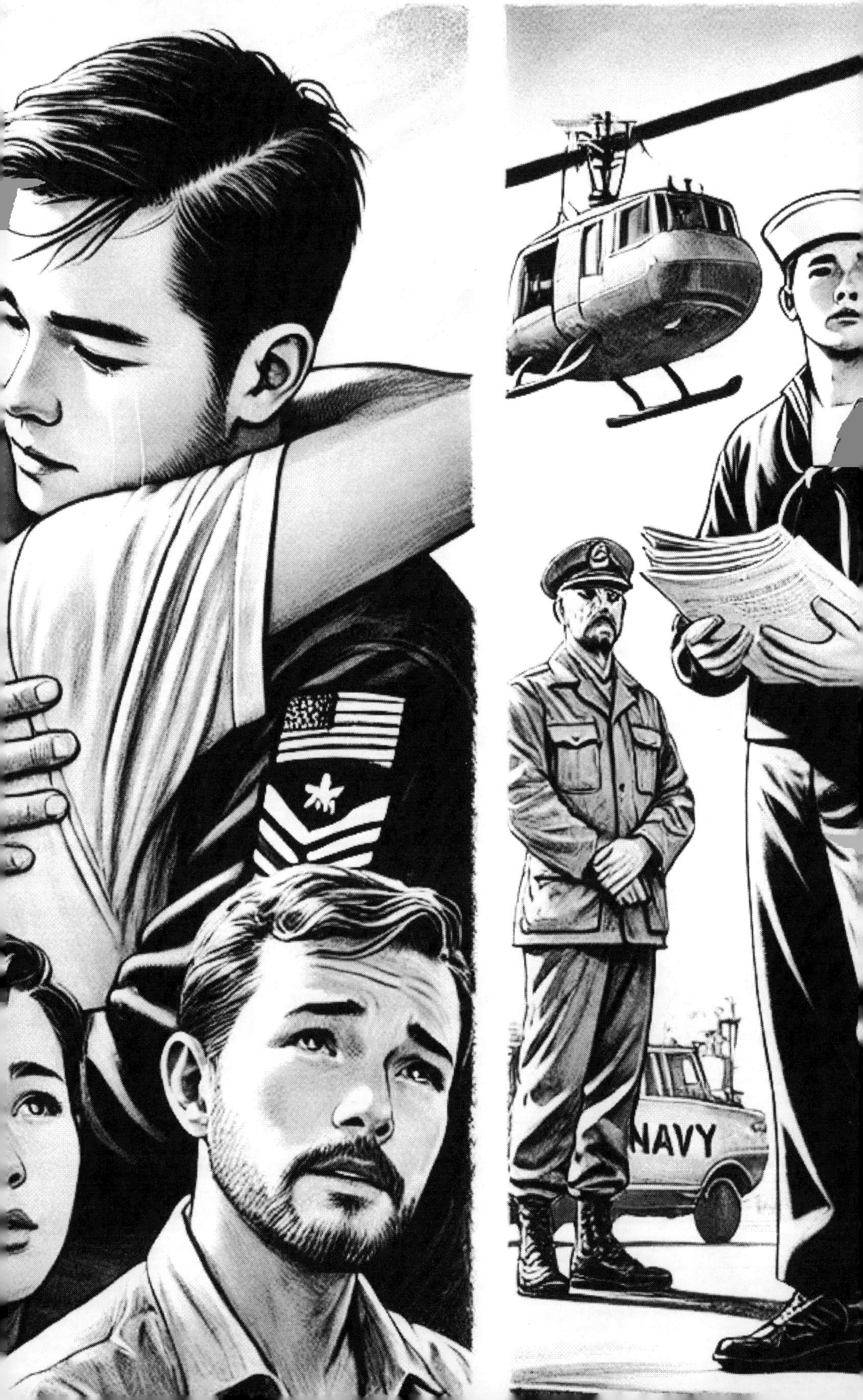
NAVY

Farewell Hugs and New Frontiers: Off to Vietnam

December seemed to fly by, and before I knew it, it was time for me to head to Travis Air Force Base in California for my flight to Vietnam. On the morning I left, the Barracuda was safely parked in the garage, and Tator had taken us all to my parents' house so I could say my goodbyes. I'll never forget that moment. Dad did something he had never done in his life—he gave me a hug. I was so shocked that I just hugged him back, savoring the rare gesture. Tator then drove me to Columbus Airport, while Hideko and the kids stayed with my parents. I departed for Vietnam on December 27, 1968.

Unlike my previous flights to Vietnam, this one was a direct flight from California to Da Nang. Upon arrival, I was greeted by someone from the Division Surgeon's Office. When they saw from my record that I was a cardiopulmonary technician, they immediately determined that I needed to be assigned to the Medical Battalion. I remembered what the Commanding Officer at Saint Albans had told me when he presented me with the commendation letter: "If you get assigned to anything other than cardiopulmonary work, let me know immediately." The Navy had a rule that school-trained technicians had to work in their field of training, and I wasn't going to let that slip through the cracks.

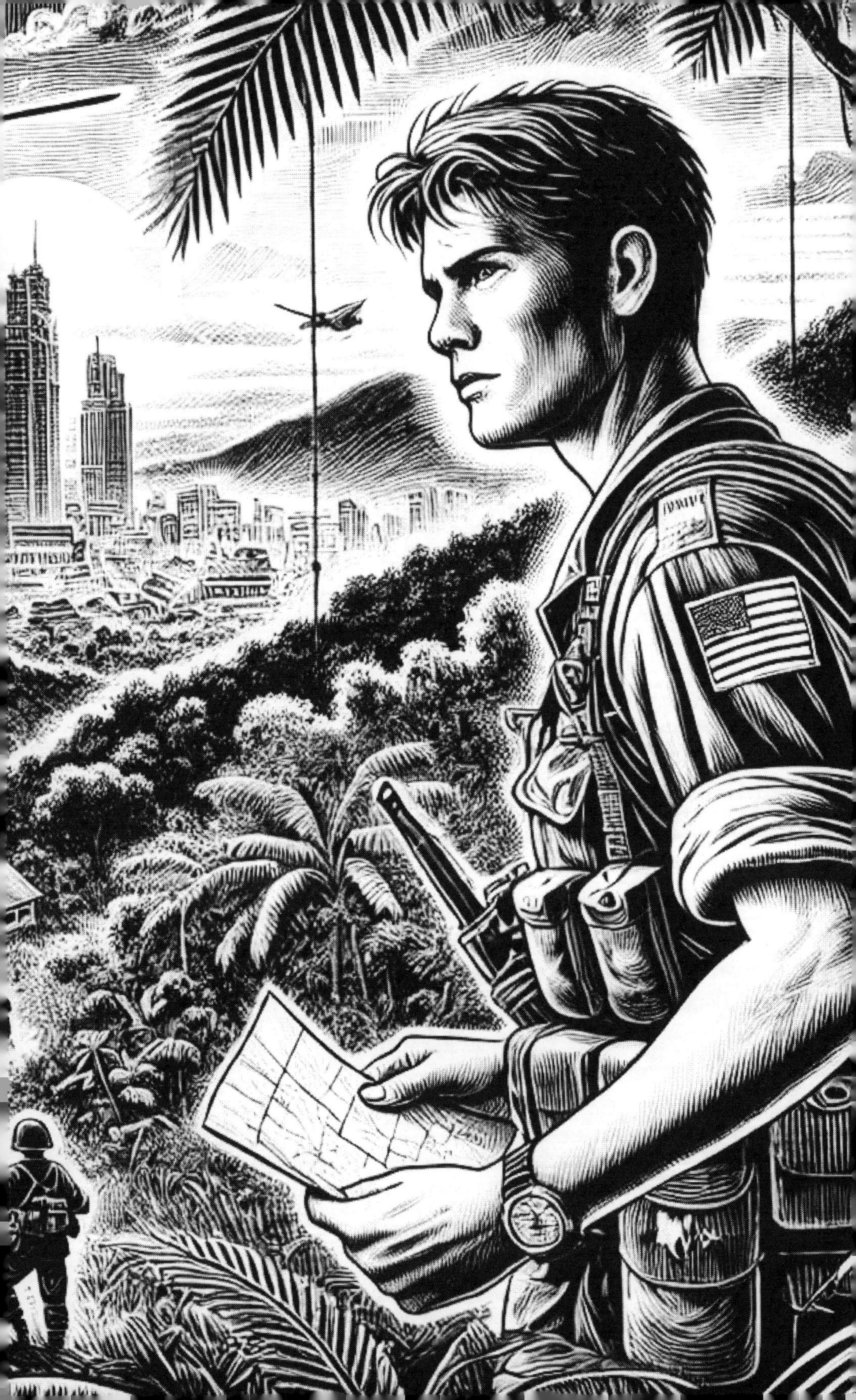

From New York to the Boondocks: Navigating a New Role in Vietnam

When I checked in at Medical Battalion, I was given the choice of two jobs. One was to be the Petty Officer in Charge at AN HOA Battalion Aid Station, about 10 miles out in the boondocks. The other was to be the Chief Medical Regulator at the Naval Support Hospital (NSA), located across from the Marine Corps Helicopter Landing Strip. Curious, I asked what the medical regulator's job involved. They explained that I would be in constant radio contact with both Army and Marine medevac helicopters and would determine which medical facility was best equipped to handle the wounded on board.

I had no experience operating a two-way radio, but after years in the Navy, I had learned the "see one, do one" approach to just about anything. It was getting late in the day, so they assigned me a bunk for the night. Tomorrow, someone would take me to my new job. The bunk was one of eight canvas cots in a building with a wooden floor, screen walls, and a metal roof.

By 10 PM, I was already asleep when the crack of rifle fire woke me, echoing just inches from my head. I instinctively rolled out of bed and tried to flatten myself as much as possible on the floor, heart racing. I could hear voices, but nothing made sense in the chaos. After what felt like an eternity of lying still, nothing else happened, so I cautiously climbed back into bed. The next morning, I learned that a junior corpsman had been reprimanded by the First Sergeant the day before and had come back with the intention of shooting him. Thankfully, no one had been in the building next to mine where the shooting had occurred. The corpsman was picked up in a local village the next day and placed in the brig, pending court-martial.

This wasn't cardiopulmonary work, but it was a far cry better than living in New York, so I didn't say a word. However, the job turned out to be more complex than I had initially been led to believe. There were three radios constantly running, and I had to keep track of multiple medical facilities: the Naval Hospital where I was stationed, the First Medical Battalion about 5 miles west, the Army 95th Evac Hospital 3 miles north, the Vietnamese Army (ARVN) Hospital, and one of the two Navy Hospital Ships—either the USS Sanctuary or the USS Repose, depending on which was on station.

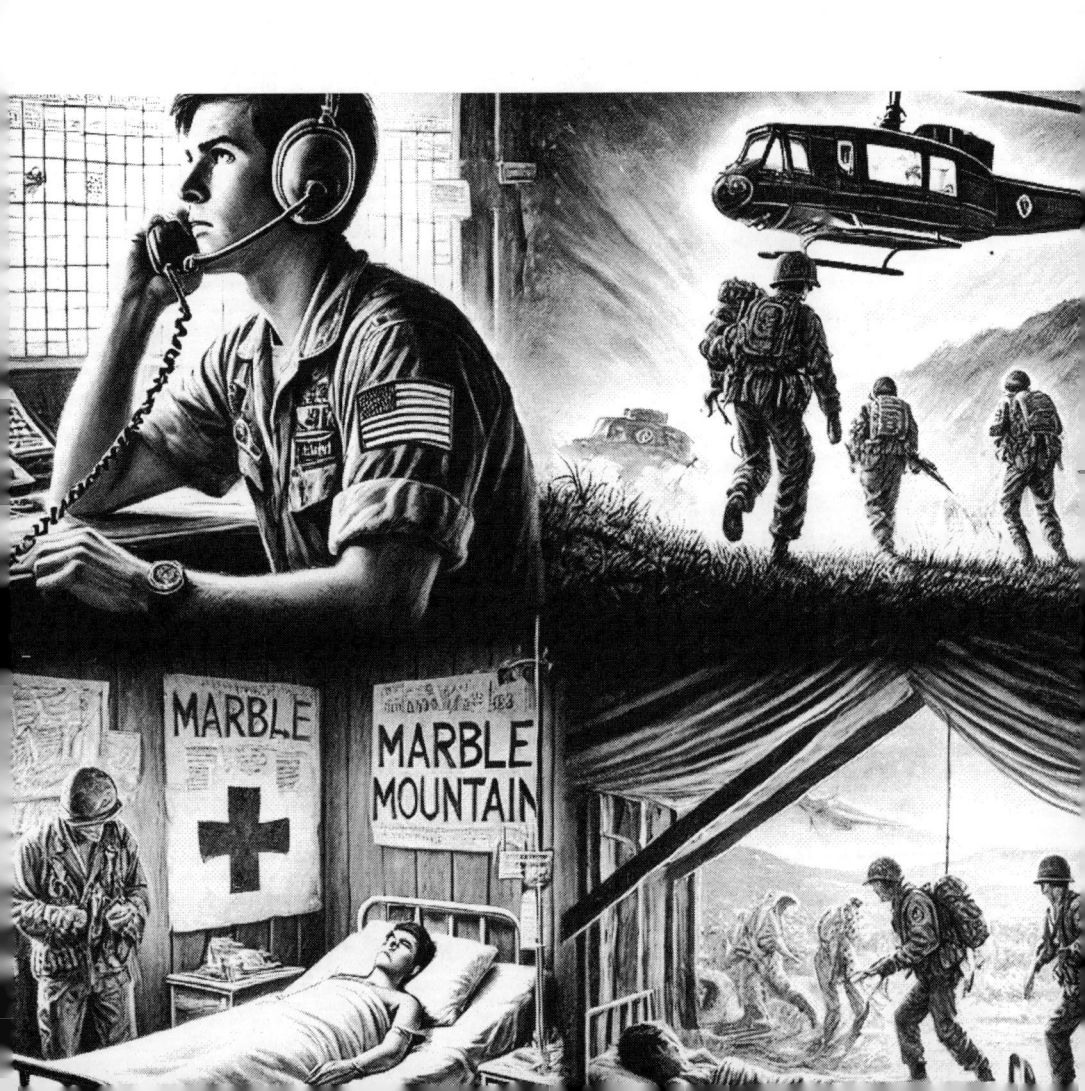

Under Fire and on Duty: Life Beside Marble Mountain

The radio room was a small, 8-foot square space with a tiny window overlooking the hospital's landing pad. One wall was dominated by a massive plexiglass-covered status board that listed each medical facility, the types of wounded they could handle, the number of operating rooms available, and those already in use. My workday stretched from 7 AM to 7 PM, seven days a week, with an occasional Sunday afternoon off.

What no one had mentioned was that the hospital and the Marine Corps Landing Strip were located just north of a place called Marble Mountain—a cluster of five limestone and marble mountains filled with tunnels, occupied by the North Vietnamese Army. In the early evening, Marine helicopter gunships would circle the mountain, spraying it with machine gun fire. Every fifth bullet was a tracer round, glowing red, which from the ground looked like a solid stream of light shooting through the sky.

Almost every night, between midnight and 2 AM, the North Vietnamese would fire rockets and mortar rounds at the Marine Air Base and the hospital. The air raid sirens would blare, and I would scramble for my flak jacket and helmet, running to the nearest bunker in just my shoes and skivvies. The hospital itself was a series of Quonset huts connected by paved walkways. During these attacks, patients who could walk would join us in the bunkers. Those who couldn't were laid on the floor beneath their beds for protection. It was a surreal routine—moments of calm punctuated by sudden chaos—but it quickly became our new normal.

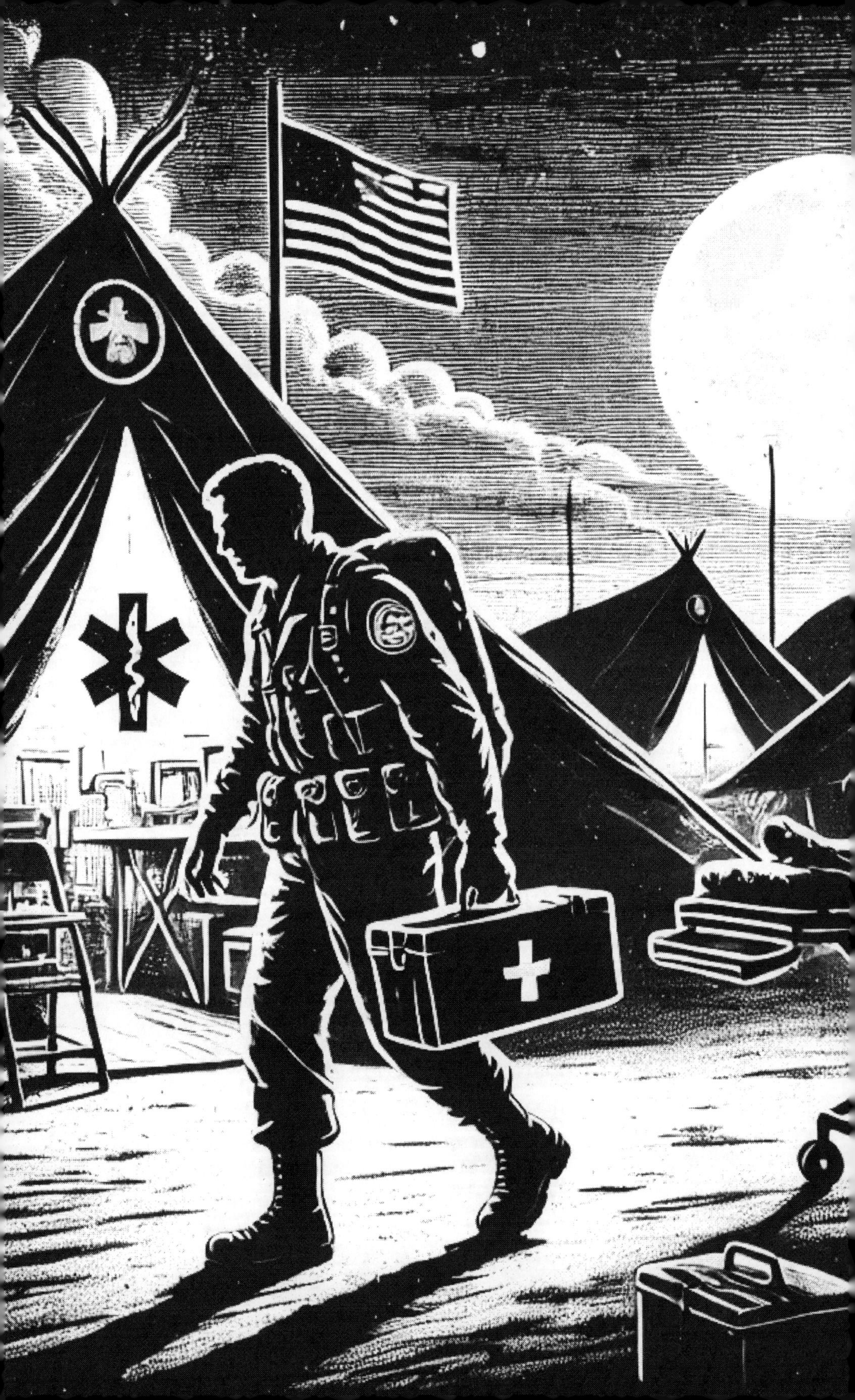

Night Shifts and Narrow Escapes: Life at the 95th Evac

In the mornings, the Explosive Ordnance team would sweep the hospital grounds, searching for unexploded shells. It became a routine part of life at the NSA hospital—a sobering reminder of how close danger always was. There was always a corpsman aboard the medevac helicopters, providing emergency treatment to the patients. I was told early on not to think of the individuals being medevaced, but instead to focus solely on the types of wounds needing treatment. Each facility had different capabilities, and not every one could handle every injury. For instance, Marines killed in action (KIA) had to be sent to First Medical Battalion, while only the hospital ships or the NSA hospital had neurosurgeons on board.

When a helicopter was inbound to my location, I would call triage and let them know the number and types of wounded they should expect. I stayed at the NSA hospital for six months before the entire operation was transferred to the 95th Evacuation Hospital, located on the beach just north of Da Nang. This time, the whole communications section was set up in a newly built bunker on the beach. The bunker had massive walls and a roof stacked with six feet of sandbags.

My shift changed to nights—7 PM to 7 AM. There was less helicopter traffic at night, but I had a new task: contacting Washington every night to get the destination hospitals for patients being flown out for further treatment. I worked alongside Frank Lewis, a junior corpsman. We usually had everything completed within six or seven hours, leaving the rest of the night to play cards or Monopoly. It was a strange existence—quiet nights in the bunker, broken only by the occasional radio call.

Unlike at the Navy hospital, we didn't live at the 95th Evac. Instead, we stayed at the 3rd Marine Amphibious Force (3 MAF) compound, about five miles away. We were provided a jeep for transportation, and the day crew would drive it back to 3 MAF Headquarters after our shift. There was a particular village we passed through every night, and it wasn't uncommon to hear small arms fire as we drove by. One night, a bullet actually passed through the windshield—right between Frank and me! I instinctively tried to make myself as small as possible, crouching down on the floorboard while Frank was driving. He just laughed and told me to get back in my seat.

Countdown to Freedom: Final Days at Saint Albans

As New Year's Eve approached, we decided to have a small party. The Christmas tree was still up in the house, so we gathered everyone for some food, drinks, and dancing. For a few hours, I could forget about the war and the constant threat of incoming fire. It was a nice break.

I had only nine months left on my enlistment, and I didn't want to uproot the family to New York again. Hideko and I agreed that she and the kids would stay in Ohio while I served out my time in New York. I had a feeling that if I went back to Vietnam, I wouldn't be coming home alive. Too many men I knew, men whose faces and names I remembered, hadn't made it back. We decided that I would spend my time in New York alone, flying home for long weekends while Hideko and the kids stayed with family.

I reported to Saint Albans Naval Hospital on January 30, 1970, only to be shocked by the news that they no longer had a cardiopulmonary lab. I couldn't believe it. "Why am I here?" was the question that kept running through my mind. Instead, I was assigned to the medical records section, responsible for scheduling physicals and processing records.

Around this time, President Nixon announced plans to reduce the size of the active-duty military. Personnel could be discharged up to three months early if they desired. My official discharge date was set for September 17, but I applied for early release.

Despite the bureaucratic shifts, there were moments of excitement. At one point, there was a rumor that President Nixon himself might visit the hospital. We were told to get everything cleaned and ready for the visit. ICU never looked better—everything was spotless, and morale was high, even if only for a few hours. Unfortunately, for security reasons, no one ever came.

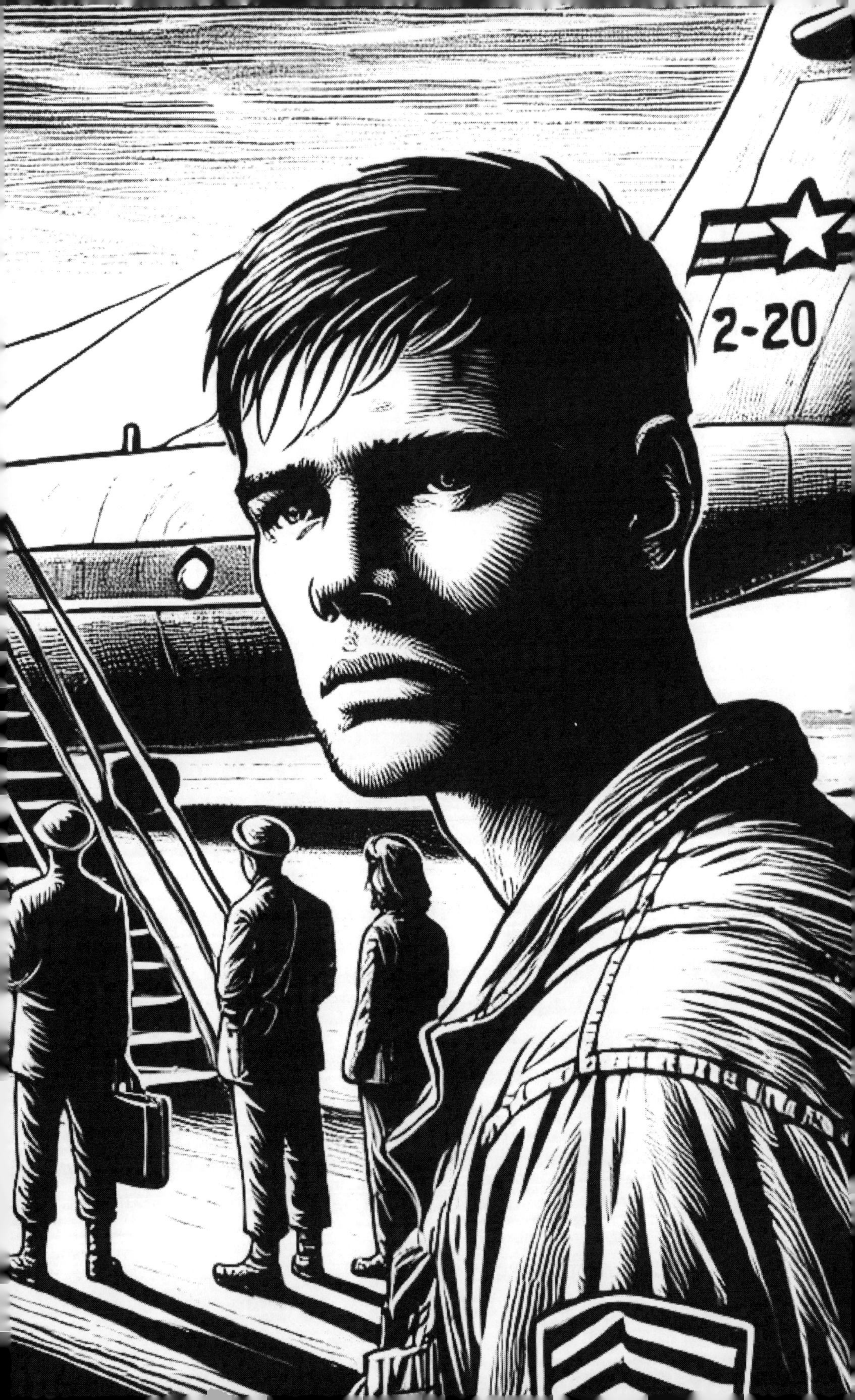
2-20

Unwelcome Home: The Final Flight from Vietnam

Finally, I received my transfer orders, and my departure date was set for December 27. I was to fly to Okinawa for three days of processing and then on to Edwards Air Force Base in southern California. I was grateful for the stop in Okinawa—it gave me one last chance to visit Hideko's grandmother. Saying goodbye to her was as tear-filled as ever, but this time, some of the tears were mine too.

I landed at Edwards Air Force Base on December 30 and took a bus to Los Angeles Airport for my flight back to Ohio. Of course, I was in my uniform, and while waiting for my flight, a hippie-looking guy approached me. He asked if I had just come from Vietnam. I responded with a simple "yes," and then he hit me with, "How many babies did you kill?" I was stunned, caught off guard by his hostility. All I could say was, "Get away from me, man." I had not expected a welcome home like this.

Homecoming Reflections: A Year Lost, A Life Rebuilt

That year in Vietnam now seemed like a lifetime ago. Patrick was now 4 ½, and Chiemi was 1 ½. I had missed so much over the past year. Hideko had done an outstanding job managing our finances, keeping the house in order, and taking care of everything in my absence. I didn't tell her outright, but I was incredibly proud of how she had handled it all.

Even while I was gone, life moved forward. Tator had gotten married, and Patrick had been the ring bearer at the wedding. Friends and their families stopped by the house on their way to new duty stations, and Hideko welcomed them, handling it all with grace. She truly was amazing.

It was around this time that I received my next set of orders. I was to be stationed at Saint Albans Naval Hospital in New York. There was no way I wanted to go back there. After spending nights calling Washington during my time in Vietnam, I had learned how to navigate the phone system, so I tried calling the Corpsmen Detailer to see if I could be transferred anywhere else. But no matter how much I pleaded, the answer was a flat no. I was to report to Saint Albans by the end of January 1970.

Meanwhile, the number of troops in Vietnam was being reduced, and more and more corpsmen were being sent home early. Day after day, I seemed to be losing coworkers. I had hoped to be transferred before Christmas, but no such luck. We had heard that Bob Hope was scheduled to come to Vietnam that Christmas, performing just a few miles down the road from Medical Battalion. It was rumored that he always stopped by to see the worst of the wounded, and we thought maybe he would come to our battalion. We spent half a day preparing 60 beds, getting everything cleaned and ready. We were so sure he'd stop by, but for security reasons, it never happened. Still, for a few hours, morale was high, and the ICU looked better than ever.

Part 6

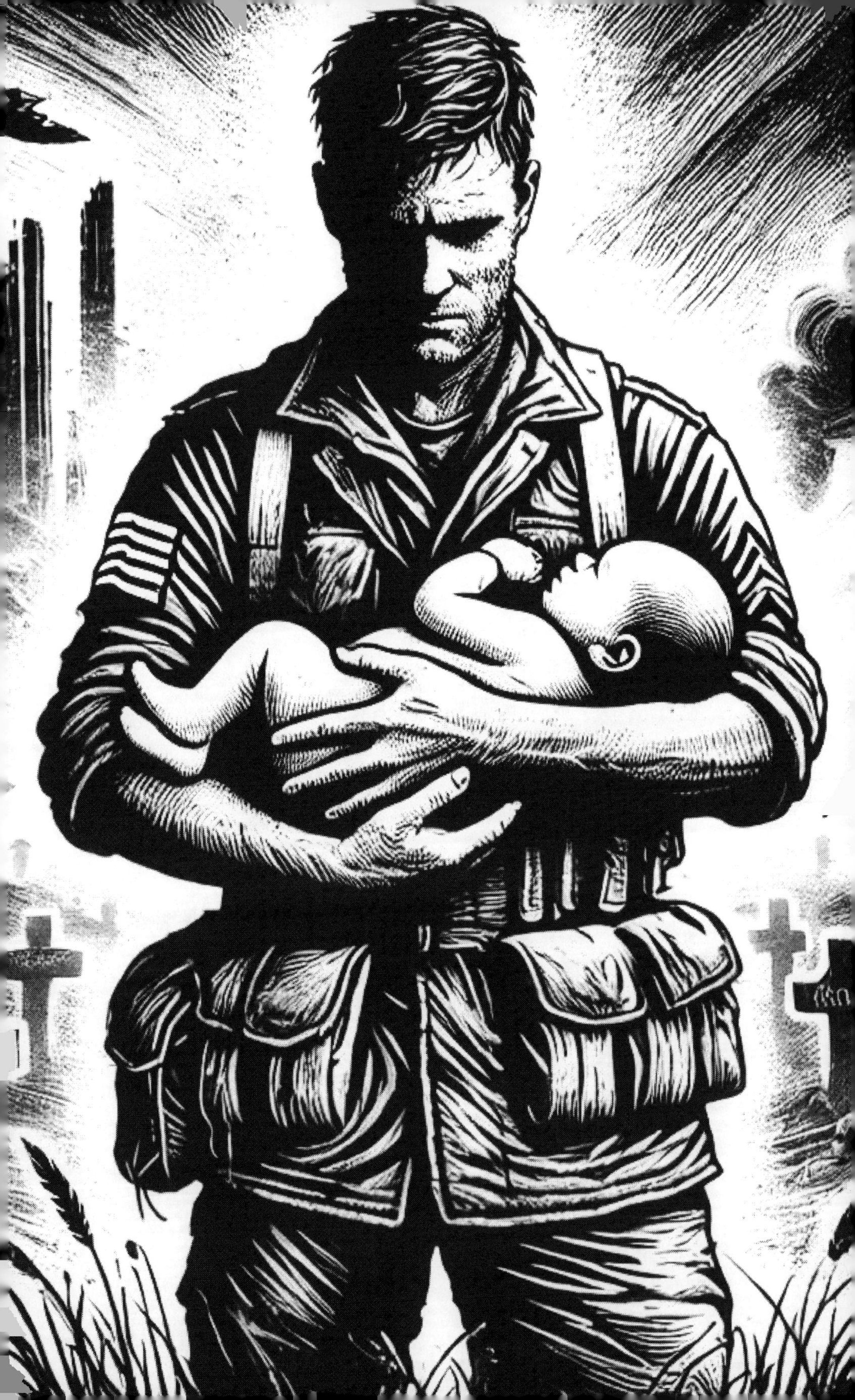

From Battlefields to Birth: A Test of Faith

One of the most difficult things during my time in Vietnam was seeing the wounded arrive. Outside our back door was Graves Registration, where all the KIA were processed. I now had faces to put with the wounds I'd been hearing about over the radios for the last ten months. The words "Don't let me die, Doc!" are etched into my brain. I heard them often, but sometimes, there was just nothing more we could do. In triage, those most likely to survive were treated first, while those with lesser chances were made as comfortable as possible and treated later, if at all.

In early December, a young pregnant Vietnamese woman came in with shrapnel wounds to her abdomen. I remembered enough of my Vietnamese language training to understand her when she said, "My belly hurts." Because she was pregnant, I told the corpsman to check her every 15 minutes for bleeding. I left for evening chow, and when I returned, I asked how she was doing. One of the corpsmen told me he was just about to check her. Suddenly, he shouted, "There's a big black spot!" I rushed over and called for the crash cart and for another corpsman to get the doctor on duty. By the time I got my gloves on, the baby's head was already crowning. I ended up delivering the baby myself.

We did have an incubator on hand, and I immediately suctioned and got the baby breathing. Once the baby was stable, I placed it in the incubator. By the time the doctor arrived, everything was under control. That was one of those moments where training kicked in, and we all did our jobs without thinking twice.

But over time, I became increasingly disillusioned with what we were doing in Vietnam. The average Vietnamese citizen didn't seem to care about the government—they were more concerned about having enough food for tomorrow. The nightly air raids and the ever-growing number of casualties made it clear that we needed to leave Vietnam and let these people live their lives. I began to blame God. If He existed, how could He let such terrible things happen to innocent people? I no longer believed in a supreme being. God, in my mind, had abandoned us all.

Rest, Reunion, and Unspoken Tensions

In late September, I became eligible for five days of Rest and Recuperation (R&R), and I chose to visit Okinawa to see Hideko's grandmother. It was a one-day trip each way, but it was worth it. We landed at the Marine Corps Air Station, which wasn't far from her grandmother's house. When I arrived, she greeted me with a tearful hug, just like I was the prodigal son returning home. It was as though all was forgotten. For those few days, I experienced a sense of peace and joy, a welcome break from the chaos of Vietnam.

Back in Vietnam, Frank had been transferred to the States, and I had a new coworker. We barely had time to get acquainted before I was transferred again, this time back to Medical Battalion in late October. I was now assigned as the Petty Officer in charge of the ICU and recovery unit, which was housed in a long, air-conditioned Quonset hut.

One thing that kept morale up was the mail—always a booster, even though it was slow coming from the States. My cousin Eileen sent me a journal every week, full of good stories about life in Stoutsville. Mom, on the other hand, wrote often but usually complained— mostly about the kids at home or about Hideko. She would gripe about Hideko going out for driving lessons and leaving the kids at home by themselves. I wrote to Hideko about it, and her reply reassured me that one of the neighbor women always stayed with the kids while she was out.

I eventually wrote back to Mom and told her, "I don't want to hear any more complaints about anyone. If you can't write something good, don't write at all." After that, she never wrote me again. It wasn't until twenty years later that I found out Mom had taken her frustration out on Hideko after receiving my letter. I never brought it up to her again.

A NEW CHAPTER BEGINS

From Navy Blues to Civilian Shoes: A New Chapter Begins

In early March 1969, I received a one-page letter from Hideko with just two words scrawled across it in several places: "I FAILED." It didn't take long to figure out that she must have taken her driver's test and failed. Sure enough, a week later, I got another letter that simply said, "I passed." I couldn't help but smile at her persistence.

By June 17, 1970, I was officially a civilian again. We spent a few days at home before driving to visit friends in Washington, D.C., and Norfolk, VA. While in Washington, Chiemi got into Hideko's purse and ate most of a bottle of baby aspirin, which resulted in a trip to the local hospital's emergency room. The first question from the desk clerk was, "Are you going to pay for the visit?" I was taken aback—now that we were civilians, there was no more free medical care. They gave Chiemi medicine to make her vomit, and a couple of hours later, we were back home.

We returned to Ohio just before July 4th, and the family came over to our house for a cookout. After that, it seemed like every holiday was celebrated at our place. On Monday, July 6, 1970, it was time to find a job. The hospital in our hometown was too small to have a cardiopulmonary laboratory, so I headed to Columbus, a city I knew well from my Navy Reserve meetings back in the late '50s. With my discharge papers in hand, my first stop was Mount Carmel Hospital. After speaking with the personnel director, he sent me to meet the head of the Cardiopulmonary/Respiratory Therapy Department. After touring the department, he asked, "When can you start?"

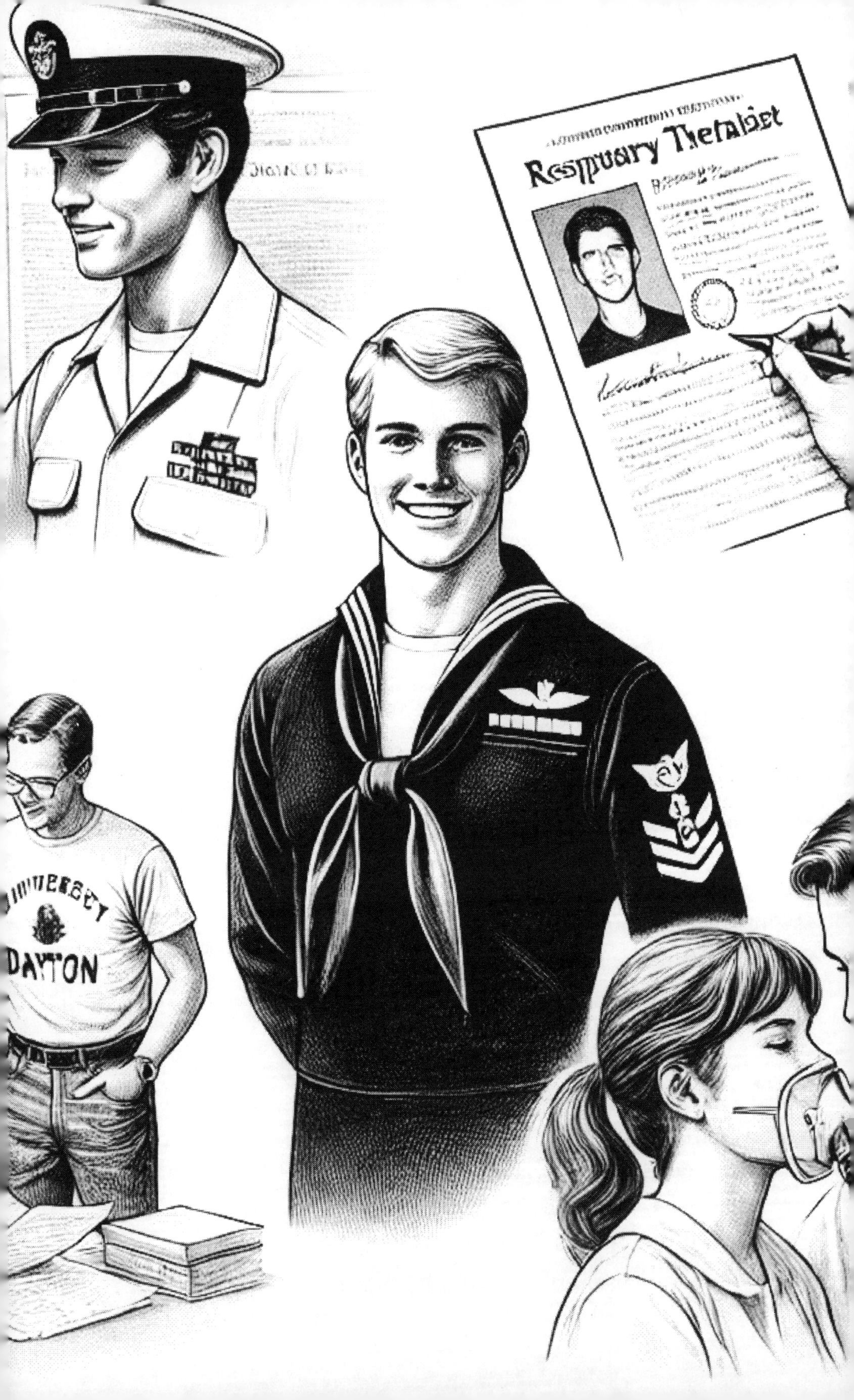
DAYTON

A Family Effort: New Beginnings in the Civilian World

I went back to the personnel office to complete the paperwork, and on July 7, I began my first civilian job. I later learned that both the personnel director and the department head were former military, so they understood the military work ethic. Of course, I had taken along the letter of commendation I received upon my discharge, and it certainly helped my case. A few months into the job, I went to the University of Dayton to take the test for national certification as a Respiratory Therapist, which I passed.

About six months later, the department head asked if Hideko would be interested in a job as a trainee. She would shadow the therapists and eventually learn how to administer gas therapy on her own. I had mentioned that Hideko had worked as a nurse's aide at the Army hospital in Okinawa, and that certainly helped. Hideko had a friend in Columbus who watched Patrick and Chiemi while we both worked. Since we worked the same hours, it made life much easier.

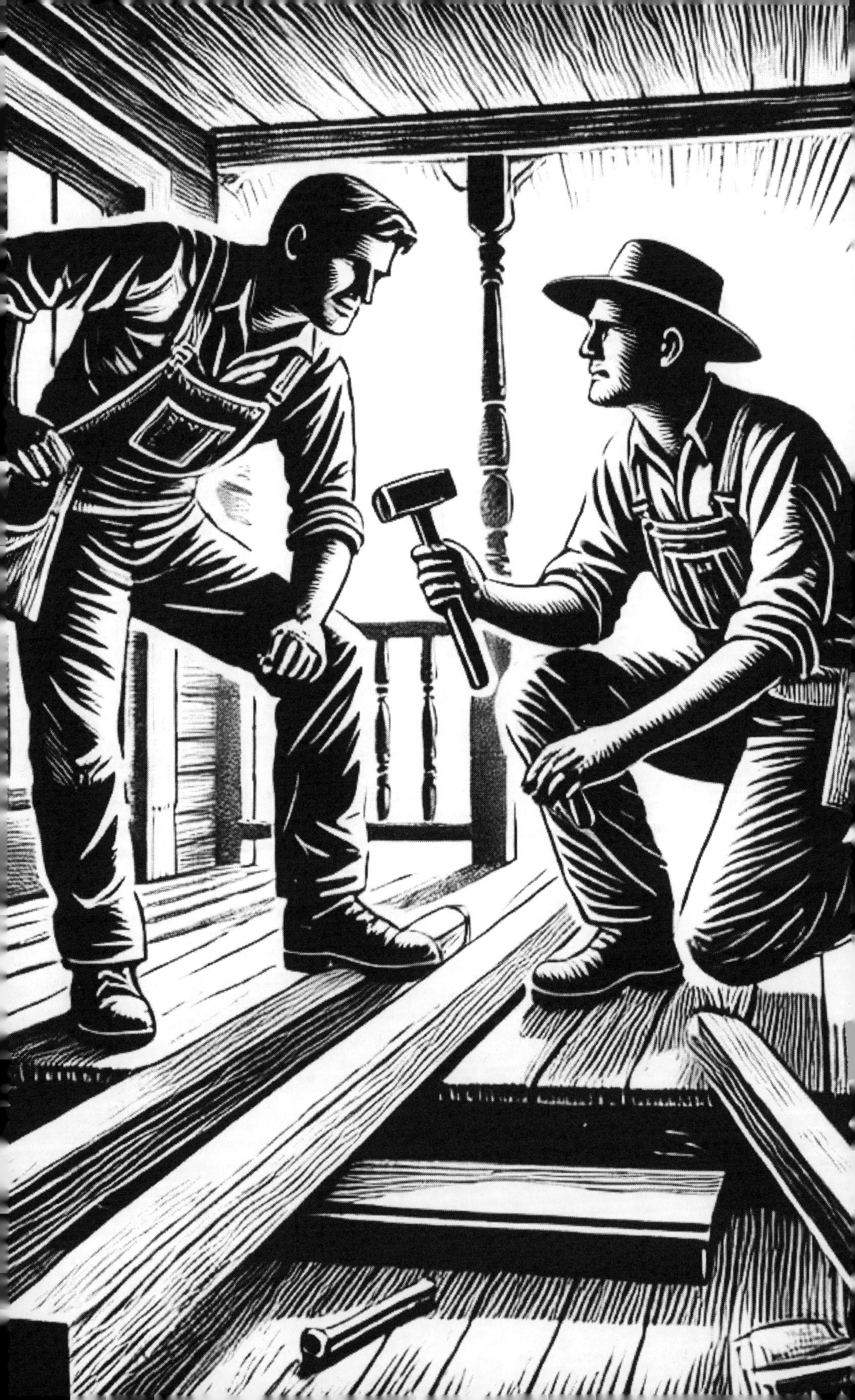

Building Porches, Battling Beliefs: A Test of Faith and Friendship

In April 1971, Tator stopped by for a visit while I was home, and during our conversation, he mentioned that his in-laws were selling their farm on Bauman Hill Road. I didn't say much at the time, but little did I know how much that piece of information would influence the next chapter of our lives.

There was a couple, Bob and Shirley Boelk, who lived three doors up from us and had been incredibly helpful to Hideko while I was in Vietnam. Bob, who had served in the Air Force in the late 1950s, understood what Hideko was going through, and that sense of empathy made a big difference. He did odd jobs to supplement his income and, after I returned, he asked if I wanted to help him after work and on weekends. I agreed.

We worked together on a few projects—first, we reroof a house, and then we rebuilt a porch on another house. It was while working on that porch that Bob invited me to come to his church. I told him flatly that I did not believe in God. The following Sunday afternoon, Bob showed up at our house with his pastor, determined to prove to me that God existed. For over two hours, they tried to convince me, but their arguments went nowhere. I just couldn't believe. I told them, "If there was a God, He wouldn't let bad things happen to innocent people."

After that, Bob remained friendly, but I never helped him again. A couple of years ago, I saw him at a concert and asked if he remembered that visit, and he said he did. I told him about the work I do now, and he just smiled. It was a silent acknowledgment of how far I had come on my journey, even if it was different from what he had hoped for back then.

From City Streets to Country Dreams:
A New Home and a New Challenge

Not long after, Tator visited. Hideko wasn't home, but I later mentioned to her that Tator's in-laws were moving closer to Columbus. She casually told me that I should see the house. She had been there once for a party before Tator and Sally got married. Curiosity got the best of me, so I called Tator and asked if we could check out the house the following weekend.

It was a two-story, two-bedroom, one-bathroom house, built in the early 1900s, but with a 15x40 kitchen/family room added in the mid-1960s. After walking through some of the 20+ acres, we decided we would buy it, and we closed on the house just before Memorial Day. The property had a half-acre, spring-fed pond, and the first thing I did—with Tator's help—was build a fence around it, with two lockable gates, to keep the kids safe.

The property also came with a tractor, which was perfect for maintaining the large garden we planted that very first year. There was a lot of grass to cut around the house, and we had six apple trees and a cherry tree to tend to. A small stream ran under the driveway in front of the house, and pine trees lined the property, making it almost invisible from the road. There was also a small barn and a shed for housing chickens. That first year, we also added a dog for the kids—giving them the full countryside experience.

Around the same time, Mount Carmel Hospital was in the process of building a new hospital on the east side of Columbus. They had already hired an administrator to oversee the construction, and I met with him several times. He offered me the position of department head for the Cardiopulmonary/Respiratory Department, a role that came with a significant increase in salary and a big challenge. I met with the architect to review the size of my department and was asked how I wanted it divided. It felt like I was shaping the future of the hospital.

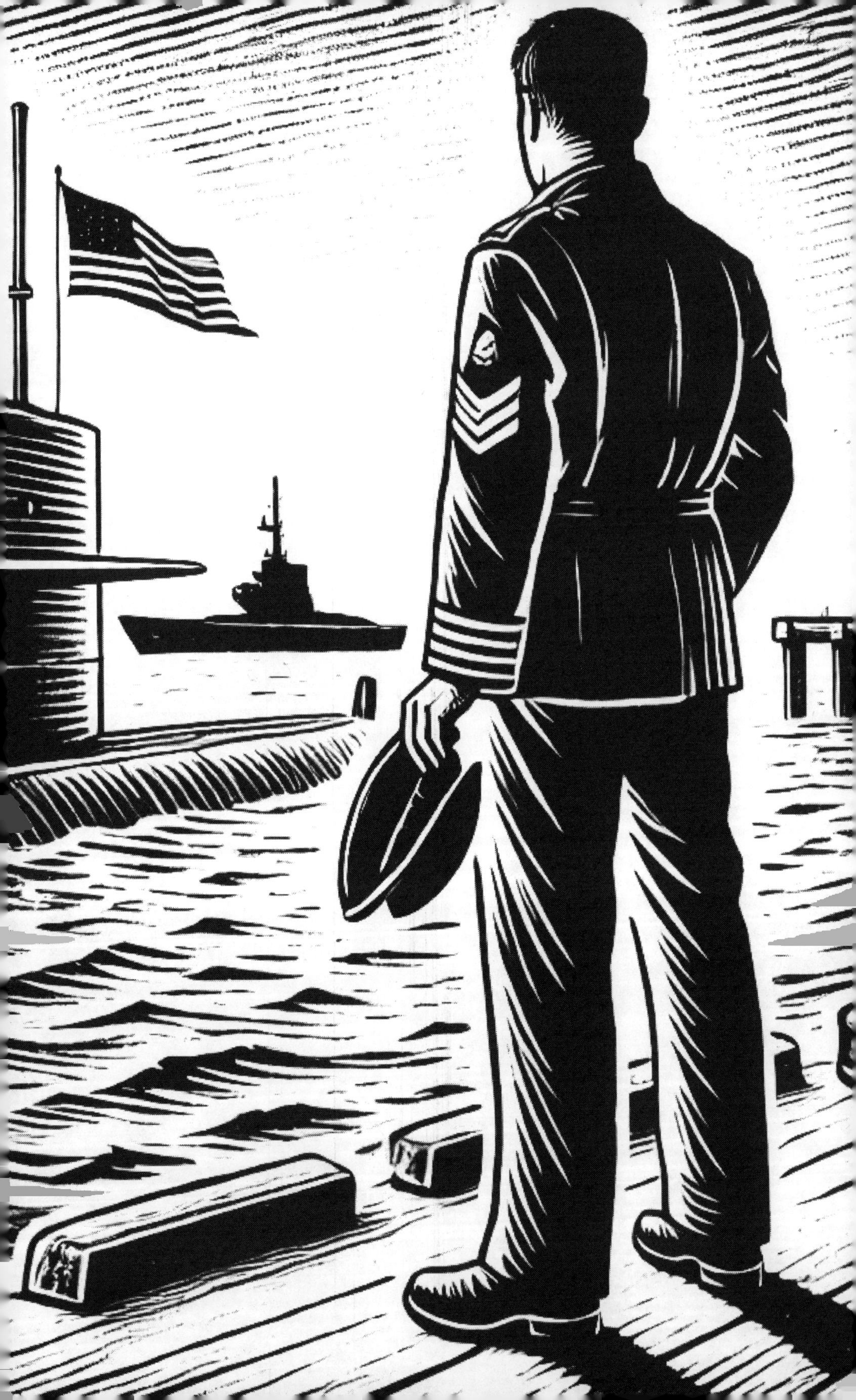

Charting a New Course: Reenlisting Without Faith

A few months before the hospital's grand opening, I began interviewing technicians to hire. Some of the therapists were going to transfer from Mount Carmel West (the original hospital) to the new Mount Carmel East. Once the new hospital opened in 1972, my life changed for the better—I no longer worked weekends, and Hideko reduced her hours to working every other weekend. It felt like we had finally found balance after years of upheaval.

In early 1973, Hideko and I began talking seriously about moving to Hawaii. I did some research at the library and found a book listing all the hospitals in the U.S. by city. I wrote to the hospitals in Honolulu, explaining that we were planning to move in the summer and inquired about job opportunities. One hospital wrote back, inviting me to visit once we were settled in Honolulu.

Our plan was to sell the house and everything else to fund the move. Then, in early March, I stumbled upon an article in the local newspaper about the Navy being short on petty officers due to the force reductions in 1970. The Navy was actively encouraging those who had been discharged to reenlist, with the promise of choosing their next duty station. I showed the article to Hideko and said, "Here's how we can get to Hawaii for free." The Vietnam War was winding down, with troops gradually being withdrawn, so it seemed like the perfect opportunity. She agreed, and the very next day, I took my discharge papers to work and stopped by the Navy recruiter's office in Lancaster on my way home. I told the recruiter that I wanted a three-year tour in Honolulu with my family and that I would reenlist for six years if that was guaranteed.

The recruiter called the Navy medical detailer in Washington, D.C., and they agreed immediately. I filled out the paperwork, but I wasn't sworn in until May. At the swearing-in ceremony, instead of saying "so help me God," I simply said, "so help me." I couldn't bring myself to say the words because I didn't believe in God anymore. When I was issued new dog tags, the space for "religion" was left blank, and instead, they stamped "NONE." I had to take a reduction in pay grade to second-class petty officer, but less than a year later, I was promoted again.

From Farm Fields to Island Life: A Family's Leap to Hawaii

The Navy sent movers to pack and ship our furniture, and we decided to rent out our farm instead of selling it. My dad agreed to act as our agent. What I didn't realize at the time was just how much the farm meant to the kids. Patrick would constantly tell everyone about "our farm back in Ohio" with its chickens, ducks, one sheep, and two ponies. The ponies were a gift from a friend of Butch and Vicki. The mother pony was very gentle, and she was the one most people rode when they visited. One day, Patrick wanted to ride, but I didn't feel comfortable letting him ride alone, so I saddled the mother pony, helped Patrick up, and led him around the field. On the way back to the barn, the daughter pony bit her mother on the rump, and she bolted. The saddle wasn't cinched tight enough, and soon Patrick and the saddle were upside down under her belly as she raced toward the barn. Fortunately, he held on until she stopped, but through tears, he said he would never ride again—and he hasn't since.

Our trip to Hawaii was the kids' second plane ride. The year before, Hideko had taken the kids to Okinawa for six weeks to visit her grandmother. As soon as we boarded the plane, Chiemi proudly showed me how to recline the seat and how to operate the music selection dial. We arrived in Honolulu late in the evening, and as we deplaned, Patrick asked, "What are we going to do next?" I must admit, I wasn't entirely sure. To my surprise, a corpsman I knew from Da Nang was there with his wife to welcome us and take us to the transient hotel. The next morning, he picked me up and helped me get checked in and familiarized with Pearl Harbor.

We stayed in transient quarters for a few days before finding a house to rent not far from the base. Our furniture wouldn't arrive for another three weeks, so we bought a couple of canvas cots and a few pots, making do for the time being. My uncle and his wife lived about thirty minutes away, and they were a huge help, showing us around and helping us find a car.

New Beginnings: Life on the Peninsula and School Days

The summer flew by, and Hideko took charge of getting the kids enrolled in school—Patrick in second grade and Chiemi in kindergarten. They had spent the summer taking swimming lessons and were getting comfortable with life in Hawaii. In October, military housing became available, but it meant the kids would have to change schools. Since we were going to be there for three years, we figured it would be best to move sooner rather than later. The new school had a lot of military families, and the housing was on Pearl City Peninsula, which was perfect for us. I was now the senior corpsman and petty officer in charge of the Ford Island Dispensary, located in the middle of Pearl Harbor.

One of the perks of living on Pearl City Peninsula was a paved bike trail that wrapped around Pearl Harbor. That Christmas, Hideko bought me a ten-speed bike, and I started riding the 7 miles from our house to the Ford Island ferry. It was a simple, yet peaceful way to start each day.

We were always busy every weekend, either heading to the beach or checking out local tourist attractions. The kids were happy because the neighborhood was filled with other military families. There was always someone to play with, and it felt a lot like living in Stoutsville, where everyone knew everyone else. We never had to worry about them.

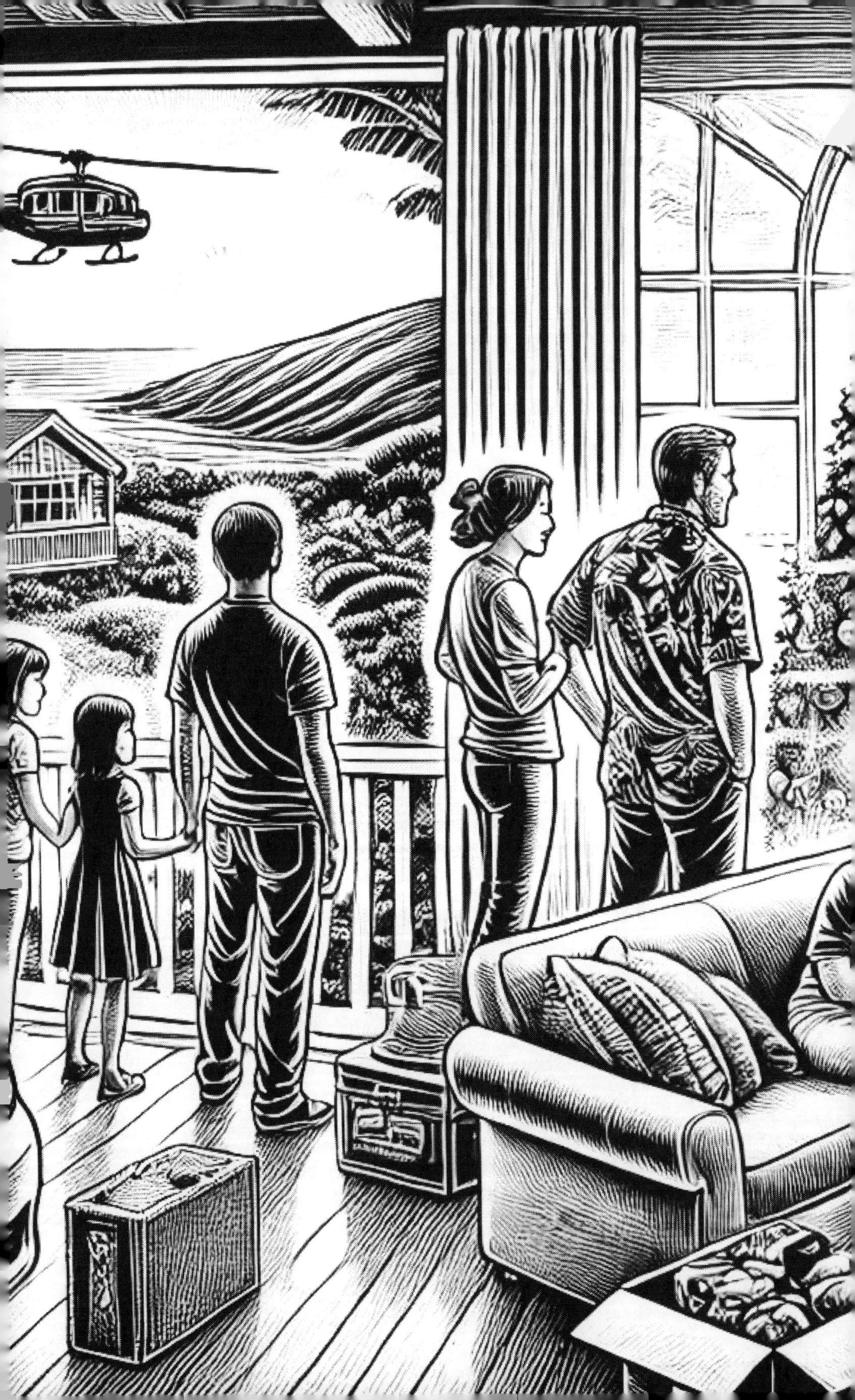

Seasons of Change: Family Visits and Fresh Starts

Daddy started visiting regularly. The first year, he came right after Christmas and stayed for a couple of weeks. The second year, he arrived before Christmas and stayed until the end of January. By the third year, he came before Thanksgiving and stayed until March. We had other visitors too, which made life even more exciting. A girl I worked with at Mount Carmel East came with her mother and cousin for two weeks. Tator, Sally, and their two girls also visited for ten days. It was nice to have people visit, and we enjoyed showing them around Hawaii.

In 1975, Hideko started working evenings at a psychiatric hospital. We never worried about leaving the kids alone for a couple of hours before I got home since there were plenty of adults around in our housing area to keep an eye out.

Our time in Hawaii seemed to pass at warp speed, and before we knew it, I received orders to transfer to the First Marine Division at Camp Pendleton in Oceanside, California. We shipped our Toyota Corolla and household furnishings at the end of June and flew to Ohio to visit family. I stayed for just a couple of weeks, but Hideko and the kids stayed longer until I could get base housing and the furniture arrived. Finally, in early August, everything was settled. Our new apartment had four bedrooms, two bathrooms, a second-floor laundry room, and a one-car garage. There were plenty of kids in the neighborhood, and Patrick and Chiemi quickly made new friends.

Transitions and Travels: From Marines to Family Adventures

Normally, corpsmen serve three years of shore duty and three years of sea duty. My time in Hawaii was counted as shore duty, so my time with the Marines at Camp Pendleton was considered sea duty. We knew we would only spend two years at Camp Pendleton before transferring again.

During our second year in Hawaii, we got Chiemi a Siamese kitten, which she named Nosey. Chiemi was very responsible and kept her room clean, making sure Nosey was well taken care of. We didn't think to get Nosey spayed, and sure enough, within a year, we had five more cats. Luckily, we were able to get them all adopted, and Nosey went to the vet to get fixed.

Then came another transfer—this time to Okinawa, to join the Third Marine Division. I had been promoted to Petty Officer First Class and was assigned as the Administrative Assistant to the commanding officer of the First Medical Battalion. I often joked that my job was to keep the CO out of trouble. He would tell me what he wanted done, and I would pass it along to the right people.

Hideko got the kids enrolled in school—Patrick in fifth grade and Chiemi in third. The school was close enough for them to walk, and most of the students were military dependents, so they fit in easily. We made it a point to explore as much of Southern California as we could, showing the kids places like the San Diego Zoo, Disneyland, Universal Studios, and the beach, which was just a mile away.

Sally and her girls, Rebecca and Robyn, came by bus with Sally's mother and stayed for a few days. We enjoyed showing them the highlights of Southern California.

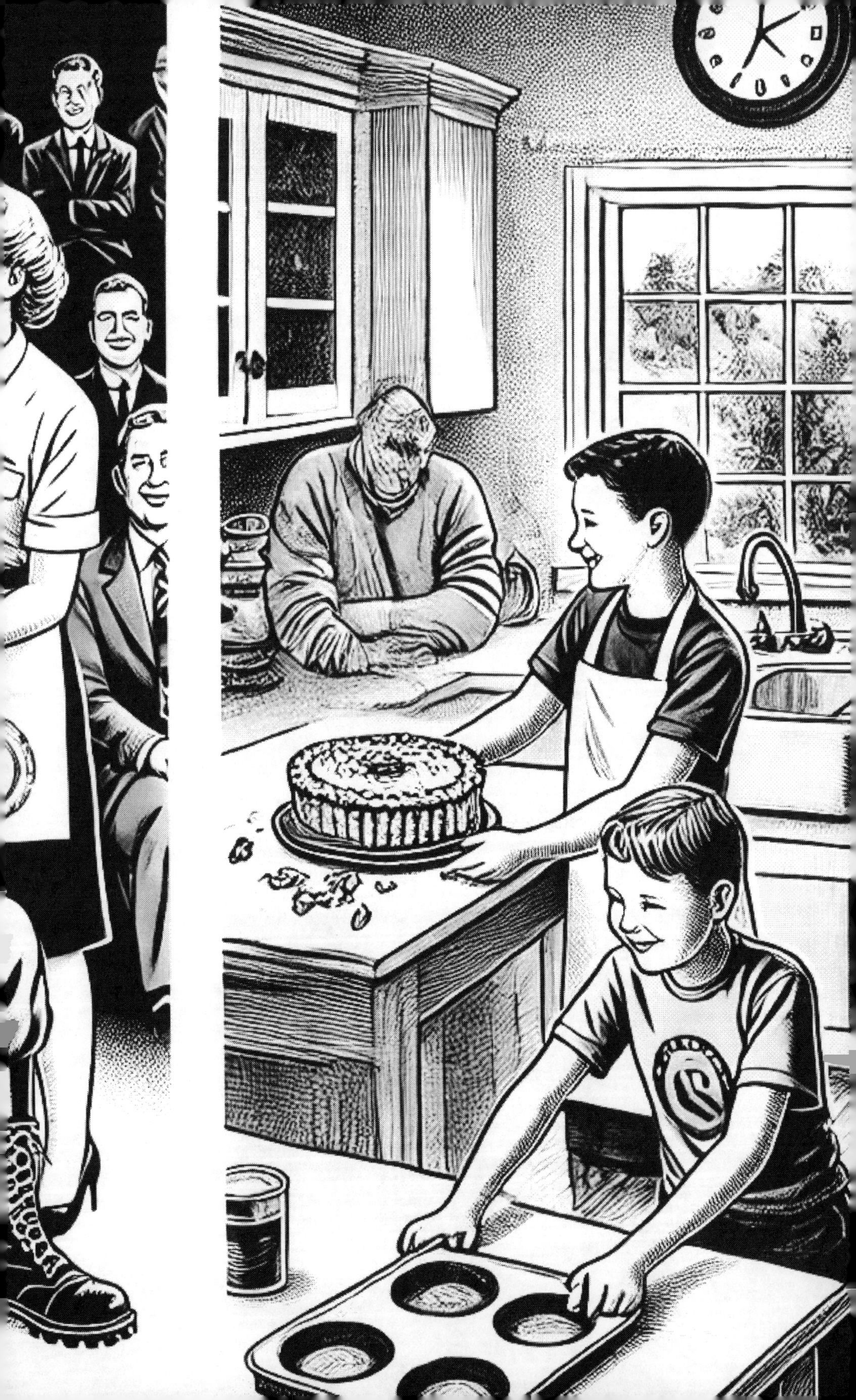

Pie Fights and Life Lessons: Navigating Promotions and Parenthood

During my time at Medical Battalion, I was promoted to Chief Petty Officer. At my initiation ceremony, the other chiefs had me dressed as the CO's secretary—complete with a wig, skirt, and combat boots. One skit I participated in involved me standing in for one of the chiefs during an argument. At one point, the chief was supposed to get smacked with a shaving cream pie, but at the last second, my instincts kicked in, and I ducked. The pie hit the other chief instead. The audience roared with laughter, but I had messed up. On the second take, I took the pie right in the face—this time, to applause.

During our second year at Camp Pendleton, Hideko got a job working evenings at an airplane factory. She did this to establish California residency and earn free tuition at the community college. She got a library card, a California driver's license, and we bought a second car, a '64 VW Bug titled in her name. Unfortunately, when she went to register for school, she found out she needed all of that done six months before enrolling. Meanwhile, I enrolled at Mira Costa College for a nursery management class—free of charge since I was military.

When Hideko was working, the kids would be home by themselves for about an hour or so before I got back. One day, I bought a tool to trim the grass along the sidewalk that ran in front of our unit and told Patrick to take care of it after school. When I got home, nothing had been done. He said the edger didn't work well, and he couldn't use it. I tried it myself and saw it was fine, so I asked him to do the job the next day. The following day, the sidewalk was perfect. When I asked how he managed to get it done, he admitted he had to use the meat cleaver to finish the job. That was a bit unconventional, but the job was done, so I let it go.

Later, while I was preparing dinner, I noticed some deep nicks along the edge of the kitchen counter. I asked Patrick if he knew what happened. He denied knowing anything about it. After the kids went to bed, I was unloading the dishwasher, and as I placed the meat cleaver back in the drawer beneath the nicks, it clicked. The cleaver had left those marks. I went to Patrick's room and asked him to come to the kitchen. Showing him the cleaver and the cuts, I asked if he had made the marks. He admitted that, in anger, he had used the cleaver on the counter. I told him he needed to be punished for lying. I took him into the pantry and gave him a light smack on the rear. I felt terrible afterward. That was the only time I ever used physical punishment on either of the kids.

Desert Drives and Cat Claws: The Journey Back to Ohio

Soon after, it was time for me to transfer to the 3rd Marine Division in Okinawa, and luckily, our farm was vacant. The Navy shipped our furniture, we sold the VW, and we prepared for another cross-country drive—this time with two kids and a cat.

It was almost July, and we were driving across the Southern California desert. Our Toyota didn't have air conditioning since it wasn't necessary in Hawaii, and the heat was intense. The cat was miserable and started crying, so Chiemi let her out of the carrier. Suddenly, the cat climbed up the back of my neck, her claws digging in. I yelled, and the cat went right back into the carrier.

I tried to make the trip interesting for the kids, showing them some of the sights I had seen during my many cross-country journeys. We took our time and spent five days on the road before reaching Ohio.

We stayed with Tator and Sally until our furniture arrived a few days later. Once we were settled in, Hideko flew to Okinawa to visit her grandmother, while I stayed home with the kids. At the end of July, it was time for me to leave for Okinawa, but Hideko wouldn't return for another week. During that time, the kids stayed with Tator and Sally until she got back.

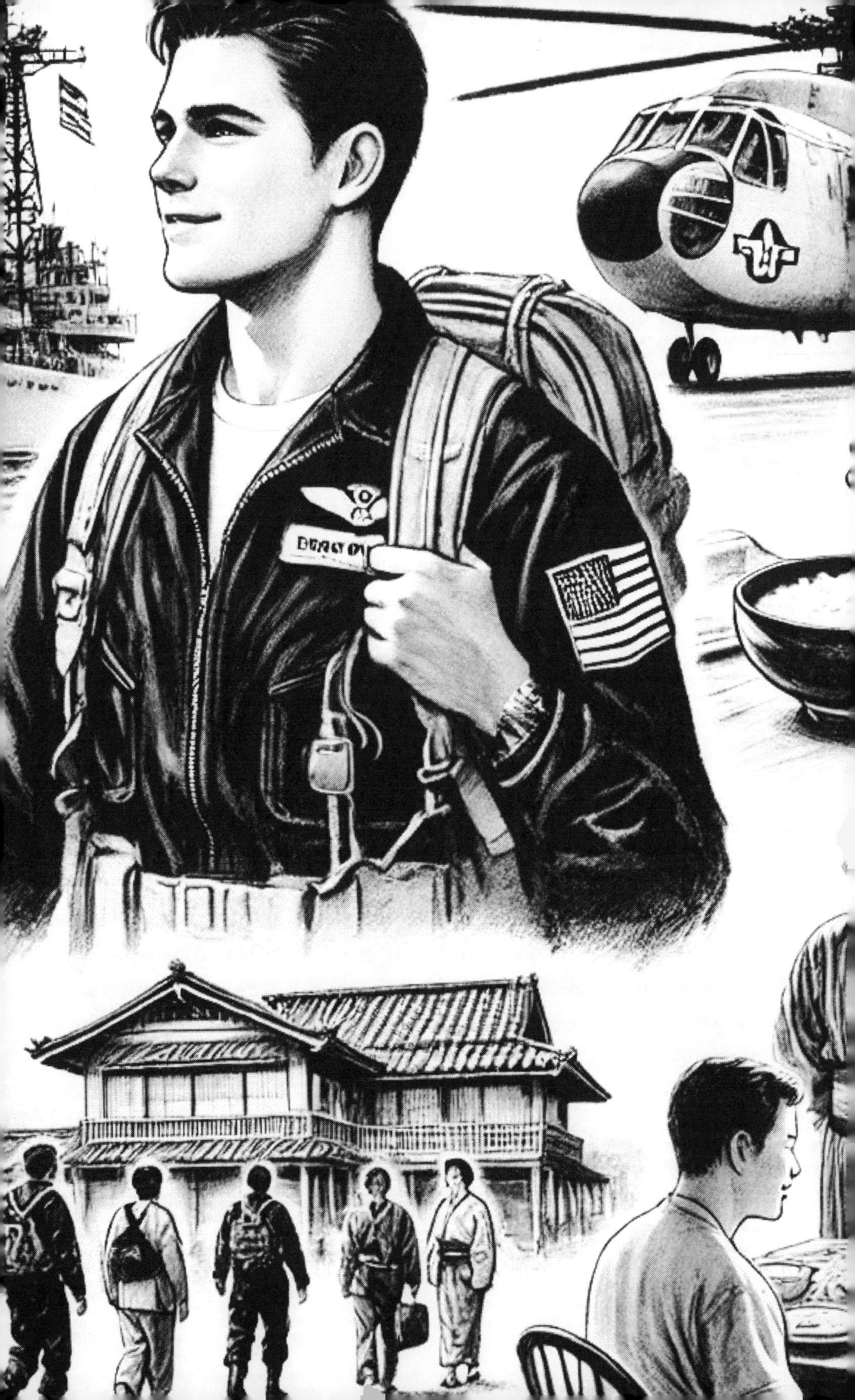

From Okinawa to Oakland:
A Year of Duty and a Birthday Treat

It was now near the end of July, and it was time for me to fly to Okinawa. Upon arriving at Kadena Air Force Base, I was met by someone from the Division Surgeon's Office and escorted to Camp Courtney, the headquarters of the 3rd Marine Division. Before my arrival, the commanding officer from the Medical Battalion at Camp Pendleton had called ahead to the Division Surgeon and praised the work I had done as his Administrative Assistant, recommending me for the same position with the Division Surgeon. I ended up filling that role for my one-year tour.

Hideko was still at her grandmother's for the first week of my tour, so I had the chance to visit her several times before she returned home. During one of my visits to Grandma, I managed to ask her, along with Hideko's two aunts, if they would cook sukiyaki for me and three of my coworkers for my birthday in 1978. With my limited Japanese, I made the request, and they kindly agreed. I gave them some money to buy the necessary supplies, and it turned out to be a real treat, not only for my friends, who had never been inside an Okinawan home, but also for me, as I got to show off a little.

My work at the Division Surgeon's Office was quite similar to what I had been doing at the Medical Battalion, except now, I was dealing with higher-ranking officers. The year on Okinawa seemed to fly by. Outside of work, my main after-hours recreation was running 5 to 7 miles a day and spending an hour in the gym. In June 1979, I received new orders to transfer to the Naval Hospital in Oakland, California for six months of training at the Navy Environmental Health and Preventative Medicine School. This school was affiliated with Merritt College, so I would also earn additional credit hours. At the end of June, I flew home and spent the month of July with my family. We decided that Hideko and the kids would stay in Ohio until I was assigned to a permanent duty station after my schooling.

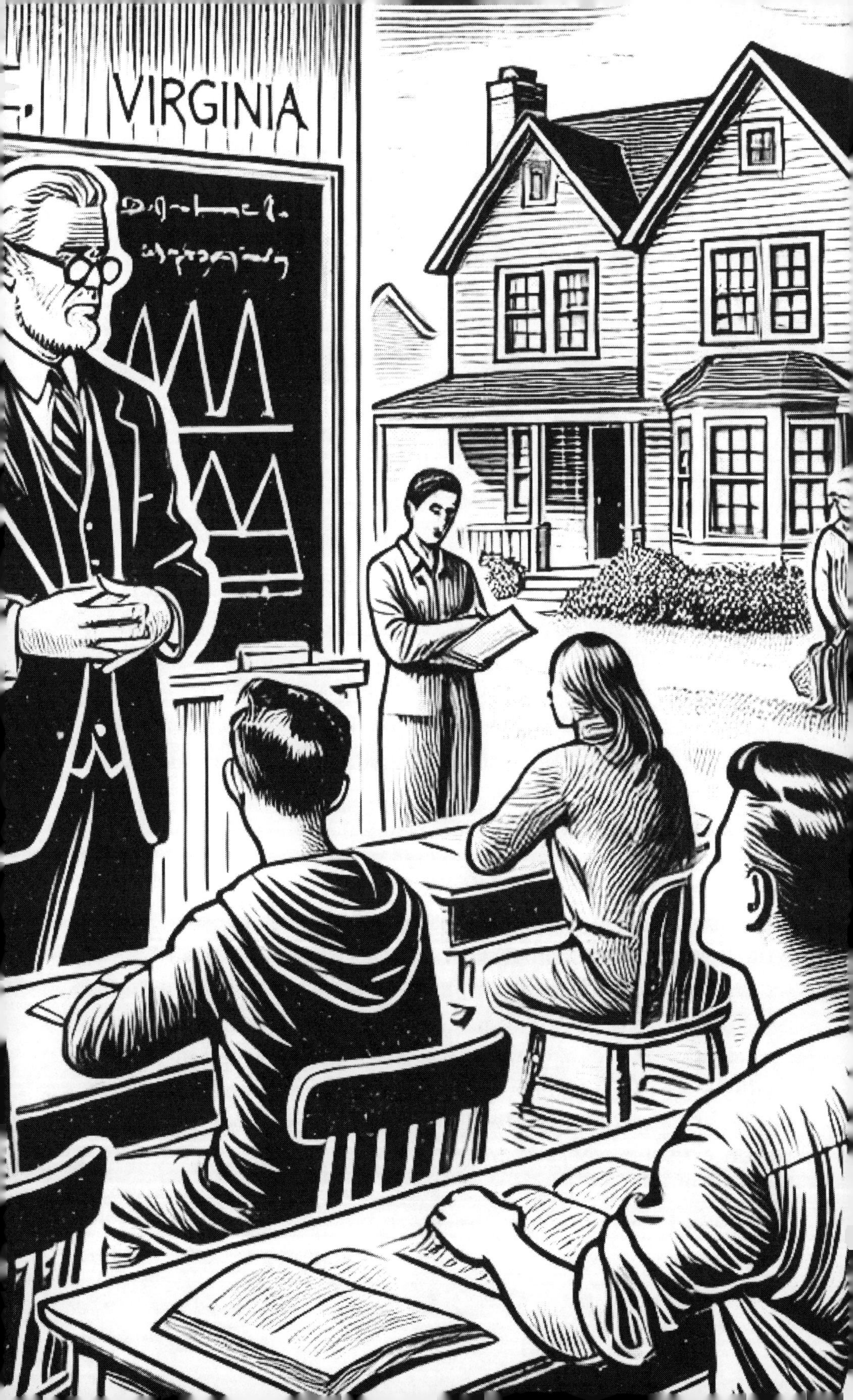
VIRGINIA

Leading the Class: From Study Sessions to a New Life in Virginia

By the end of August, I reported to the school and was informed that I was the senior-ranking student in the class, responsible for overseeing the 32 junior enlisted students enrolled. It wasn't a difficult job, as everyone had to be smart to have been selected for the program. Very few had their spouses with them, and none had brought their families.

In the second week of class, I started a study group with four other students to review what we had covered in class during the previous week. It really helped me, as I had to go over the material thoroughly to ask questions. Over time, our group grew to 15 students, and we met every Sunday morning at 10 AM to work for two hours. Several students already had college degrees, including one who had been a high school biology teacher for four years before joining the Navy. There was stiff competition to see who would get the highest test scores. I ended up with the highest score in Entomology, but overall, I came in third place.

I now had orders to the Navy Environmental and Preventive Medicine Unit Number Two (PMU2) in Norfolk, Virginia. I flew home at the end of February and spent most of March with the family. We decided that Hideko and the kids would stay in Ohio until the end of the school year. In the meantime, I would search for a house in the area, which I eventually found in Chesapeake, VA, near Portsmouth. Once the paperwork was completed, we had our furniture shipped, and Hideko and the kids moved in by early August 1980.

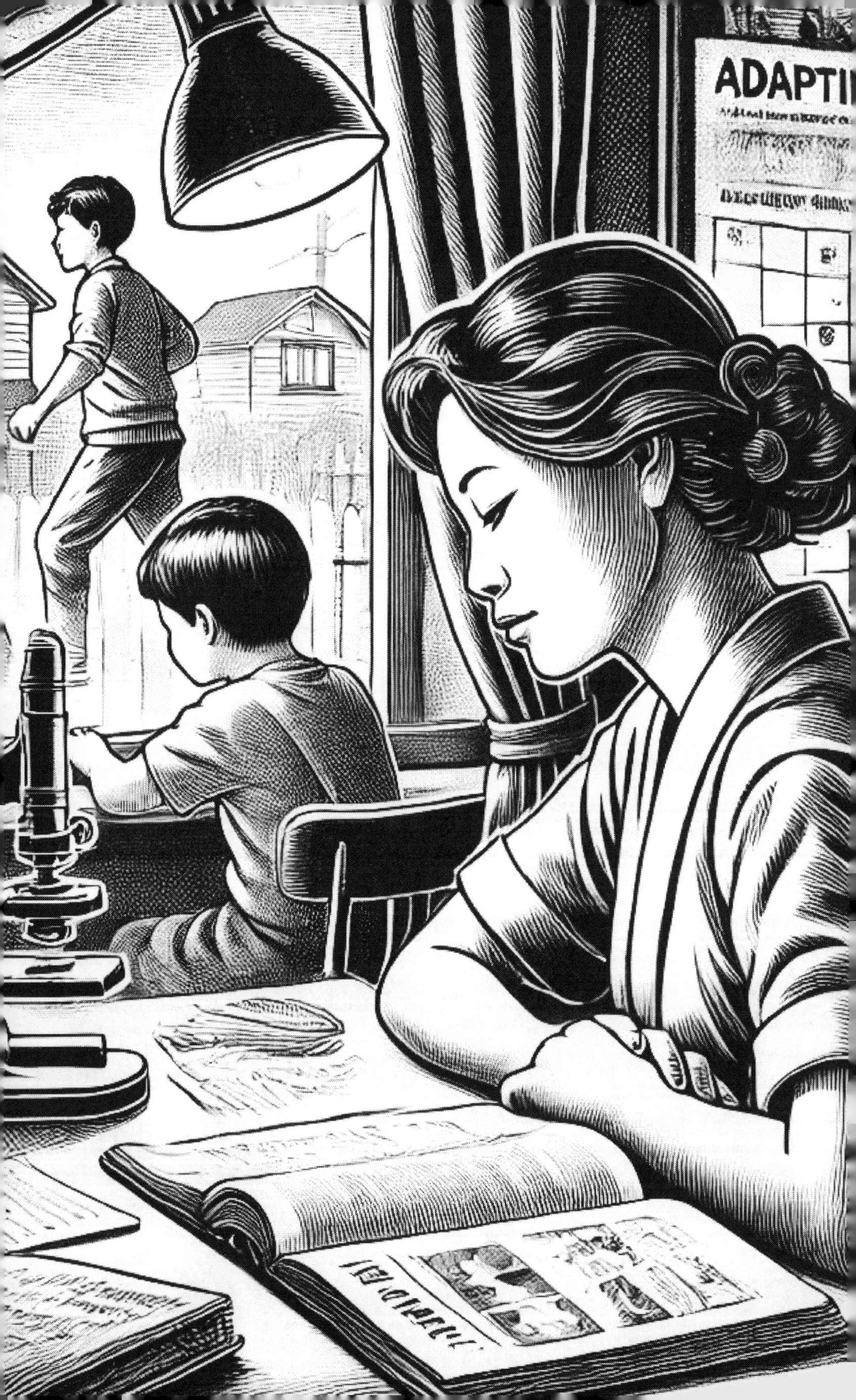
ADAPTI

Adapting to Change:

Settling Into Life and Supporting Hideko's New Path

As always, Hideko took care of getting the kids settled into school—Patrick was now in 7th grade and Chiemi in 5th. There were plenty of kids in the neighborhood, some of them close in age to Patrick and Chiemi, which made the transition a bit smoother for them.

My job at PMU2 involved teaching food service sanitation and shipboard water sanitation twice a week. I also conducted inspections in food warehouses and aboard ships. Once a month, I was part of a team that flew to Navy bases along the Gulf Coast and the East Coast to perform inspections at the bases or on ships stationed there. Occasionally, I conducted heat and noise level surveys in various spaces while the ship was underway. Asbestos was still found in some of the piping on certain ships, and sometimes crew members would bring samples to PMU2 for identification. Using a specific microscope, we could determine if the sample contained asbestos, and if so, what type. The Navy had strict standards for handling and mitigating any positive results.

In November 1980, Hideko had surgery to remove tumors in her uterus, which required her to spend several days in the hospital. By 1981, we discussed her enrolling in nursing school. The kids were old enough to be on their own for a little while, even if I was away on inspection trips. So, she enrolled at the Norfolk School of Practical Nursing. The program was 18 months long, and upon completion, she would be eligible to take the Virginia Licensed Practical Nursing Exam. Many evenings were spent with Hideko studying quietly in our bedroom, as there was a lot of homework involved.

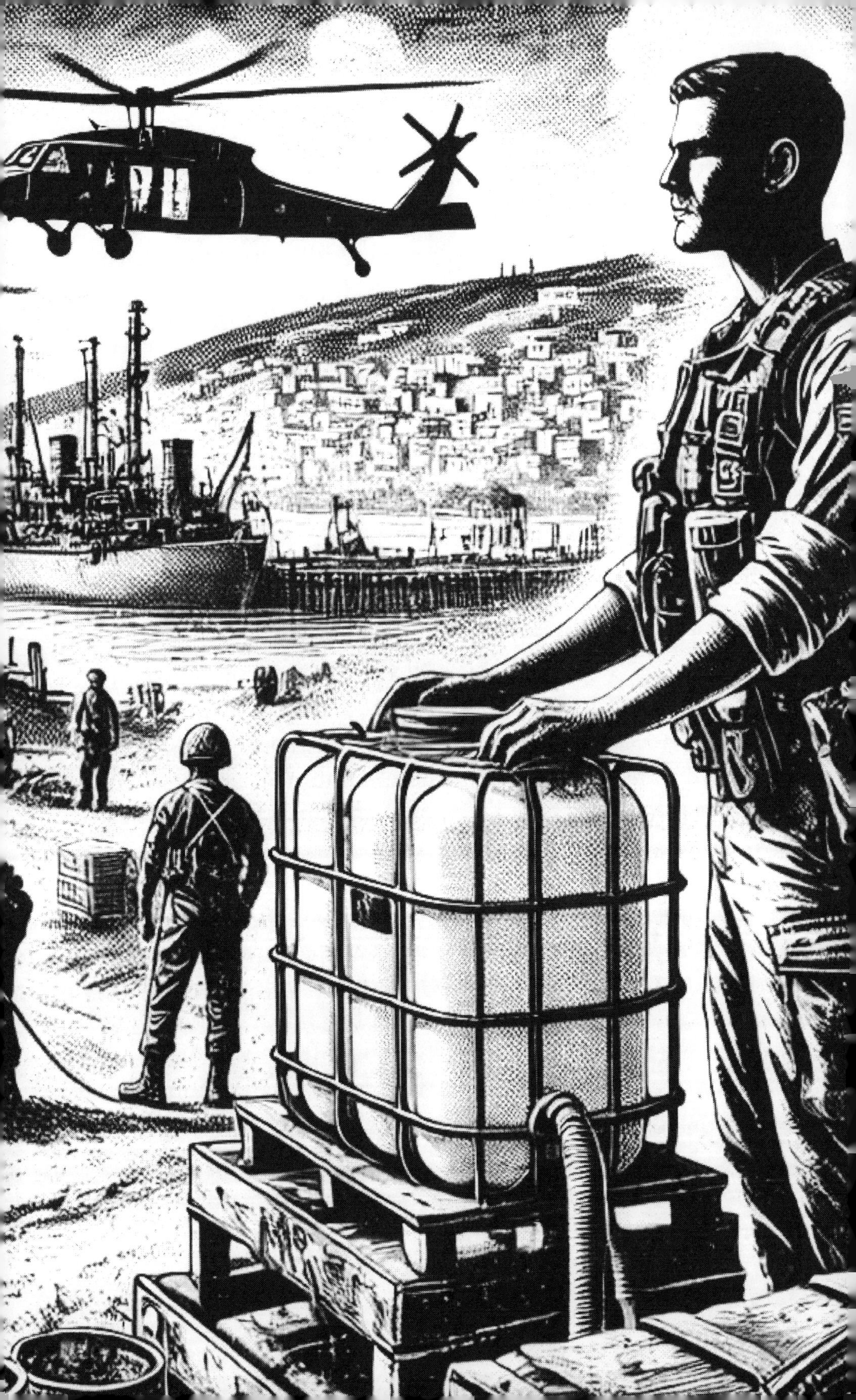

Conflict in Beirut: A Sudden Return to the Frontlines

In August 1981, tensions escalated between Palestinian Muslims and Lebanese Christians in Beirut, Lebanon. A contingent of U.S. Marines aboard the USS Iwo Jima in the Mediterranean Sea was deployed ashore to help keep the warring factions apart. A Preventive Medicine team was needed to ensure the health of the Marines, and I was selected as part of a six-member team to fly to Cyprus and then be transported by helicopter to Beirut.

We ended up stationed in the Beirut port area with the Marines who had come ashore from the Iwo Jima. Our job was to make sure their drinking water was properly disinfected and that sewage disposal methods were adequate. After about two weeks, most of the Palestinians were evacuated to Libya, and the Marines returned to the Iwo Jima, allowing us to fly back to the United States.

However, my time back in Norfolk only lasted 10 days before I received orders to return to Beirut. There had been another conflict between the Lebanese Christians and the few remaining Palestinians, resulting in several deaths. The Marines were sent back ashore to keep the factions apart, and I was called back to assist. I had just three hours to get home, pack, and catch a flight to JFK in New York, where I was to meet the rest of the team.

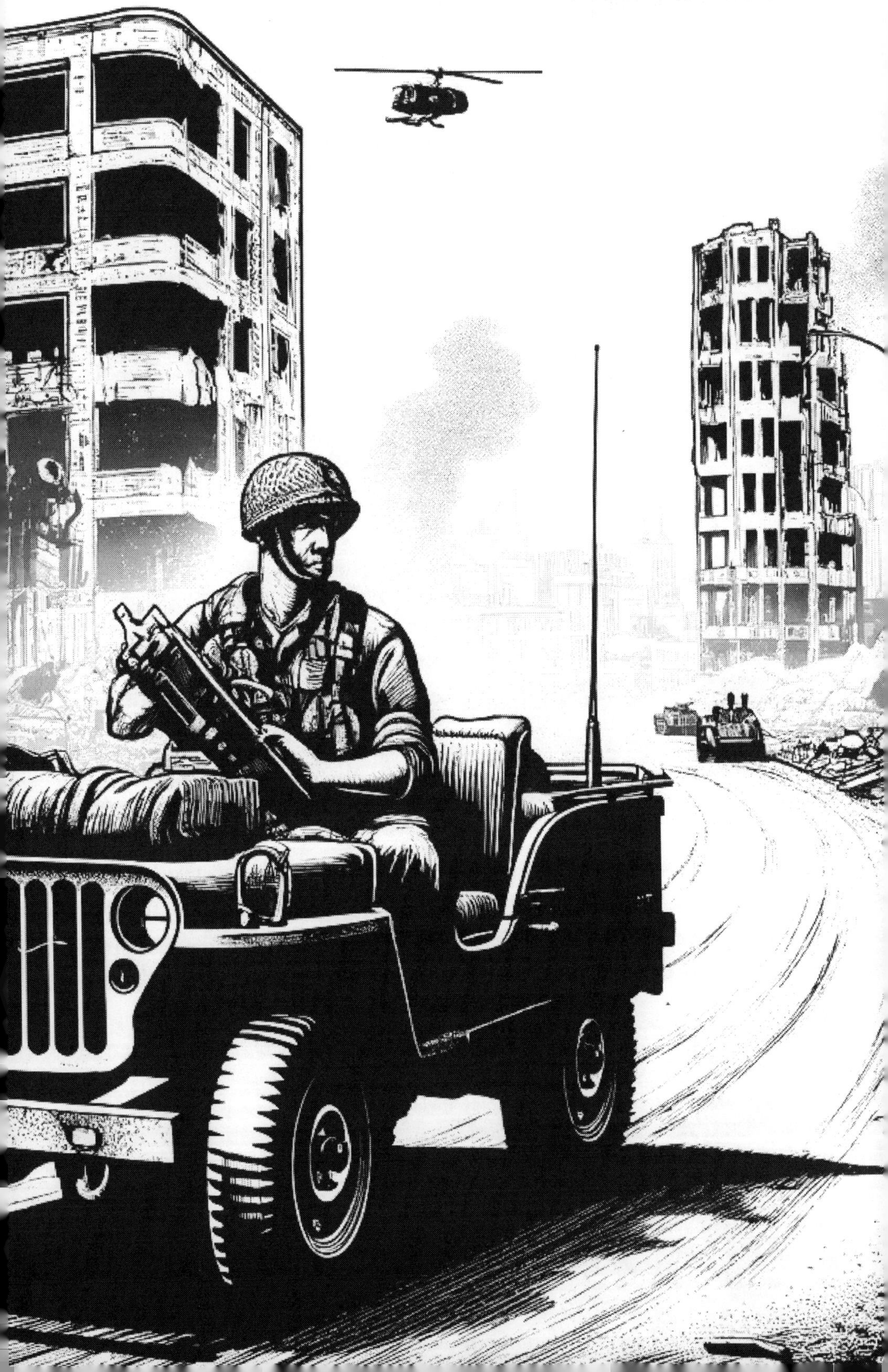

Amidst Ruins:
Navigating a War Zone in Beirut

As part of her schooling, Hideko was doing clinical practice at Norfolk General Hospital several days a week. I stopped there on my way home to say goodbye before heading out on another mission. This time, we were told that our time in Beirut was open-ended, with no return date in sight.

We flew from New York to Athens, Greece, and then took a local flight to Crete. From there, we waited for a helicopter to fly us to the USS Independence for a refueling stop, and then we headed on to Beirut. This time, we were stationed closer to the Beirut airport, but the Marines were spread out in squads of eight to ten, positioned all around the outside of the airport. Many of the nearby buildings had been bombed or burned, leaving only their shells. We made one of these ruined buildings our living quarters.

My job was to make daily rounds to each Marine outpost to check on their living conditions. I was assigned a jeep and a Marine driver who was armed with a rifle, though the Marine was never given any ammunition. My rounds usually took about four or five hours each day.

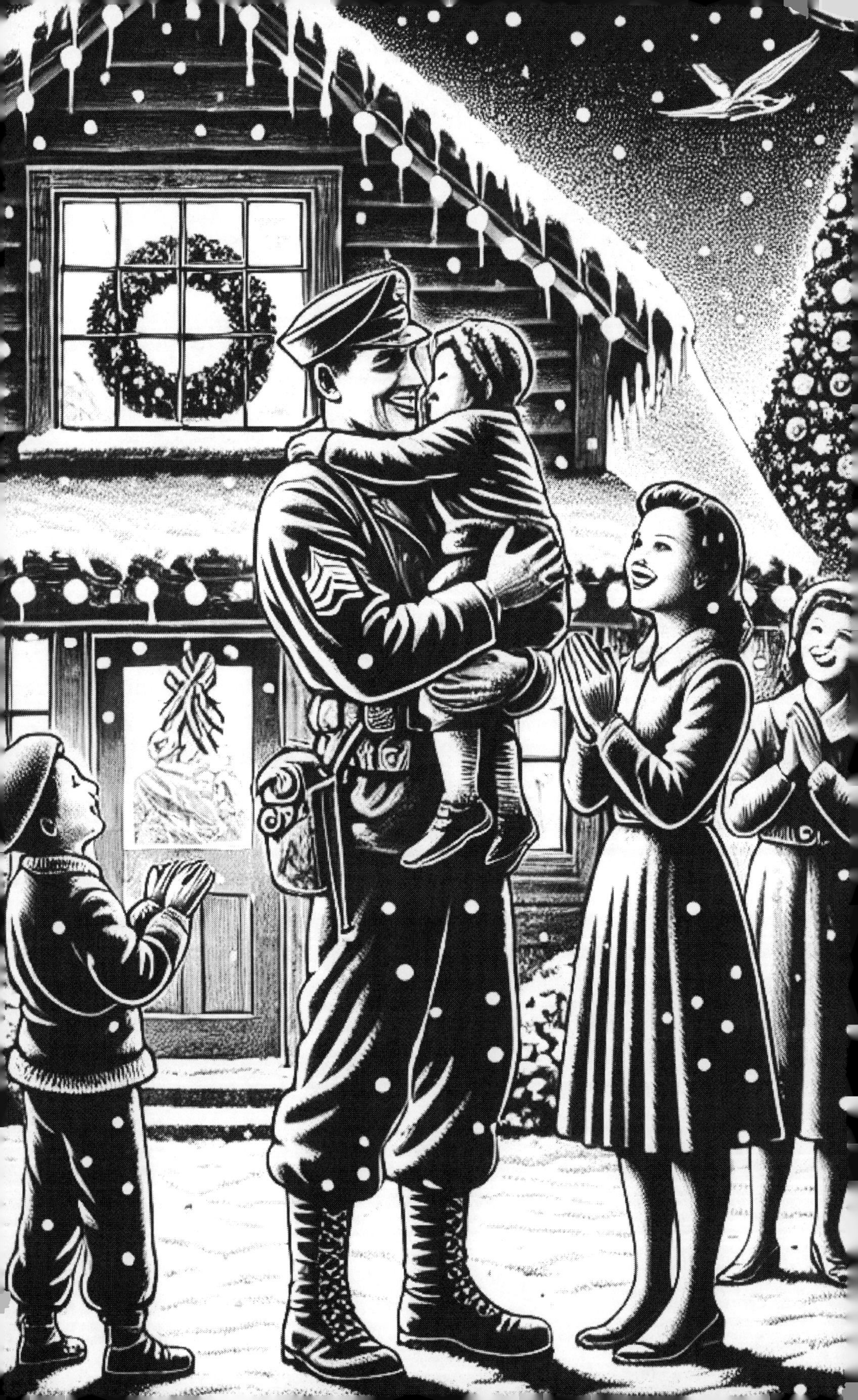

From the Frontlines to Family: A Christmas Reunion

The days turned into weeks, and soon August became September, then October. Every day, we wondered how long we would be staying there. The Marines were busy cleaning up and fixing things to improve their living quarters. One of the buildings they occupied was a five-story office building that had been burned and was filled with debris. It served as the main barracks, with the medical section on the top floor. Our Preventive Medicine Team stayed in a smaller building about 500 yards away, which had once been a school. It, too, had been burned, but it still had three solid concrete walls and a decent roof. We filled the open wall with sandbags to make it more secure. Our living space consisted of canvas cots for beds, along with makeshift chairs and tables.

When we weren't making rounds to check on the Marines, we spent our time reading anything we could get our hands on. Our meals mainly consisted of Meals Ready to Eat (MREs)—beef stew in a pouch, dehydrated fruit, instant coffee, powdered hot chocolate, and powdered creamer. Even though the meals were high in calories, I managed to lose fifteen pounds during my stay in Beirut.

During one of my rounds to a Marine outpost, I was stopped by a group of people and told to turn around due to an anti-American demonstration up ahead. Tensions were high, but we kept going as usual.

Then, in mid-December, we received orders that we would be relieved before Christmas. I arrived back in Norfolk just a few days before the holiday and was granted leave for both Christmas and New Year's. The kids were out of school, so we went to Ohio to spend time with family. It was the first time in years that we were all together at my parents' house for the holidays. On New Year's Eve, most of us went out drinking and dancing at a local nightclub, which brought the family even closer.

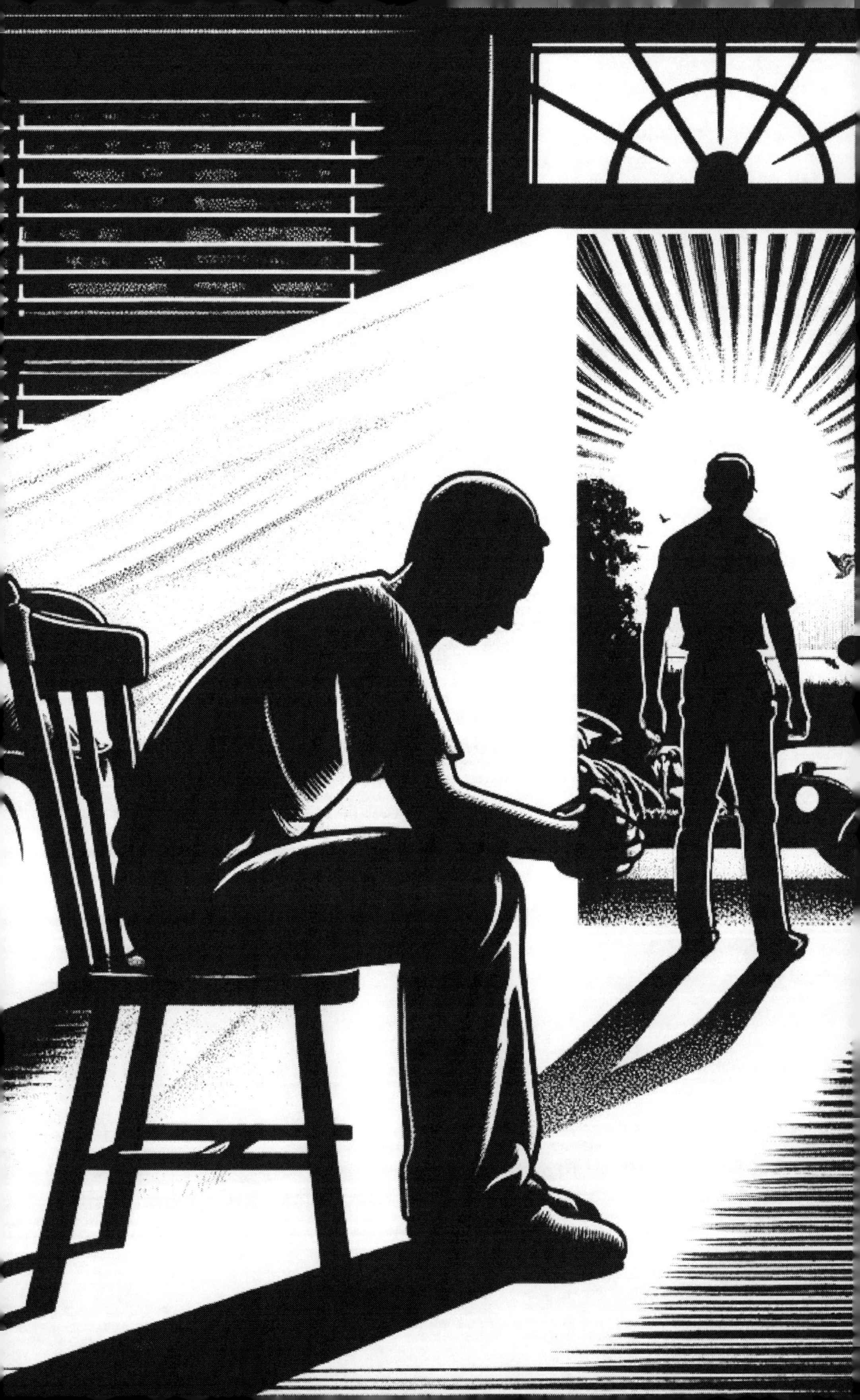

Facing the Shadows: A Journey to Healing and Letting Go

As 1982 began, it was back to work teaching and conducting inspections. In April, the selection list for Senior Chief was released, but my name wasn't on it, even though some of my fellow chiefs, who were junior to me in rank, were selected. Not being promoted led me to question my life and my purpose. I sank into a deep depression, even contemplating suicide as a way to end my misery. I stopped eating, lost weight, and spent most of my time in bed when I was at home.

Finally, I got tired of feeling the way I did and called the mental health clinic to schedule an appointment. After speaking with a psychologist, I was admitted to the locked psychotherapy ward at Portsmouth Naval Hospital. There, I worked through my feelings of inadequacy in group therapy. When I first arrived, I didn't feel proud of anything I had accomplished in my life and considered myself a failure. But after two weeks, I was discharged with a renewed sense of purpose. It was time for me to take control of my life and live with intention.

During the summer of 1982, Patrick asked if he could move back to Ohio to finish his last two years of high school with his friends there. He had always done well in school, and his report card showed him near the top of his class. He was driving now and becoming a responsible young adult. After making a few phone calls to my parents about Patrick's request, we decided to let him move in with his grandparents in late summer and enroll in Lancaster High School. It was difficult to leave him behind, but we knew he would be in good hands.

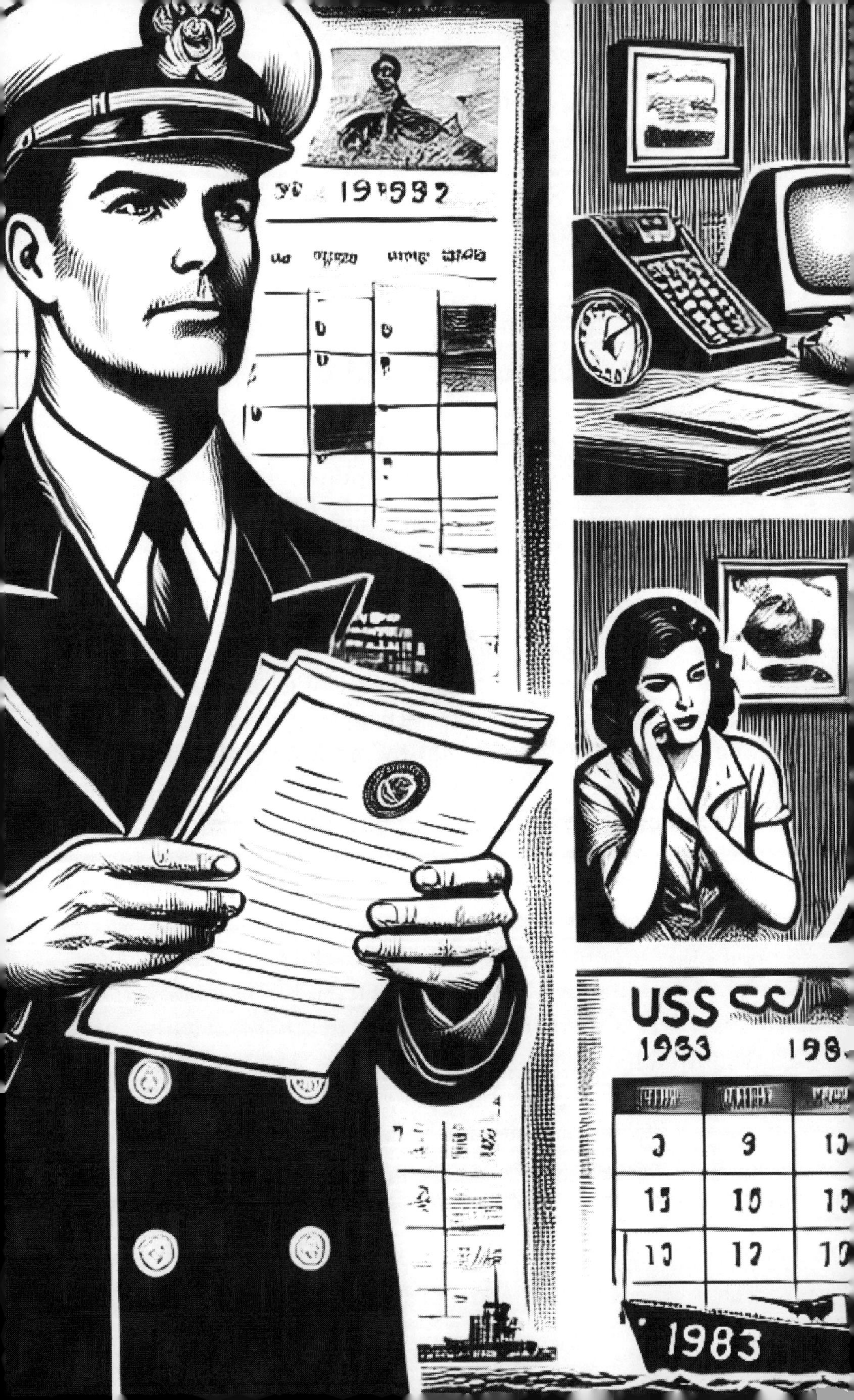
USS
1983

Taking Charge:
From Self-Evaluation to Senior Chief

My annual evaluations always mentioned that I was a hard worker and a dependable guy, but they never highlighted my actual accomplishments. For my next evaluation six months later, I decided to take matters into my own hands. I wrote my own evaluation, listing all the specific things I had achieved in the past year. I handed it to my immediate supervisor and told him he could use any part of it when submitting it to the Commanding Officer. To my surprise, he sent it forward without changing anything, only adding a numerical grade of 4.0. I had received a 4.0 before, but this time I finally felt like I had something to justify that mark. This time it was different, and in April 1983, I was selected for promotion to Senior Chief.

The Senior Chief at PMU2 was transferred at the same time, and I moved into his office as the head enlisted representative of the command. I was now responsible for all the junior corpsmen, both male and female. Then, in October 1983, a bomb-laden truck blew up at the Marine barracks in Beirut. There was one corpsman from PMU2 assigned to the Marines in Beirut, and I received a call early Sunday morning from his wife, who was frantic that her husband might be one of the casualties. I spent the entire day glued to the television, trying to gather as much information as possible. I tried to reassure her that unless something had changed, he wouldn't have been in that building. Information from Beirut was slow to come, but three days later, we were notified that he was okay, and she finally got a phone call from him.

I was scheduled to transfer in December, and another tour with the Marines seemed to be on the horizon. While doing an inspection on one of the ships, I learned that the Senior Chief there was transferring, and I made some calls to Washington. By early December, I had arranged to be assigned to the USS Mount Whitney (LCC 20), reporting aboard on December 17, 1983.

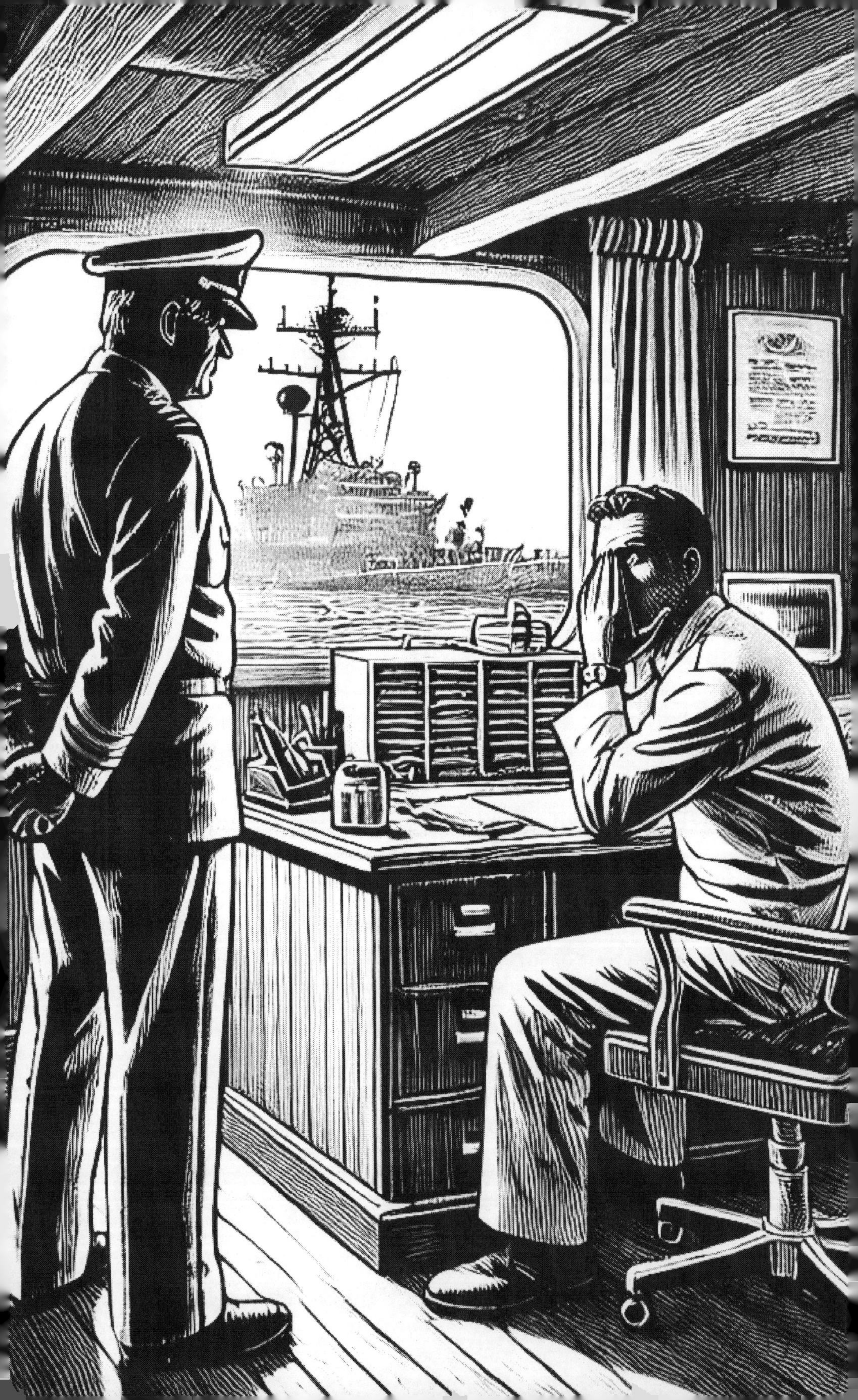

Uncovering the Truth: A Doctor's Confession

We had bought a house in Chesapeake, VA, and Chiemi was doing well in school. By staying in Norfolk, we could be there until she graduated, which was a relief. I reported aboard a week before Christmas. Although we had a doctor on board, I was responsible for managing nine junior corpsmen. The Mount Whitney was a command and communications ship, responsible for coordinating Marine amphibious operations. We were preparing for a North Atlantic NATO operation scheduled for February 1984.

In late January, the pharmacy technician and the leading petty officer approached me with concerns. They said that the pharmacy wasn't receiving prescriptions for narcotics the doctor was ordering. Apparently, the doctor would request large quantities of narcotics to keep in his office, dispensing them as needed, but the pharmacy wasn't being given any record of who was receiving them. I asked where the doctor kept the narcotics and was shown a locked file cabinet. As the Senior Chief, I had access to keys for everything. The doctor had been on board for six months and had been ordering large quantities of narcotics since the beginning of his tour. An examination of the locked drawer revealed only a small amount of several types of narcotics, but there were no prescriptions in the pharmacy for what might have been dispensed. There were also no prescriptions in the drawer.

When a crew member came to sick call, their name, work location, and complaint were logged in a record book. I copied the names of those who had reported pain severe enough to warrant a narcotic prescription. Then, I checked their medical records to see the treatment they had received. Some had received narcotics from the pharmacy technician, but others had received them directly from the doctor.

I then interviewed each patient to ask about their treatment and whether they received pills from the doctor or from the pharmacy. The next day, I went to see the Chief who served as the drug and alcohol counselor on board and asked for his advice. After talking with him for a while, we decided to go see the Executive Officer (XO), the second-in-command on the ship. After listening to my story, the XO said, "So, you're accusing your doctor of doing drugs?" "No, Sir. I just want to find out what happened to the drugs that the pharmacy cannot account for." I asked, "Is there any way we can get Atlantic Fleet Headquarters to do a surprise audit on our pharmacy?" He looked at me, shook his head, and said, "Dismissed."

The next morning, right after 0800, a Navy Lieutenant and a Senior Chief from Fleet Headquarters walked into my office, announcing they were there to perform an audit on the pharmacy. It only took them a few minutes before they came back to my office and asked to see the doctor. I knocked on his door and told him there were people to see him. They were only in there for about fifteen minutes before the doctor came out with them and said he would be leaving for the day, which he did.

The next day, I was already at my desk when the doctor came in and called me into his office. He said, "I've been accused of using drugs, and I have to admit that it's true. I started using drugs while I was in medical school, and I've continued up until today." He asked me to assemble all the corpsmen so he could make an announcement. He openly admitted to them that he had been using drugs and that he was leaving the ship.

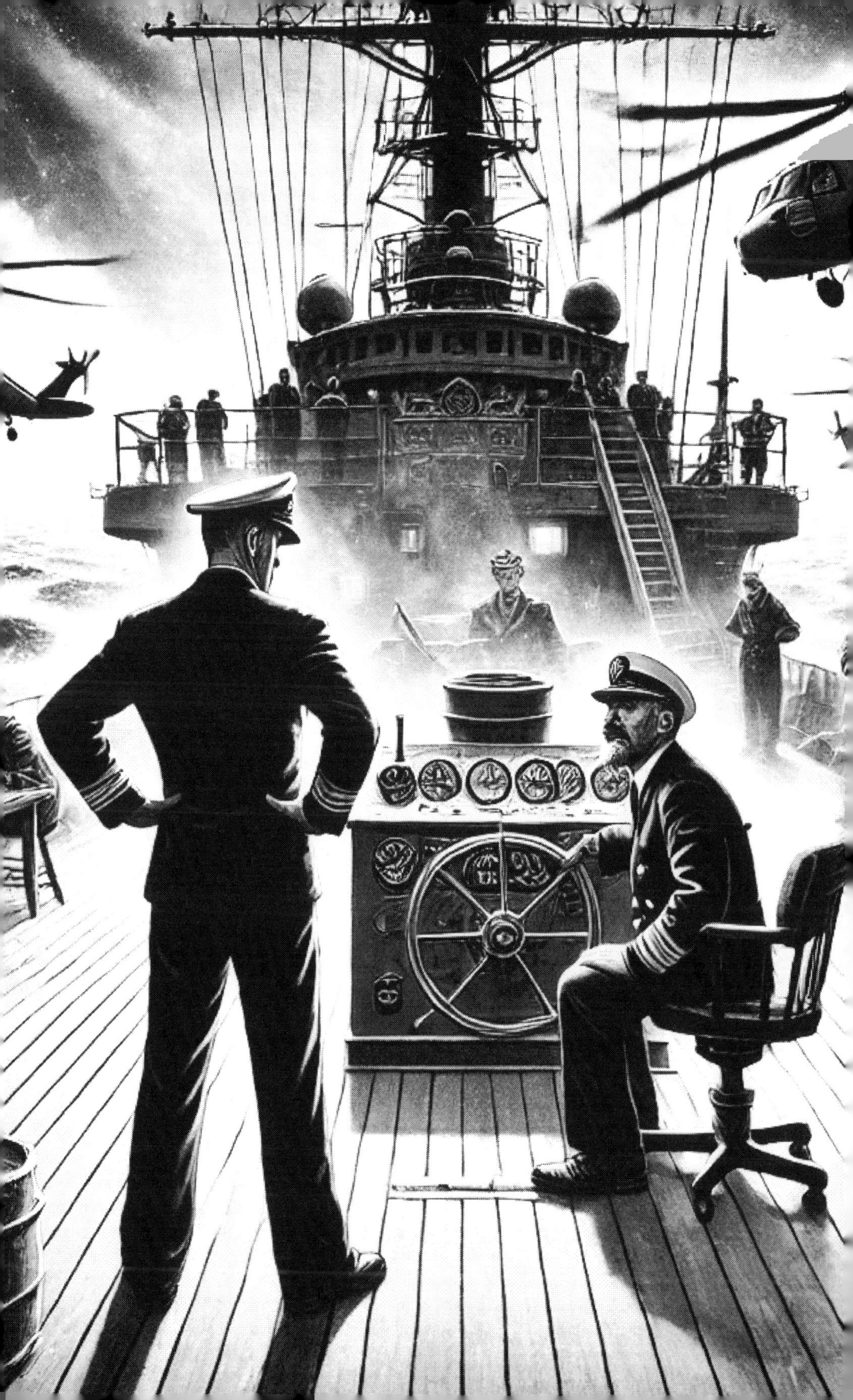

Navigating Turbulent Waters: Command, Crisis, and Unexpected Solutions

The Mount Whitney was scheduled to be the command ship for a NATO exercise and was set to lead the Norfolk flotilla in two days. Since we had so many high-ranking officers on board, we needed a medical doctor before we could sail. However, when the day arrived, the other ships scheduled to participate in the exercise departed on time, while we were still tied to the pier—sans doctor. It took two days for us to get a volunteer from one of the medical clinics in Norfolk, who agreed to serve as the medical officer, but only on the condition that I would be responsible for the overall operation of the medical department. This meant I had to attend twice-daily meetings with the Commanding Officer (CO) and other department heads. Surprisingly, this arrangement worked well, and I became better acquainted with officers from other departments. The Senior and Master Chiefs' berthing compartment consisted of ten bunks, all filled, a small sitting area, and a washroom with two sinks, one shower, and one toilet. Reveille was at 0600, so to avoid waiting in line for the sink or shower, I would get up at 0500 and be in the Chiefs' Mess having coffee before anyone else was awake.

One morning, when the ship was located above the Arctic Circle in Northern Norway, I was having coffee when the phone rang in the Chiefs' Mess. Someone answered and then said, "Senior Chief Moore, the Commanding Officer wants to see you on the bridge." I knocked and requested permission to enter the bridge. As soon as I stepped in, the CO started chewing me out from top to bottom and back to top again. I had never been talked to like that in my life. There had been helicopter operations planned earlier that morning, but no helicopter can take off or land unless a medical corpsman is on-site for emergencies.

I wasn't aware there were supposed to be helo operations, and my apology was going nowhere. By the time the Commanding Officer (CO) finished, I had never felt so worthless in my life. He threatened me with every consequence he could think of. My first task was to find the corpsman who was supposed to be on station. Eventually, I found him in the shower in his berthing compartment. His apology was sincere—he had simply forgotten. I told him we'd talk about it after the start of the workday. That was the first time I truly felt responsible for the crew and everything they did, both good and bad.

During this time, the pharmacy technician came to me and said that the CO wanted Mylanta tablets, but we only had the liquid version, which was what regulations allowed. It seemed that the Senior Chief before me had done some trading to acquire the tablets for the CO. The pharmacy tech asked if I could call the CO and tell him we only had the liquid, which I did. "But I don't like the liquid," the CO replied. I needed to keep this man happy. Since the Senior Chief Radioman slept in the bunk above me, I asked if he could send a message to one of the larger ships in our flotilla to ask if they could spare any tablets and send them over during the next helicopter operation.

The next morning, the Radioman presented me with a bottle of 100 Gaviscon antacid tablets, which I promptly took to the CO, apologizing that they weren't Mylanta. A couple of days later, I asked the CO how the tablets were working, and his response was, "I like them better than Mylanta." Once the NATO exercise was finished, the ship was scheduled for some port calls, allowing the crew liberty time.

Our first stop was Bergen, Norway, and I took advantage of the ship's scheduled tours of the country, knowing I'd likely never return. It was an impressive place—so clean, not a single piece of trash anywhere—and I learned a little history along the way.

Across the Seas: Beer, Castles, and a Court Martial

Our second stop was Portsmouth, England, where we tied up next to a British aircraft carrier. While we were in the Arctic, we had an overabundance of upper respiratory infections among the crew, and we had used up all of our cough syrup. I discussed the situation with the doctor, and we decided I should go to the carrier to see if they could spare any. When I arrived at the quarterdeck of the carrier, I was met by two Chiefs from their medical department. To my surprise, they took me to the Chiefs' Mess instead of the sickbay. Unlike American vessels, some British ships allowed beer on board, and the British carrier was one of them. Behind the bar was a Plexiglass board with all the Chiefs' names listed, and at the top, it said Pints and Quarts. A mark was made next to a name when a Chief had a beer. I had always heard the expression "mind your P's and Q's," and that's where it came from.

After having a beer, we toured the medical spaces, and I was given a gallon of cough syrup to take back to the Mount Whitney. The next day, the British Chiefs came to the Mount Whitney and invited me to go with them to a pub for fish and chips, served in a cone of newspaper. A few months later, the British carrier came to Norfolk for a port call, and I went aboard and invited the Chiefs to my house for an evening meal, which they accepted. I served them American beer—Miller Lite.

While in Portsmouth, the ship sponsored a three-day bus trip to Edinburgh, Scotland, which I went on. It was incredible to see the castles and landmarks I'd only ever read about. I did feel guilty, though, because I was getting to experience so much while Hideko was home with Chiemi.

The next port after leaving Portsmouth was Lisbon, Portugal, where we stayed for five days. Once again, I took advantage of the ship's sponsor for sightseeing, hopping on a bus to soak in as much history as I could. It was now early May, and the ship headed back to Norfolk. Once docked, we lost our temporary doctor, but by June, we finally got one full-time. In August, I was the chief witness at the Court Martial of our drug-addicted doctor. I felt so sorry for him. His wife, also a Navy doctor, apparently had no idea about her husband's addiction. He was fined five thousand dollars and received a Bad Conduct discharge from the Navy.

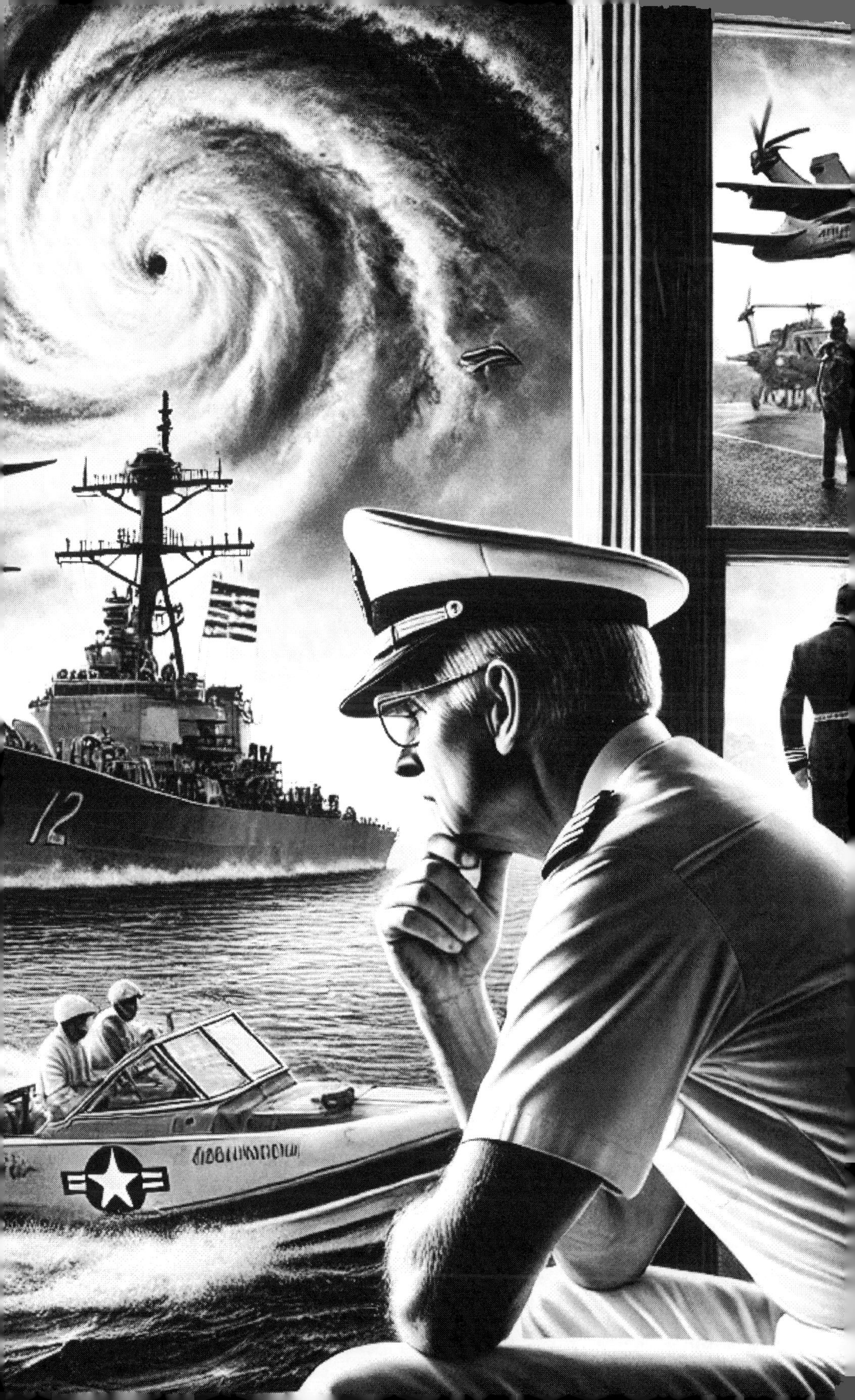
12

Hurricanes, War Games, and the Road to Retirement

The rest of 1984 and early 1985 consisted of four to six-week trips to the Caribbean, including the Bahamas, Saint Thomas, and Puerto Rico. By late summer of 1985, the ship was in dry dock at the Portsmouth, Virginia Navy Yard. Then, in September, Norfolk got hit by a hurricane, and all hands had to be on the ship. This meant Hideko and Chiemi had to ride it out by themselves. I didn't know until I got home two days later that they had driven to Charlottesville, more than a hundred miles away, and stayed in a motel. I would never have thought of that.

After getting out of the shipyard in October, we went to the naval station at Guantanamo Bay, Cuba, for crew training and playing war games while underway. It was intense, with many sleepless nights.

During this time, I began seriously considering retirement from the Navy. The names for promotion to Master Chief were going to be announced in April, but if I requested retirement, my name would be stricken from the list. Chiemi would be graduating from high school in June, just before my retirement date, and Patrick was two years out of school, living on the farm, working, and going to college part-time.

The ship returned to Norfolk on December 24, and the crew was anxious to get home to their families. Unfortunately, I had duty that day, so I had to stay on board until Christmas. The next day, Hideko came to pick me up, and I told her about my desire to transfer to the Fleet Reserve. She was very quiet. She loved Navy life—the moving every three years, seeing new places, and getting to know new people. She was now a licensed practical nurse in Virginia and had a good job. If we moved, it would mean she'd have to take the state licensing exam in Ohio and start over.

After Christmas, I submitted my request to transfer to the Fleet Reserve. In the Navy, one doesn't officially retire until they have completed thirty years. I would have completed twenty-six years total. Anything less than thirty but over twenty is still considered retired, but it's called Fleet Reserve, meaning you are subject to recall in case of a national emergency. I submitted my request, and it was approved by the Commanding Officer before the end of December, making my retirement date official.

Patrick was happy that we were coming home. Chiemi, however, wanted to stay in Virginia after her graduation in June. She had taken cosmetology classes during her junior and senior years in high school and would be a licensed cosmetologist upon graduation.

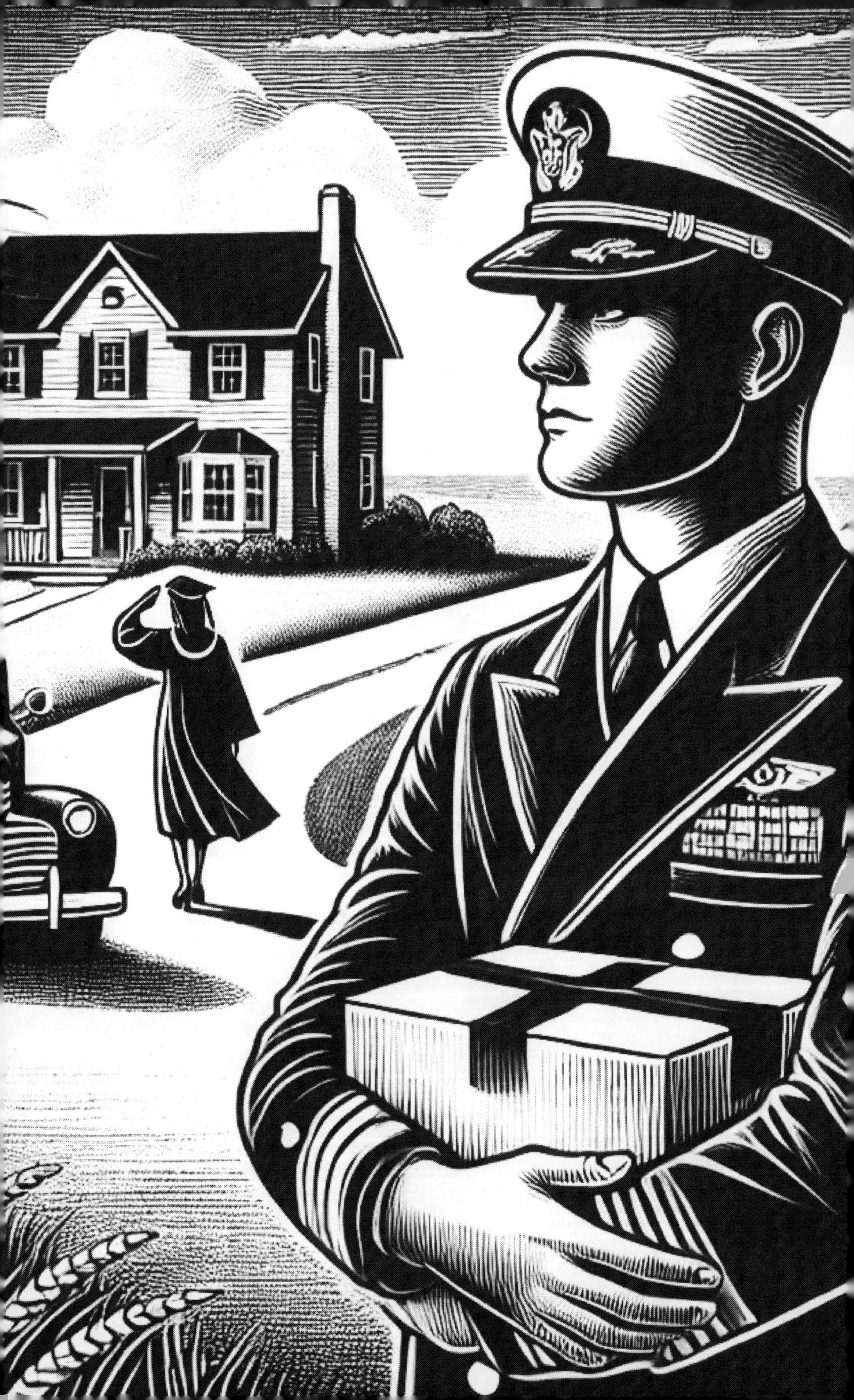

Closing One Door, Opening Another: From Service to Home

My last six months on Mount Whitney seemed to fly by. There were a couple of short cruises to the Caribbean, but most of the time was spent in our homeport of Norfolk. During this time, I spent a lot of hours in the classroom and with other Chiefs, studying for the Enlisted Surface Warfare qualification exam. I passed and was awarded the Surface Warfare (SW) pin in April 1986.

Our next-door neighbor was a realtor, so we asked him about selling our house. He advised us to list it sooner rather than later. We rented a storage locker, cleared out the closets and garage, and filled the locker. In early March, we had him list the house for sale. We did everything we could to make it look bigger and better. To our surprise, the very first couple who toured it made an offer at our asking price. Our closing was set for late April, and the couple allowed us to rent the house back until Chiemi's graduation and my retirement in mid-June. Though my official retirement date was June 30, I was using up all the leave I had saved. Chiemi's high school graduation marked the last time I wore my Navy uniform.

Chiemi had already been hired by one of the national beauty shops and had rented an apartment with a friend. The day before her graduation, the movers came, packed everything, and loaded it to ship to Ohio.

One of the hardest things I've ever done was driving off and leaving my daughter standing on the corner, waving goodbye. We had given her the old Toyota wagon that we bought in Hawaii, so at least she had some transportation, even if it wasn't the best in the world.

We were on our way to Ohio and a new chapter of our lives. But I kept having to pull over every hundred miles or so because I would start crying so hard I couldn't see to drive. I wasn't in control of my life anymore. Did I make the right decision, passing up my chance for promotion to Master Chief? Chiemi had just turned 18 a few days ago, and now she was in Virginia, while I was in Ohio. How could I protect her? If I were a religious man, I could have prayed for guidance, but all I could do was hope for the best.

We were only home for a few days before we went off with Butch and Vicki to visit some retired Navy friends in Wisconsin and South Dakota. Butch and Vicki knew them from Camp Pendleton and their visits to us in Virginia. Seeing friends showed me that there could be a fulfilling life after leaving the Navy.

My intention was to go back to school and get my teaching certificate for elementary education. Our first order of business, though, after we returned from vacation, was to add a third bedroom and another bathroom to the house, along with a 2 ½ car garage. We had made a considerable profit from the sale of our house in Virginia, but we still had to watch our pennies. We hired a contractor for the bedroom and bathroom, but the garage was a family affair. Butch was a draftsman, and he drew up the plans for the garage, a two-story structure. The contractor looked at the plans and told me what kind and how much lumber to buy.

Butch laid out and built the foundation and cement floor. The lumber was delivered the Wednesday before Labor Day, and that Friday, all my brothers, my dad, and my cousin came with their families, tents, and campers to spend the weekend. All we had to provide was the food and drinks.

Part 7

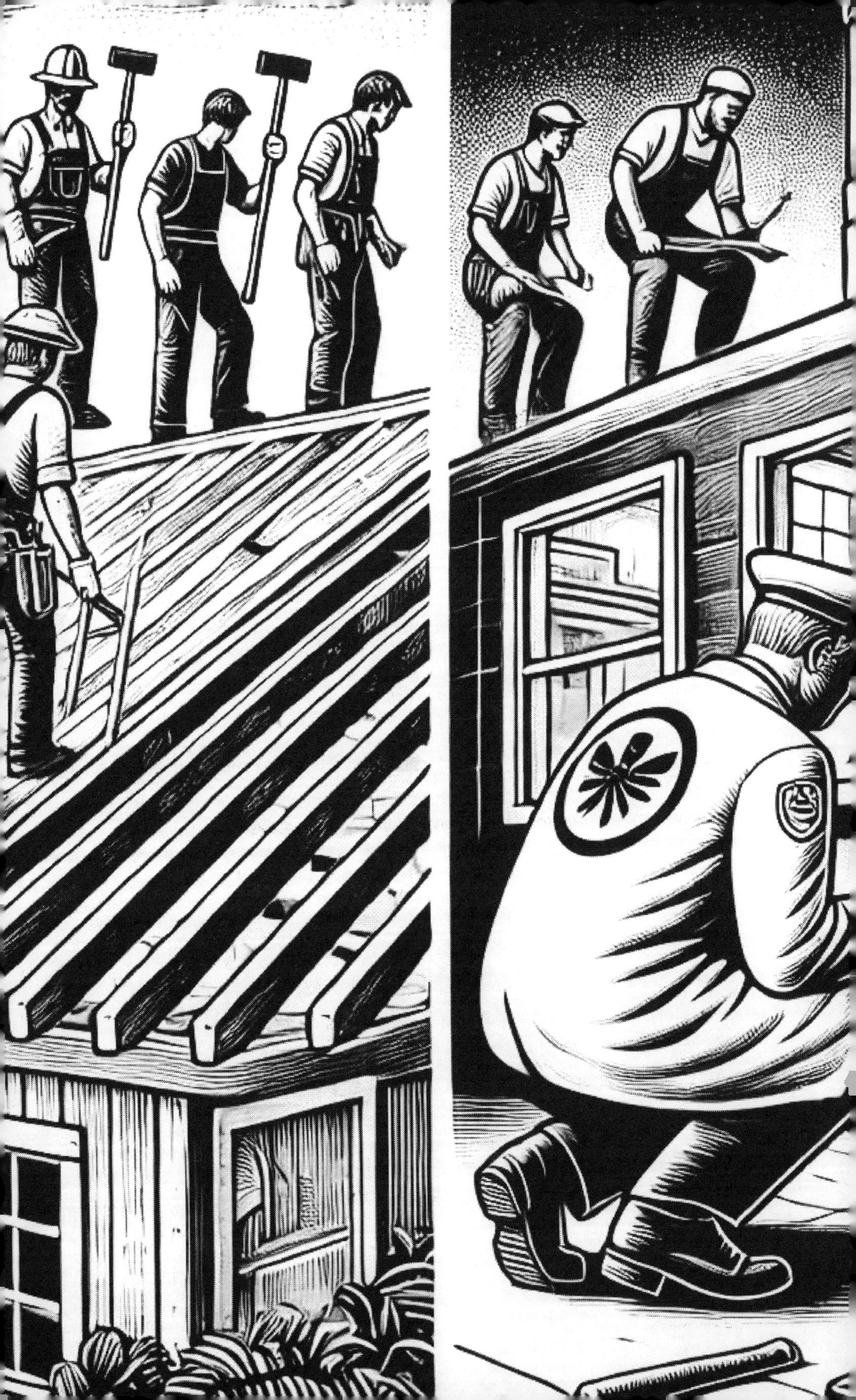

From Hammer to Health: A New Path Unfolds

Early Saturday morning, we started with thirteen men, hammers in hand, and by Labor Day Monday, we had finished installing the roof. There was still some finishing work left, but it looked like a garage, complete with a second-floor storage loft. When the contractor came back with his crew on Tuesday, he was surprised by how much we had accomplished in such a short time. That experience was a good learning opportunity for the family because, over the next eight years, we worked as a family on six projects, building or remodeling houses for different family members.

In late August, I went to the Lancaster Branch of the university to see what classes I needed for a teaching certificate. I enrolled and started after Labor Day. However, in my second week of school, some of the teachers in my classes painted such a dismal picture of teaching that I started having second thoughts about making it a career. At the same time, I saw an ad in the local newspaper for a sanitarian position at the Hocking County Health Department. I talked it over with Hideko and hand-delivered my resume.

I withdrew from school, returned all my books, and started working as the Director of Environmental Health—a fancy title for the chief health inspector. Shortly after starting, I got licensed as a Registered Sanitarian. There was only one other sanitarian in the department at the time, but she quit two weeks after I started because she hadn't been promoted to Chief Inspector.

At that time, state regulations required that food service establishments only be inspected once a year, which was all the sanitarian before me had done, no matter how bad the establishments looked. On my first day, she took me to inspect what she considered the worst and then the best restaurant in Logan, the county seat. The worst had many violations, but the best was even worse. During the meeting with the owner of the so-called best restaurant, as I pointed out the discrepancies, he stated, "I knew I was in trouble when the inspector got down on his hands and knees and looked under the equipment."

I instituted a program where all food service establishments would be inspected once a quarter and more frequently if needed. By working with the owners and managers, we only had to suspend one establishment's food service license in my 14-year tenure at the health department.

Expanding Horizons in Public Health

In addition to food establishments, the environmental health section was responsible for inspecting campgrounds, swimming pools, schools, home sewage systems, and water wells. A short time after starting, I was able to hire Kelly Montgomery, a recent Ohio University graduate. Together, we nearly quadrupled the number of inspections done in all areas. In my third year at the health department, the administrator and the Board of Health allowed me to hire a summer intern to help with inspections that were mainly done during the summer.

It was during this time that the State of Ohio registered and licensed all sanitarians working in environmental health. With the new requirements, there was now a shortage of qualified people to work in the field. As a result, Kelly and I frequently received job offers from other city and county health departments. Hocking County was mostly rural, and at first, I had to rely on maps and ask for directions when making appointments. Eventually, I knew every square inch and back road in the area.

Both Kelly and I became State Licensed Public Pest Control Operators, and in the summer, we would fog for mosquitoes in selected areas of the county. I was already familiar with the fogging equipment from my time in Beirut with the Marines.

The State of Ohio required all registered sanitarians to receive 18 hours of continuing education annually, and the state health department would sponsor a few days of classes at Ohio State University to fulfill that requirement. After about a year at the health department, I convinced the Board of Health that we needed an additional full-time sanitarian due to the increasing number of inspections Kelly and I were doing each month. The growth of tourism in the county, including more campgrounds and tourist cabins, led to more food service places that needed inspection.

Cleaning Up and Moving Forward

One area neither Kelly nor I liked was nuisance complaints. Often, it was a neighborly dispute, but we were the ones who had to settle it. One memorable complaint was from a neighbor who said the house next door smelled bad, and rats were running in and out. Kelly and I went to inspect. The house was occupied by a middle-aged man who had lived with his parents before their passing over 25 years ago. The calendar on the wall still showed the date of their deaths. He didn't cook and would walk to fast-food places for his meals, which he brought home. He never threw anything away. Everything that had entered the house over the past 25 years was still there. The stench was overwhelming, and you could walk through the house without ever touching the floor, as trash in most rooms was knee-high, wall-to-wall. We managed to get him some psychiatric help, and the city of Logan hired a crew to clean out the house, filling several dumpsters with garbage.

A local high school teacher once asked if I would give a class on food service sanitation to her home economics class. I was thrilled since I had done similar work in the Navy. But the students weren't like the sailors I had taught. Many of them talked among themselves during the class, and the teacher didn't say a word. That turned out to be a one-time class, and I was glad I hadn't pursued teaching after the Navy.

Things at the health department eventually ran smoothly. We now had three sanitarians and mapped out our day during morning meetings at 8 o'clock, making sure no two people were heading in the same direction to save on gas. I spent some of my time with township trustees and other political appointees.

Every holiday meant a family get-together at our house, especially in the summer. Everyone seemed comfortable being there, and it was always a good time. My sister, Pam, got married in our backyard garden. Patrick also got married there. We had 122 guests who spent the day fishing, playing ball, and enjoying other games. In the evening, we had a cookout, followed by a DJ and dancing in a tent. The whole thing was supposed to end at 10 PM, but the DJ and everyone else were having such a great time that it went on until closer to midnight.

From Farm to Garden: Crafting Our Retirement Sanctuary

Chiemi had moved back to Ohio and worked as a beautician for a few years before transitioning to a lab position at Ralston, analyzing breakfast cereal. In a short time, she saved enough money to make a down payment on her own house. Patrick had bought a farm about a mile from us. After all those years of being away from the family, now everyone was close by.

Hideko was working nights at the Fairfield Medical Center, while I worked days at the Hocking County Health Department. In October 1999, after much discussion, Hideko and I decided that we would retire in early 2000. At the next Board of Health meeting, I informed them that I would be retiring effective April 1, 2000, but that I would be gone most of the time after December 31, 1999 due to accumulated vacation and comp time from mosquito spraying. Hideko also informed her supervisors of her intention to retire before April.

In March 2000, Hideko and I enrolled in the OSU Master Gardener course at the county extension office. This helped us better manage our already large garden and in pruning our shrubs and fruit trees. We also volunteered, planting shrubs and flowers at the courthouse and other public places in the city. At home, we spent time clearing hiking trails in our woods, making the paths large enough for me to drive the tractor to keep them mowed. Building footbridges across the small stream in the front of our property caused a lot of stress between us, but we eventually got it done. I tore down an old garage next to the driveway and replaced it with a gazebo, inspired by a design I had seen in a Better Homes and Gardens Outdoor Projects book. That project turned out so well that I constructed a second gazebo, this time of my own design, further up the driveway. Under the shade trees overlooking the pond, I built a small Tea House for Hideko to entertain her Japanese friends. Once we had everything just the way we wanted—with hiking trails and the grounds looking like a park—we hosted a meeting of the county Master Gardeners, just to show off a little.

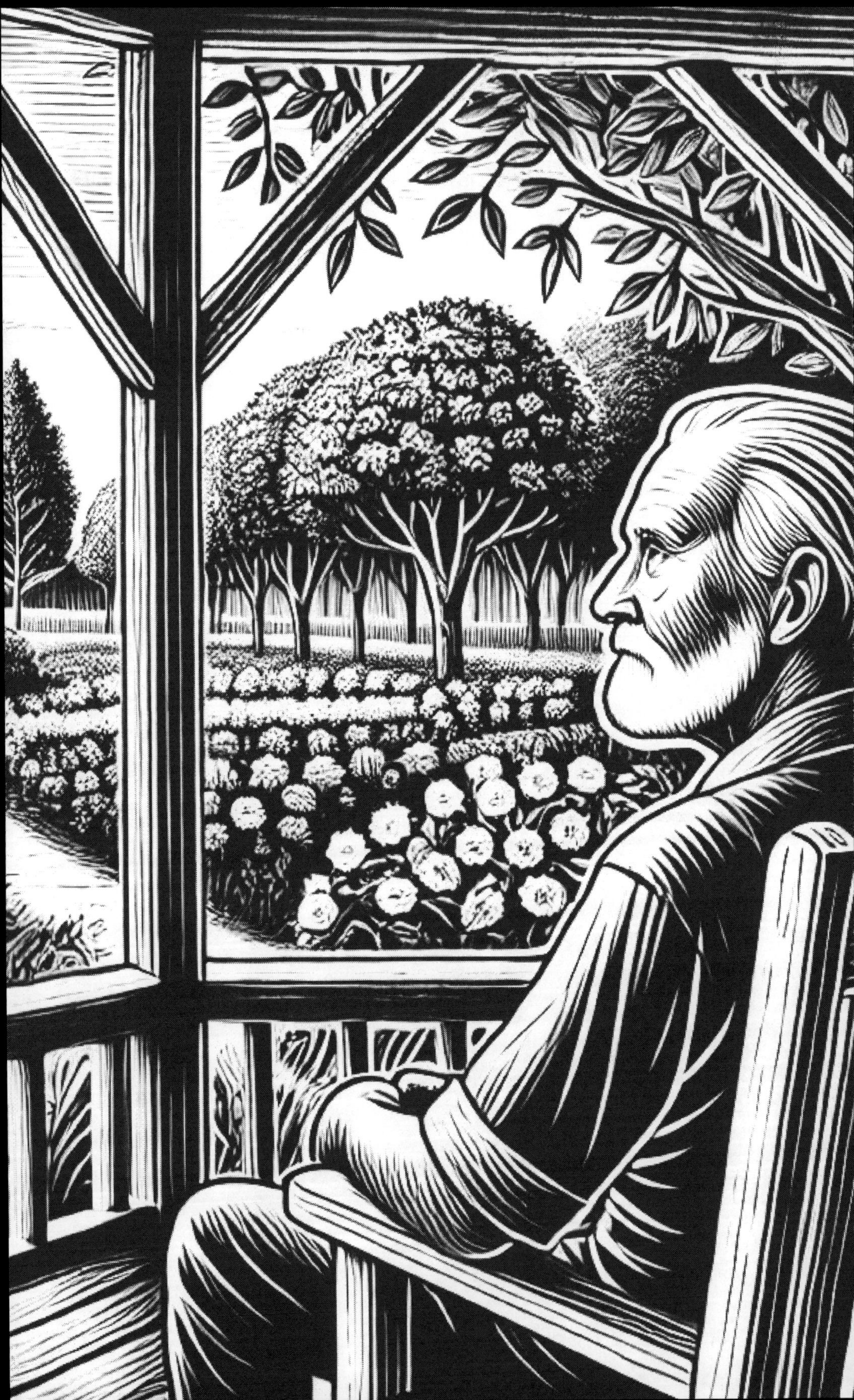

Searching for Purpose in the Quiet of Retirement

In addition to the volunteer work we did for the Master Gardeners, I worked three days a week at the Berne Union in the 6th grade class, helping students who were struggling in reading and math. Every year, I worked one-on-one with students in those areas where the teacher didn't have enough time due to the size of the class. Through her contacts at the hospital, Hideko started attending religious services at Saint Paul's, a small Lutheran Church a short distance from our house. Although the congregation was small, they were very active, with twice-yearly rummage and bake sales and other community activities. We volunteered with another couple to clean the social hall and kitchen once a week, and we took one month out of the year to clean the sanctuary.

I got to know most of the members of the church and would occasionally attend services with Hideko, although not frequently. Every time I went, if they were having communion, the pastor would look at me and extend an invitation to participate. I never did. I just didn't feel it was the right thing for me to do.

Everything in my life seemed to be in order. I had a convertible sports car, a truck, and another car that Hideko was driving. I didn't have any bills except for monthly living expenses, yet I felt like something was missing. I'd often take a walk around the yard, sit in one of the gazebos, and just think. What was I supposed to do now?

A Return to Faith: Finding My Way Back

It was late summer 2009, and Hideko and I had just finished cleaning Saint Paul's in the morning—the kitchen and social hall. On our way into town that afternoon, I blurted out, "I want to go back to church!"

She looked at me, surprised, and asked, "What did you forget?" thinking I'd left something at Saint Paul's.

"No, I want to go back to Saint Mary's," the Catholic church where I'd been baptized in 1957. She gave me her blessing, and we didn't say anything more.

The next day, I stopped by Saint Mary's and knelt in the last pew. I was afraid to go any further. For the first time in many, many years, I prayed and asked God to help me and to lead me where He wanted me to go. On my way out, I picked up a copy of the weekly bulletin to take home and read. Over the next few days, I looked at it several times, surprised to see that only one priest was listed. When I joined the church in 1957, there had been three priests assigned to Saint Mary's. Finally, I mustered the courage to call the number listed for the parish office. Cathy Shumaker, the parish secretary, answered. I told her who I was, that I had been away from the church for quite some time, and asked what I needed to do to return. She scheduled an appointment for me to meet with Father Donald Franks, the pastor.

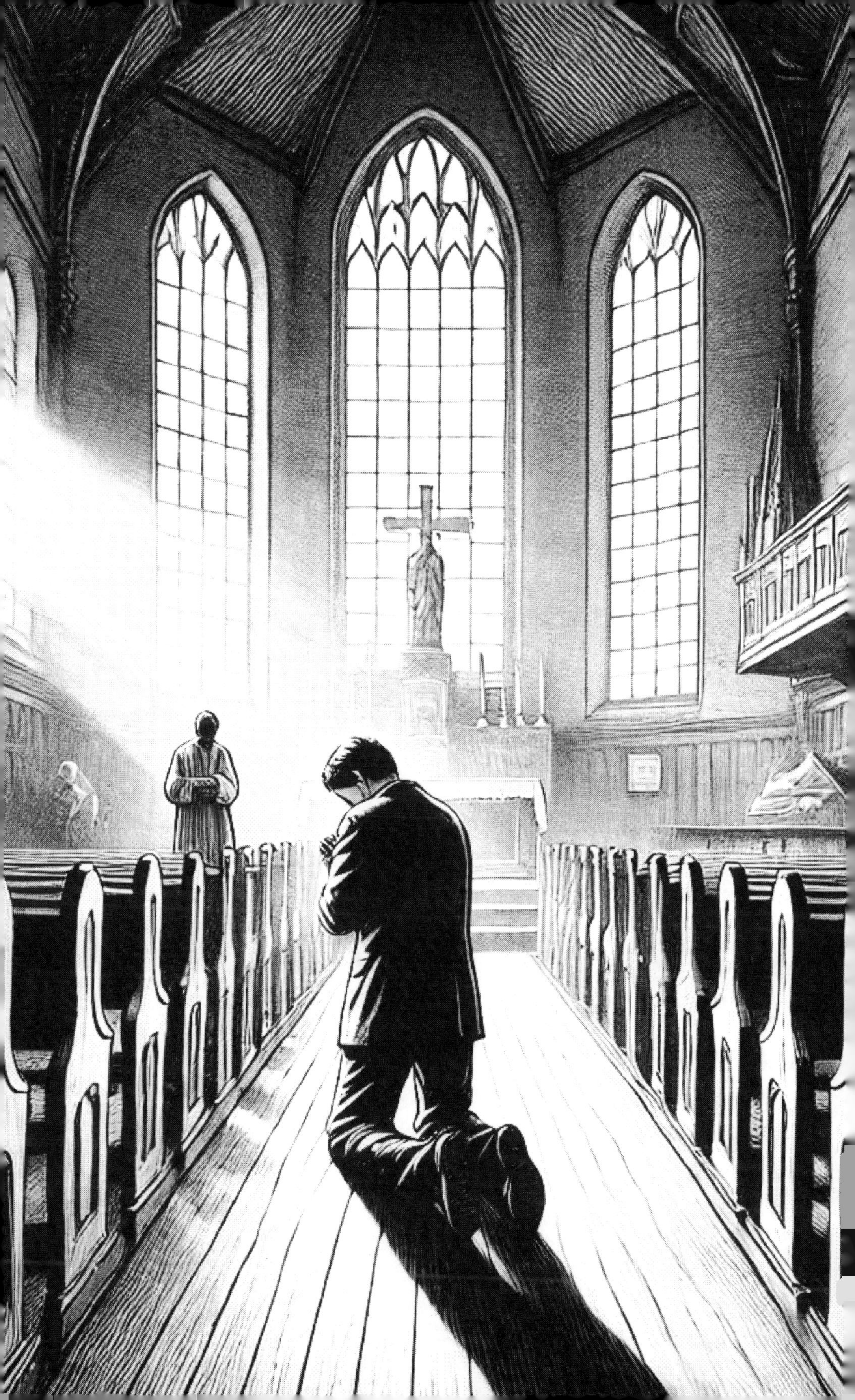

My 10 AM appointment came faster than I expected. True to my training, I was there a little early. Father Franks was in a meeting, so I sat in the hallway and waited. Finally, I heard the voices quiet down, and Father opened the side door and welcomed me into his office. I introduced myself, and we sat in two chairs, facing one another, about three feet apart. "Tell me about yourself," he said. It was an easy invitation to start the conversation, and I began to tell him about my baptism in 1957, my time in the Navy, my work with the Hocking County Health Department, and how I was now retired and helping Hideko at Saint Paul's. After talking for a while, Father Franks said I was more than welcome to return to the church, but first, I needed to go to confession. We could do it now, or I could wait until the Saturday confessions at the church. That really shocked me—confessing face-to-face with a priest was something I hadn't thought about. All my previous confessions had been behind a screen. I thought for a moment and then said, "Let's do it now."

He knew I wouldn't remember every sin I'd committed, but by asking me questions, he helped me along. After a while, he could tell I was getting worn out, so he said he'd help me with an Act of Contrition. He had me stand and repeat the words after him. He put one hand on my head and one on my shoulder and said, "This is going to be pretty powerful." We began, and by the time we finished, I was shaking all over, tears running down my cheeks, and snot running down my nose. After he said the Absolution, he smiled and said, "I told you this would be powerful."

We talked a few more minutes, and he suggested I sit in on the Rite of Christian Initiation for Adults (RCIA), which would start the following week. Father Franks then took me back to the office, where Cathy Shumaker registered me as a member of Saint Mary of the Assumption. Before leaving the church, I knelt again and thanked God for allowing me to return to His church.

The following Sunday, at my first Mass, I sat in the middle of the church so I could watch what people were doing and follow their movements. I figured this was why Father suggested I attend RCIA classes—I needed to learn more about my faith.

Embracing a New Mission: A Journey of Faith and Service

The following Monday was my first RCIA class, taught by Brian McCauley, a former high school teacher. My name was on the list of attendees, and he was expecting me. Although I didn't have a sponsor, several Catholics offered to be there for me. The two-hour class was so full of information that I wondered what he would say at the next one. There were always handouts and papers to review for the next class. The nine months flew by quickly, and I was glad to witness those individuals who entered the Church at Easter.

The following year, I asked Brian if I could sit in on the class again, and he gave me permission. After the first couple of sessions that second year, Hideko asked if she could attend as well, even though she wasn't planning on becoming Catholic. She just wanted to know more about the Catholic faith. Brian gave his permission, and for the rest of that year, the two of us went to class every Monday night. In the third year, I was asked if I would be a sponsor for a man entering the Church. I said yes, and I was a sponsor every year for the next nine years.

About three months after I returned to the Church, I told Hideko that I couldn't just be a Sunday Catholic—I needed to do more. So, I started going to daily Mass a couple of times a week. Then, I volunteered to go once a month on a mission project to Beaver, a town in southern Ohio. I also volunteered to work in the kitchen when there was a funeral luncheon. I was always welcomed by the people working at the mission or in the kitchen.

On one mission trip to Beaver, just before Christmas, the man who was supposed to dress as Santa Claus called at the last minute to say he couldn't make it. The Sister in charge told me they had a suit but no one to fill it, and asked if I would consider being Santa. I must have done a good job because the following year, they didn't even have to ask—they knew I was it. Though the mission has since closed, I'm still in the kitchen, fifteen years later.

It was about my third year working in the kitchen when one of my female coworkers asked why I wasn't an Extraordinary Minister and distributing communion. I had never given it a thought and didn't feel qualified. Around the same time, Brian, who was in charge of training Extraordinary Ministers, asked if I would take communion to the homebound. Of course, I said yes. Over the years, I've visited many parishioners after Sunday Mass, carrying communion to the homebound. It wasn't long before I also started distributing communion during Mass.

About six months after I returned to the Church, I told Father Franks during one of my confessions that I couldn't begin to describe the peace and joy I had felt since allowing God to direct my life in my pursuit of happiness.

Full Circle: Finding Faith, Home, and Purpose

About five years after returning to the Church, I had a conversation with Dale Murphy, a coworker in the kitchen, as we were preparing for a meal. We started talking about the Rosary, and I mentioned that I had a rosary given to me by my godparents when I was baptized in 1957. I had carried it with me all over the world in my travels, but I had never used it and didn't know how. The very next time I saw him, Dale gave me a CD from the Mary Foundation on how to pray the Rosary.

I started listening to the CD only when I was in the car, but after a few weeks, I began saying the Rosary at home, always praying the Joyful Mysteries since they were the only ones I could remember. Eventually, though, I made it a point to go to Mass 45 minutes early so I could spend that time praying the Rosary.

In 2012, we moved to a condominium in Lancaster, right next door to Saint Bernadette Catholic Church. Now, I could walk to daily Mass in just two minutes and attend every day. Though I still belonged to Saint Mary's, my daily Mass schedule became centered around Saint Bernadette's due to its proximity.

We left the farm because taking care of the property had become a chore, but Hideko missed having a garden, which was forbidden in the condo. Our daughter, Chiemi, and her husband, Brian, had moved into our farmhouse, and Hideko would go there in the summer to work in the garden and yard. However, after four years of doing that, she said it was too much work. So, we began looking for a small house in Lancaster where she could work outdoors for a while and then rest indoors when needed.

After four years in the condo, we bought a house on the far west side of Lancaster, and it seems like a perfect fit. It has a garden big enough to give away vegetables, and Hideko still has enough to can or put in the freezer. I can no longer walk to daily Mass, but Saint Mary's is only about a mile and a quarter away, just a seven-minute drive. So far, the streets have been clear in the winter, making it easy to get there.

Part 8

~ The Grace of Age ~
A Life Well Lived: Reflections at Eighty-Four

I'm now eighty-four, and as I look back at the memories I've put to paper, I wonder why it all seems to have happened just a short time ago. I realize that life doesn't always go as planned, but we must work with what we have at the moment. The key to happiness is to be content with the situation you're in at the present time. That doesn't mean you can't strive to change things, but it does mean accepting where you are in life and being determined to work for the change.

When I found out that I wasn't going to nursing school in August 1962, I cried and ran away. Fortunately, I had a place to run to and people who cared. My return to the Navy was the best thing that could've happened to me because it led me to meet my wife and gave me two wonderful children whom we see and talk to several times a week.

I can't begin to describe the pleasure I get from going to Mass or saying the Rosary, and I regret that for so long I did neither. As a result, Patrick and Chiemi were never baptized as infants and had no religious education. I just didn't think it was important at the time. Both Patrick and Chiemi have attended Mass with me on occasion, as has Hideko, but not enough to pique their interest in becoming Catholic.

Becoming a father is not like babysitting for a few hours. You're in it for life, responsible for their safety and guiding them with your actions and decisions. When giving advice, do it once, then stay quiet. When my grandson was offered a PhD scholarship, he wasn't sure he wanted to accept it because it would take five years to finish, and he would be 32 by then. I asked him how old he would be in five years if he didn't accept the scholarship—then I shut up. He'll graduate in six months.

I'm struck by how quickly the years have passed. Memories that once felt so distant now seem to have happened just yesterday. Life, as I've learned, rarely goes exactly as we plan, but there's a beauty in working with what we're given in each moment. The key to happiness, I've come to understand, lies not in getting everything we want but in being content with where we are while still striving to make things better.

I also reflect on my spiritual journey. In the earlier years, I neglected the importance of faith. It wasn't until later that I rediscovered the peace and purpose that come from attending Mass and praying the Rosary. While I regret not raising Patrick and Chiemi with that foundation, I realize now that faith is a personal journey, and my role is to live as an example—offering guidance, but ultimately respecting their path.

Fatherhood has taught me patience and the importance of leading by example. As a parent, you're in it for the long haul. It's not about controlling their lives but guiding them when needed, then stepping back. When my grandson debated over accepting a PhD scholarship, I offered my advice just once. I simply asked him, "How old will you be in five years if you don't take it?"—and then I left the decision in his hands. Now, he's set to graduate in six months.

The lesson I carry with me is that life, in all its unpredictability, gives us opportunities to grow, to learn, and to love more deeply. Every twist, every unexpected turn, has its purpose. The joy isn't just in the destination, but in the wisdom gained along the way.

~ The Strength of Loyalty ~
Enduring Bonds: Fifty Years of Friendship

We called my best man from our wedding, Richard, and his wife, Julene, who were friends when we lived at Camp Pendleton and San Diego in 1965 and 1966, and told them we were going to San Diego for a vacation. We hadn't seen them in over forty years, although we talked on the phone a couple of times a year and sent Christmas cards and letters. They flew from Seattle and met us there, and it was as if we hadn't seen them for only a week. We laughed, joked, and toured places we frequented when we lived there. It was a wonderful week together. Then, on the day of our 50th wedding anniversary, a florist delivered two dozen roses to our house from the Mallea. When we called to thank them, we found out that Julene had passed away just a week before. They had talked about sending the flowers before her passing, and Richard didn't want to tell us before our anniversary to avoid spoiling the surprise.

When I was to undergo open-heart surgery to replace my aortic valve, Richard was there for me.

Steve Horst, a Navy friend now living in South Dakota, drove to Ohio a few days before my surgery. He stayed with Hideko during the surgery and remained for a couple of days after my recovery was assured. True friendship is something that transcends time and distance.

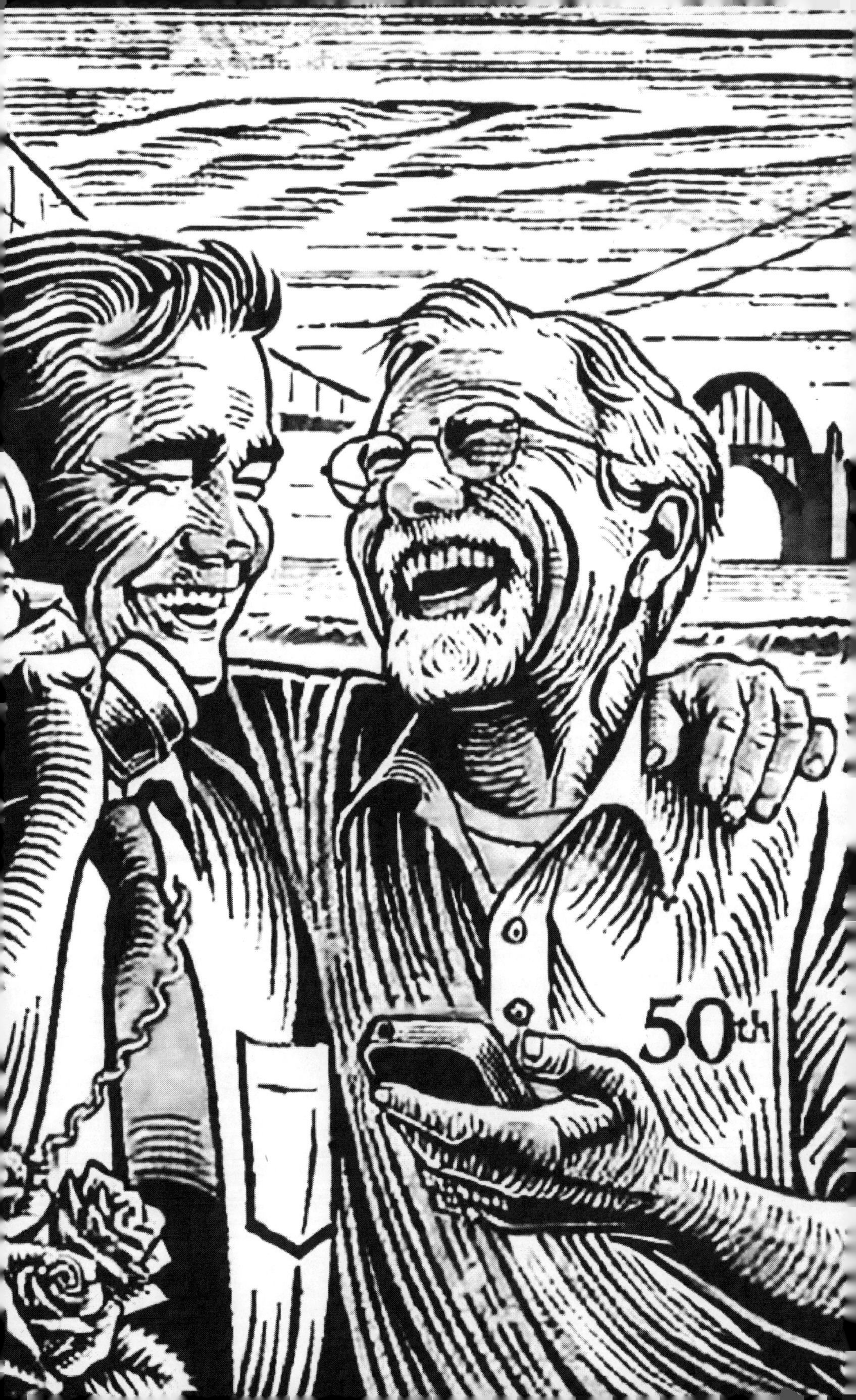
50th

Fifty years of friendship teaches you that true bonds never fade. Even when time and distance separate us, real friendships pick up as if no time has passed. When we met Richard and Julene after forty years apart, it felt like we had only been away for a week. We laughed, reminisced, and visited familiar places as though we'd never left. The joy of reconnecting was so effortless, a testament to the depth of our friendship.

I'll never forget the day we received two dozen roses from the Millers on our 50th wedding anniversary. It was such a beautiful surprise, only to learn later that Julene had passed just a week before. Richard had kept the sorrow to himself so that it wouldn't overshadow our celebration. That selfless act reflected the kind of loyalty and love that has always been the foundation of our friendship.

True friendship also shows itself in times of need. When I was facing open-heart surgery, Richard was there for me, and Steve, another Navy friend, drove across the country to stay with Hideko and support her through those anxious days. Their presence reminded me that real friends walk with you through life's hardest moments.

In reflecting on these bonds, I've learned that true friendship isn't measured by how often we talk or see each other, but by the unwavering support and loyalty we give when it matters most. Time and distance may separate us, but friendship rooted in love and loyalty endures.

~ Lessons in Leadership ~
The Journey from Command to Compassion

In my years in the Navy, I realized that I can tackle any job I'm given as long as I'm shown how to do it. Whether it was learning to suture a cut or operating a shortwave radio to communicate with medevac helicopter pilots, I always managed to handle my tasks well. I wouldn't call myself an expert in everything, but I did a damn good job at everything I was assigned.

One thing the Navy didn't teach me, however, was how to be a better father. While stationed at the Naval Hospital in New York in 1967-1968, Patrick, who was the proud owner of a new Nerf football, would wait for me to get home so we could play outside. We would chase each other and pretend to tackle, and we did this every day, weather permitting. He was only 2 ½ then. By the time I got home permanently in 1970, Patrick was almost 6, and Chiemi was 2. That closeness we had never fully returned. It wasn't until Patrick got married and had sons of his own that we rekindled our bond.

Looking back, I could have been a better father instead of a dictator. I didn't always take their feelings into account as they were growing up. I was too focused on being authoritative rather than listening to them. Now, they are two outstanding adults, loved by everyone in spite of my shortcomings. It was always a challenge to be separated from family while serving in the Navy—first from my parents, brothers, and sister, and then from Hideko and the kids. A lot of important milestones happened to them while I was away. I always stressed the importance of honesty to Patrick and Chiemi, always telling them to tell the truth. Patrick even received a whipping for lying to me once.

One time, while the ship was in Guantanamo Bay, the Officer of the Day asked me about the status of a crew member who had been admitted to the Naval Hospital. The ship was leaving for Norfolk in a couple of days, and we needed to know the crewman's condition. I went to Sick Bay to get the hospital's phone number and was confronted by a second-class Corpsman on duty. He thought I was checking up on him and refused to listen to why I was there. We began to argue, and in frustration, I ended the conversation with "F*** you, Frank! I have a job to do, and I'm not going to stand here and argue." What I meant to say was "F*** it, Frank," but the words didn't come out right. The next day, the Corpsman complained to the doctor, who called me into his office. When he asked me if that's what I said, I denied it. Now, 39 years later, if I could, I would apologize to both the Corpsman and the doctor. This incident has stuck with me all these years, and writing about it makes it feel like it just happened. Honesty cannot be compromised.

Today, I am most thankful for my wife and children, and I'm especially proud of how they've matured. Both of them put others before themselves. They never leave without giving a hug and saying, "I love you." I don't know if things would have been any different had I worked a 9-to-5 job and been home every night, but they managed well, and they've made a difference in this country. An added bonus is that Patrick's sons emulate their father and always put others first.

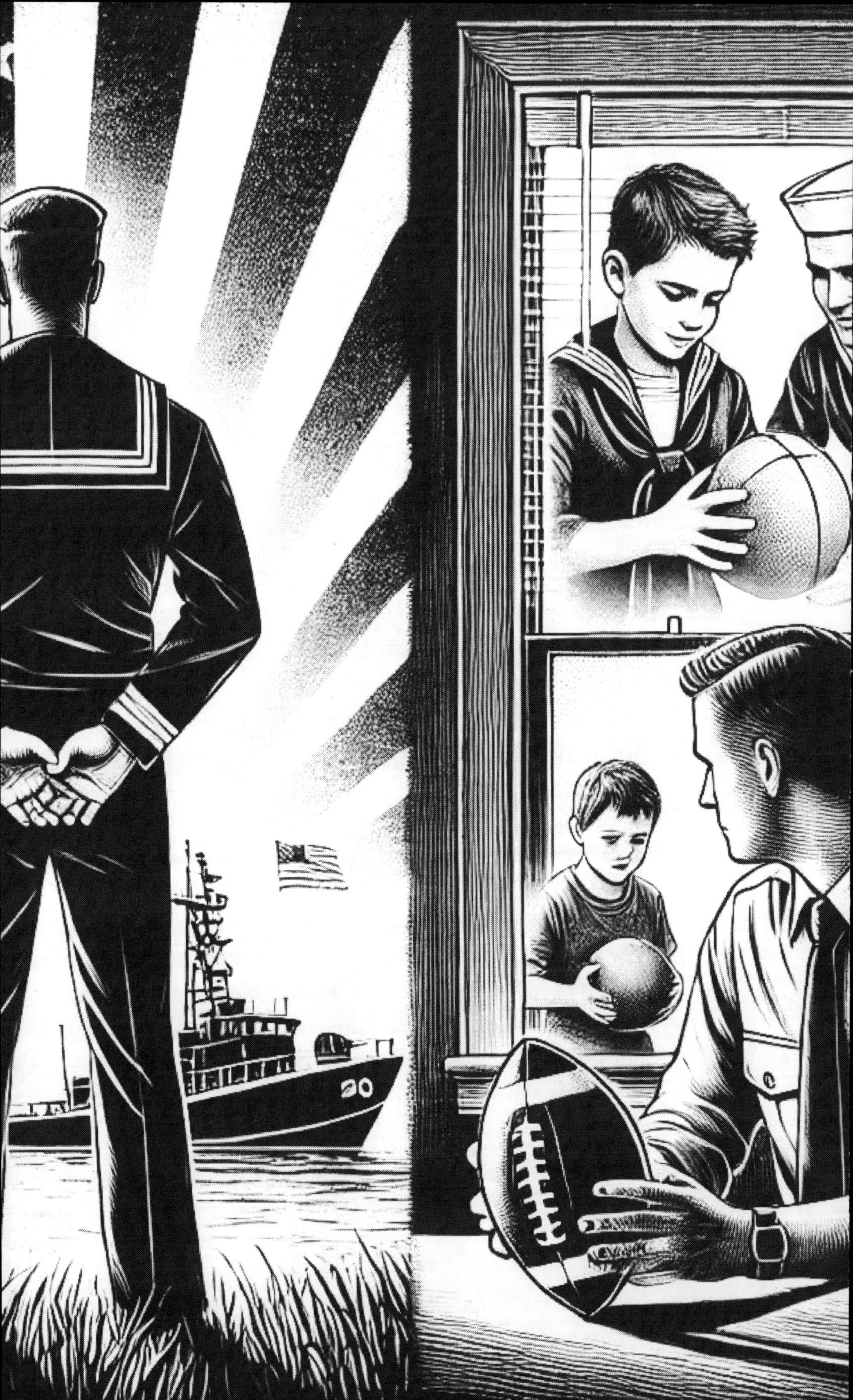
20

Looking back on my Navy years, I realize that I was able to tackle any job as long as I was shown how. Whether it was stitching a wound or communicating with medevac pilots, I handled each task with determination and a commitment to do it well. But while the Navy taught me many skills, it didn't teach me how to be a better father. That's something I had to learn through time and reflection.

Being away from family during my service was one of the greatest challenges. I missed important milestones, both with my parents and siblings, and later with Hideko and the kids. It's something I can never get back, but I am deeply grateful for the incredible adults Patrick and Chiemi have become despite my shortcomings. They're both kind, compassionate, and always put others before themselves. That, to me, is the greatest testament to their character—and an outcome I'm proud to have witnessed.

As I reflect on my life today, I am most thankful for my wife and children. They have grown into individuals who truly care for others, and I see that same quality passed down to Patrick's sons. Although I wonder if things would have been different had I been home more often, I know they have done well in spite of my absences. At the end of the day, the love and respect we share now is what matters most, and for that, I am deeply grateful.

Looking back on my Navy years, I realize that I was able to tackle any job as long as I was shown how. Whether it was stitching a wound or communicating with medevac pilots, I handled each task with determination and a commitment to do it well. But while the Navy taught me many skills, it didn't teach me how to be a better father. That's something I had to learn through time and reflection.

Being away from family during my service was one of the greatest challenges. I missed important milestones, both with my parents and siblings, and later with Hideko and the kids. It's something I can never get back, but I am deeply grateful for the incredible adults Patrick and Chiemi have become despite my shortcomings. They're both kind, compassionate, and always put others before themselves. That, to me, is the greatest testament to their character—and an outcome I'm proud to have witnessed.

One moment that has stayed with me all these years was a confrontation with a Corpsman in Guantanamo Bay. In my frustration, I said something I shouldn't have, and when asked about it later, I denied it. Even now, 39 years later, I wish I could apologize to both the Corpsman and the doctor. It's a reminder that honesty should never be compromised, even in difficult moments.

As I reflect on my life today, I am most thankful for my wife and children. They have grown into individuals who truly care for others, and I see that same quality passed down to Patrick's sons. Although I wonder if things would have been different had I been home more often, I know they have done well in spite of my absences. At the end of the day, the love and respect we share now is what matters most, and for that, I am deeply grateful.

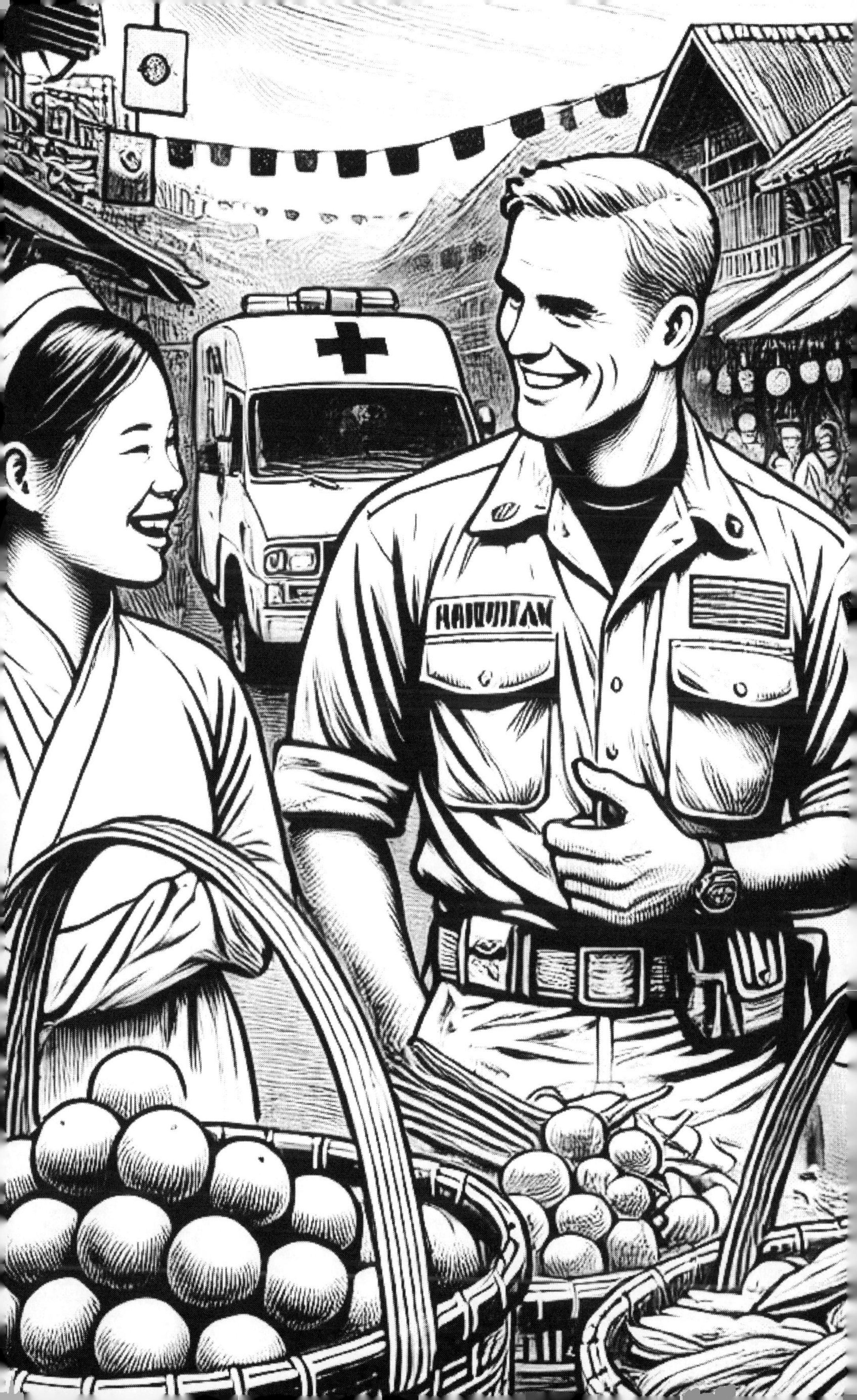

~ Lost in Translation ~

Discovering Respect Through Language and Culture

If someone had told me when I was a kid that I would marry someone from another country, I wouldn't have believed them. I was always fascinated by other cultures, and I never looked down on people when I was in their country. I've always lived by the belief that you should treat people the way you wish to be treated—with respect and civility.

A simple "thank you" goes a long way. Learning a bit of the language helps you feel more comfortable in a new country. While I was in Saigon in 1962-1963, many of the other corpsmen and I took Vietnamese language lessons from the dispensary receptionist three days a week after work. After a few weeks, I thought I was doing pretty well, except that when I went to the market, the mostly female shopkeepers would giggle when I spoke to them. I assumed it was just because I was using their language.

Then, one day, I spoke to one of our male Vietnamese ambulance drivers, who spoke English, and told him that the shopkeepers would always laugh when I spoke Vietnamese. He laughed and explained that it was because I spoke Vietnamese like a female from the Central Highlands. Apparently, I spoke with a Central Highlands accent, and women say things a little differently than men in that region. That explained a lot since our receptionist was from the Central Highlands herself.

Looking back, it's almost hard to believe that my life took the turn it did—marrying someone from another country and living with such a rich blend of cultures. Growing up, that wasn't something I could have imagined, but life has a way of surprising us. My fascination with other cultures always kept me open-minded and grounded in the belief that people deserve respect, no matter where they come from. That simple act of treating others with kindness, of offering a smile and a "thank you," is universal. It's one of the few things that can bridge any cultural divide.

I learned early on that making an effort to speak the language, even just a little, can make a big difference when you're in a new place. During my time in Saigon, those language lessons with the receptionist made me feel more connected to the locals. Although, I'll admit, it came with a few humorous moments—like realizing I was unknowingly speaking with a female accent! It taught me that learning is a process filled with unexpected twists, and sometimes the mistakes are what create the best memories.

In the end, those moments of misunderstanding were a reminder of the importance of humility when stepping into someone else's world. It's not just about learning words or customs—it's about being willing to laugh at yourself, to keep trying, and most importantly, to respect the people you meet along the way. Each experience, even the awkward ones, deepened my understanding and helped me live out the simple truth: treat others as you want to be treated.

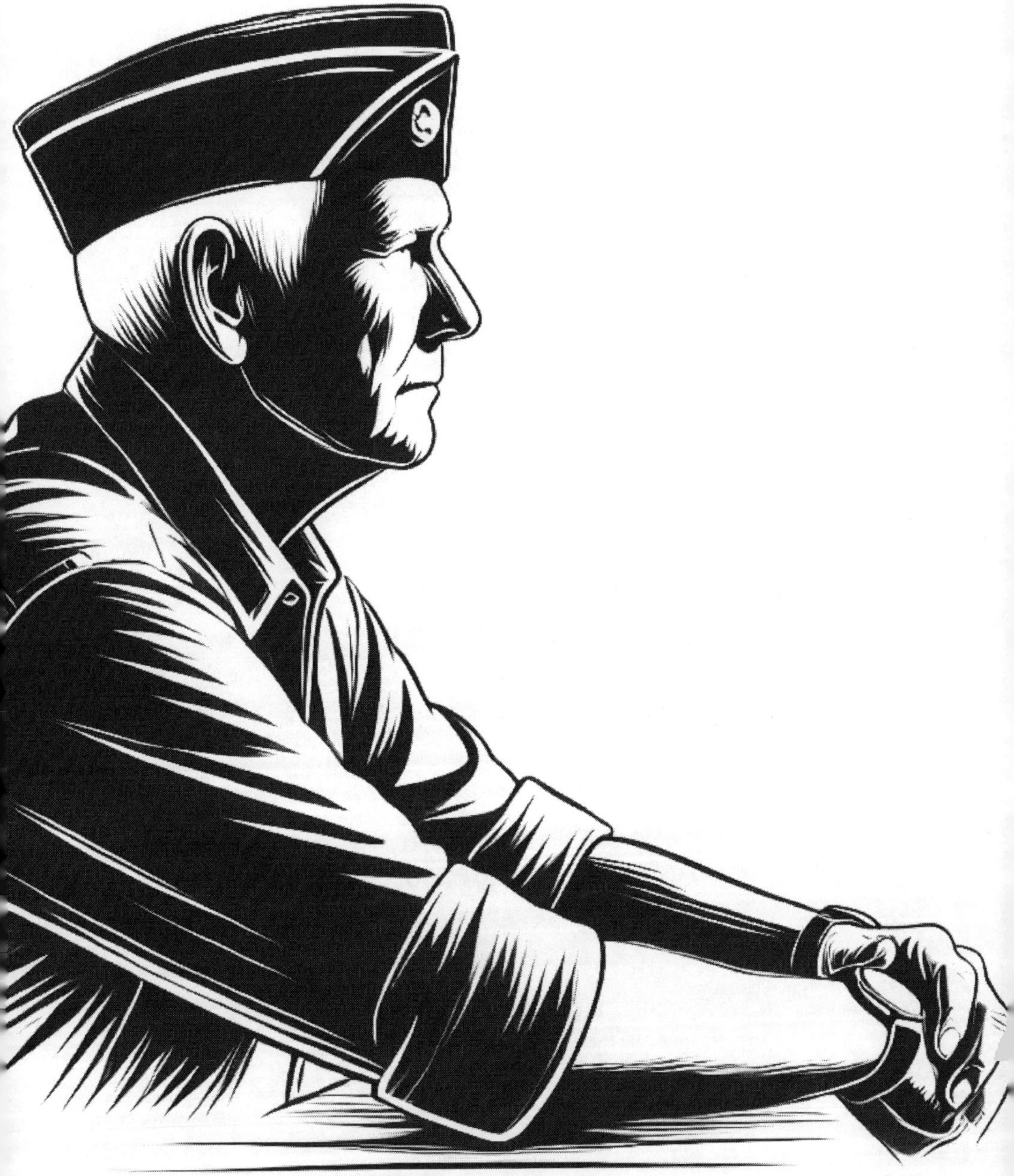

~ Matters of the Heart ~
Trust, Health, and the Lessons Learned

During my annual physical at age 72, my doctor discovered a heart murmur he hadn't heard before. After an echocardiogram at the local hospital, my doctor sent me to a cardiologist in Columbus. A thorough examination revealed that my aortic valve was failing and would eventually need to be replaced. I was told I would need an annual follow-up exam to monitor the valve's status. I had an echocardiogram each year for the next five years before needing a cardiac catheterization and eventually heart surgery to replace the valve. Initially, when the doctor discovered the heart murmur, I felt fine. But by the time I had the surgery, I would get short of breath with even minimal exertion. I felt great immediately after the surgery, and now, seven years later, I'm still doing great. It was a miracle that my family doctor was knowledgeable and knew what to look for to determine my problem. I will always be grateful to him.

I suppose trust is something I've always had with people. I would consider myself an honest person and would like to think others are honest as well, but that isn't always the case. I spent more than double what a new roof would have cost because I trusted a salesman, even though I had some doubts about his sales pitch. President Reagan once said, "Trust, but verify," and I don't always do that. I guess wisdom doesn't always come with age. Sometimes, we just become more trusting.

At 72, I never expected to hear the words "heart murmur" during a routine physical. I felt fine at the time, so it came as a surprise when further tests revealed that my aortic valve was failing. Over the next several years, my condition gradually worsened until I needed surgery. What struck me most throughout that experience was the power of early detection. It was nothing short of a miracle that my family doctor knew what to look for and caught the issue before it became life-threatening. Seven years later, I'm still grateful for his expertise—and for the health I've regained.

This experience taught me that trust is vital in life, whether it's in the hands of a skilled doctor or in everyday interactions. I've always considered myself a trusting person, believing in the honesty of others. But I've learned that trust alone isn't enough. It needs to be paired with wisdom and discernment. There were moments when my trust was misplaced—like the time I overpaid for a roof because I believed a salesman's pitch, even though I had doubts. As President Reagan once said, "Trust, but verify." It's a lesson I've had to relearn, even at this stage of life.

Wisdom doesn't always come with age, as I've found. Sometimes, we grow more trusting, assuming that experience has made us sharper. But in reality, it's important to balance trust with cautious wisdom, ensuring that we're not just relying on hope, but on careful judgment. Through both health scares and missteps, I've learned to appreciate the importance of listening to that inner voice and trusting it when something feels off.

~ From Struggles to Blessings ~
Wisdom Gained Over Time

I have always been blessed to have family I could turn to, even if we weren't on the best of terms at the time. In 1966, while stationed at the Naval Hospital in San Diego, I needed to buy gas for my car. Fortunately, the hospital gas station charged only 25¢ a gallon, but it was close to payday, and I had no money. So, I took a dollar's worth of pennies from Patrick's piggy bank to buy gas. The station wouldn't accept the pennies unless they were rolled. They gave me the paper rolls and told me to go to the car, roll the pennies, and then bring them back inside to pay for the gas.

At the time, I was a Second-Class Corpsman and didn't make a lot of money. Since then, I have been blessed to be able to care for my family without worrying about finances and have even been able to lend money to my siblings when they were in need. I am certain that life has gotten easier as I've grown older. I'm more accepting of people and conditions now than I was in my early adult years. I don't know if anyone ever gave me advice when I was younger, but if they did, I probably didn't listen. In those earlier years, I nearly always did what I wanted, but now, if things don't go my way, so what? There's always tomorrow.

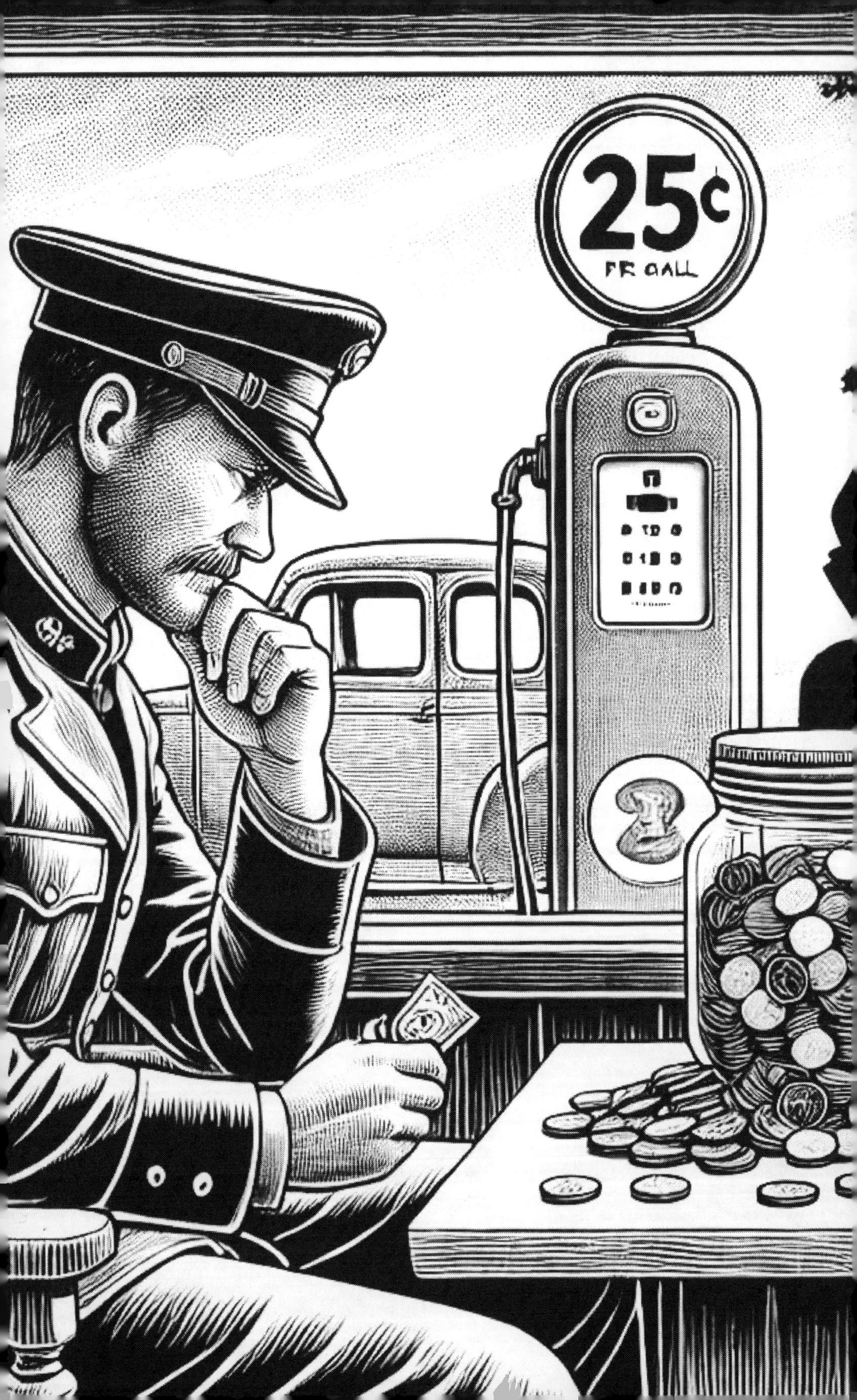
25¢

Looking back, I've always been fortunate to have family I could lean on, even in moments of tension. In 1966, when I found myself short on money, I remember the humbling experience of taking pennies from Patrick's piggy bank just to buy gas. It was a small but significant reminder of how tight finances were back then, and yet, even in that struggle, there was always a way forward.

As the years passed, I've been blessed with the ability to provide for my family without the same financial worries I had in my earlier days. I've even had the chance to help my siblings when they needed it. That's a gift I never take for granted.

With age comes perspective, and I've realized how much easier life feels when you stop resisting it. In my younger years, I was often stubborn, doing what I wanted without listening to advice— even if it was given to me. Today, I'm more accepting of people, circumstances, and outcomes. If things don't go my way, so what? There's always another day. That patience and acceptance, I believe, is one of the true blessings of growing older. Life has a way of teaching us that, in the end, everything works out as it's meant to, even if the journey doesn't unfold exactly as planned.

~ Guided by Duty ~
From Corpsman Dreams to Leadership Lessons

Many years ago, I read a quote in Reader's Digest that said, "The entire sum of man's existence is the magic of being needed by someone." I've tried to live by that, to make myself useful and enjoy life as it comes.

Since childhood, I had dreamed of becoming a doctor. But as I grew older, I realized that fulfilling that dream would require more money than my parents could make in their entire lifetime. When I was a junior in high school, one of my classmates, who was a little older and in the Naval Reserves as a Hospital Corpsman, suggested that I join and become a corpsman like him. I wouldn't be a doctor, but I would still get to work in medicine. I told my parents, and with their permission, I joined in May, two months after my seventeenth birthday.

That first summer, I spent in boot camp at Great Lakes, Illinois, followed by weekly Naval Reserve meetings in Columbus. Eventually, I was promoted to Hospital Corpsman. Over the next two summers, I went to the Naval Hospital in Philadelphia for two weeks of classroom instruction and on-the-job experience. In 1960, I went on active duty for two years, attending Basic Hospital Corps School in Great Lakes, Illinois.

The training was easy for me because of my experience at reserve meetings and my summers in Philadelphia. I stayed connected with family through weekly letters. Once I was stationed permanently and got to know my fellow workers, the Navy became like a second family. I always tried to do my best at whatever assignment I was given, and when my two years of active duty were up, I felt a bit of sadness as I headed home. I had been looking forward to nursing school, but when that didn't happen, I returned to the Navy after a two-month break.

In a way, I felt safe in the Navy. I always had a place to sleep, food to eat, and a challenging job—even if the hours were long. On my first overseas assignment, I was like a sponge, trying to absorb as much of the local culture as I could, thinking I might never be there again.

Of course, I did return to Vietnam, but this time, there was fighting everywhere. I never thought I'd be wounded by shrapnel or small arms fire, but during incoming fire, I tried to make myself as small as possible. Years later, I would have dreams about the Viet Cong and feel a sense of guilt that I wasn't a casualty when many men I knew were wounded or killed.

When I got home with less than a year left on my enlistment, I knew I had to leave the Navy. I felt that if I went back to Vietnam, I wouldn't be so lucky the next time. Then, when Hideko and I were contemplating moving to Hawaii, the Navy needed my services and offered me a duty station there. Since the U.S. was withdrawing all troops from Vietnam, the thought of going back didn't even cross my mind when I re-enlisted.

By then, my rank had risen, and I was immediately put in charge of other corpsmen. Fortunately, all the junior corpsmen under my supervision knew their jobs well and didn't need much direction. After three wonderful years in Hawaii, I was transferred to the First Medical Battalion at Camp Pendleton, California, where I spent two years as the administrative assistant to Lieutenant Commander Richard Coan, the commanding officer. Anyone who wanted to see or speak to him had to go through me first. He told me that my primary job was to keep him out of trouble—and I like to think I did. He expected 100% from the junior officers, and with the thin door between our offices, I could hear more than one of them being chewed out. I always felt sorry for the officers because they knew I could hear every word.

One time, after a particularly harsh dressing down of one of the officers, Commander Coan called me into his office and asked, "Have I ever said anything harsh to you or chewed you out?" I replied, "No, sir." He continued, "I chewed out the lieutenant because he wasn't doing his job. I know you feel bad for him, but don't. If chewing him out gets him to do his job right, then good. If not, he doesn't belong in the Navy."

As I reflect on the twists and turns of my life, one guiding principle has always remained true: the magic of being needed by someone. That simple quote from Reader's Digest has stayed with me, shaping how I've approached every job and relationship in my life. Whether it was in the Navy or in my personal life, I've always found meaning in being of service to others, in being useful, and in finding joy in the moment.

My childhood dream of becoming a doctor seemed out of reach financially, but joining the Navy as a Hospital Corpsman gave me the chance to work in medicine and help people. That role became a meaningful and defining part of my life. The Navy became like a second family, offering structure, purpose, and the opportunity to immerse myself in different cultures and experiences. I grew through each assignment, absorbing the lessons of leadership, responsibility, and compassion along the way.

Even when I faced danger in Vietnam, surviving when others didn't, I carried a sense of guilt, questioning why I was spared when so many weren't. Yet, I realized that my survival allowed me to continue serving, to help others and lead with the wisdom I gained from those moments.

As my career progressed and I took on leadership roles, I learned valuable lessons about what it means to be in charge. Working with Commander Coan at Camp Pendleton, I saw firsthand how leadership isn't just about giving orders but about holding people accountable and expecting the best from them. I'll never forget the moment when Commander Coan asked if he had ever treated me harshly. His response to my "No" was a powerful lesson in leadership: sometimes, tough love is necessary to get people to rise to the occasion. But it also underscored the importance of fairness and respect, qualities I tried to embody in every role.

Looking back, I'm grateful for the journey—filled with challenges, victories, and moments of self-reflection. My path wasn't what I imagined as a child, but it was rich with purpose. In the end, it's not about the title you hold, but the impact you make on the people around you and the fulfillment that comes from being needed and useful.

~ Family Ties, Navy Bonds ~
A Journey Across Oceans and Decades

I have to admit that when I was transferred to the Third Marine Division in Okinawa, I had tears in my eyes when I said goodbye to Commander Coan. When I arrived in Okinawa, someone from the Division Surgeon's Office met me at the airport. It turned out I was being assigned as the administrative assistant to the Division Surgeon. Commander Coan had already called ahead and recommended me for the job.

The Navy is like family. We have friends all over the United States, and we keep in touch with them. Some we talk to by phone every couple of weeks, others maybe just a card or letter at Christmas. But when we do connect, we pick up right where we left off. A few years ago, we were talking to Navy friends in Seattle who we hadn't seen in forty years. We decided to meet at the Navy Lodge in San Diego for a week. Hideko and I arrived a few hours before they did, and the only thing that had changed was our appearance. What a wonderful week it was—sightseeing, playing pinochle, and just talking. It was something I had never done with my siblings.

Traveling and meeting new people is one of the great benefits of joining the Navy, and I'm so glad I started in the Naval Reserve while I was still in high school.

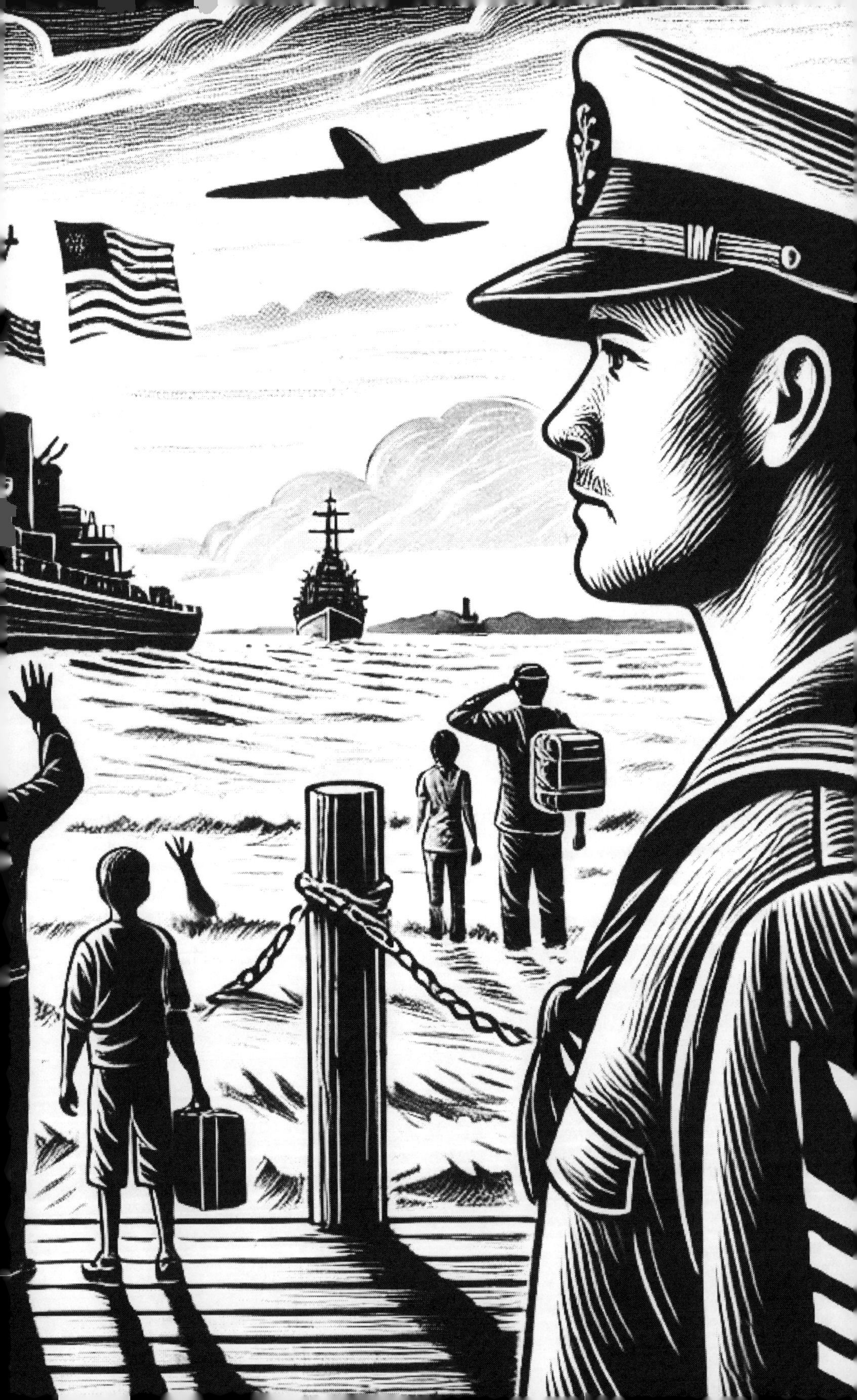

Separation from family isn't something that's often discussed when someone enlists, but being away from loved ones for months or even over a year is a reality. Nowadays, with cell phones and computers, family separation is different. Back then, all we had was U.S. Mail. When I arrived in Vietnam the last time, Chiemi was six months old and Patrick was three years old. It was a year and a half before I was permanently home with them again. I was fortunate to have a wife who took charge and handled the job of being a single parent with grace.

Thanks to my Navy training and schooling, I was able to secure a job in Cardiopulmonary at the first hospital I applied to after returning from Vietnam. I passed the National Certification Exam for Respiratory Therapy because of my Navy schooling. Years later, I was hired at a county health department and became a Registered Sanitarian, again thanks to my Navy training. Without the Navy, I probably would've ended up working in a factory somewhere. The Navy pointed me in a direction, and all I had to do was follow through.

Looking back on my time in the Navy, I realize just how much it shaped not only my career but also my relationships and sense of belonging. When I was transferred to Okinawa, saying goodbye to Commander Coan was emotional—he wasn't just a commanding officer but a mentor who believed in me. His recommendation for my new role was a reminder that, in the Navy, leadership isn't just about rank, but about lifting others up and trusting them to succeed.

The Navy truly became my extended family. No matter how many years pass between calls or letters, the connection remains as strong as ever. Reuniting with old friends in San Diego after decades apart reminded me that time may change our appearances, but it doesn't change the bonds we've formed. There's a comfort in knowing that, even after years of separation, we can pick up right where we left off, as if no time had passed.

One of the greatest gifts the Navy gave me was the opportunity to see the world and meet people from all walks of life. But with that, there was also the sacrifice of being separated from my own family. I spent long stretches away from Hideko and the kids, and it was never easy. Back then, we didn't have the luxury of instant communication—just letters that took time to arrive. I'll always be grateful to Hideko for her strength in managing everything while I was away, taking on the role of both parents with such grace.

The skills I gained through the Navy didn't just prepare me for service; they opened doors to a meaningful civilian career. Whether it was in Cardiopulmonary or later as a Registered Sanitarian, the Navy training set the foundation for my success. Without it, my life might have taken a very different path. The Navy provided direction, and I simply had to take the steps forward. For that, I'll always be grateful. It gave me purpose, resilience, and a network of friendships that span the globe.

~ From Corpsman to Commander ~
Navigating Challenges and Cultures

Early in my career as a Hospital Corpsman, I worked on hospital wards, doing the jobs of a registered nurse, licensed practical nurse, or nurse's aide. I later requested assignments to Cardiopulmonary School and Environmental Health and Preventive Medicine School. In both instances, the Navy granted my requests, and after the schooling, it was up to me to prove that they had made the right choice in taking a chance on me. One of the most difficult challenges in my Naval career was my time at Saint Albans Naval Hospital in New York. For six months, I had no particular job in the laboratory, and then suddenly, I was put in charge. It was daunting, but the Letter of Commendation I received on my transfer was a just reward for all the hard work.

Before marriage, not working weekends meant going to the Enlisted Club with friends. I must admit, we all drank too much alcohol—though that was after a run and a workout at the gym. Weekday nights were spent at the base theater or library. Holidays gave us an extra day off and a chance to sleep in. Big holidays like Thanksgiving or Christmas meant a turkey meal at noon. Once I got married, trips to the Enlisted Club came to an end, unless I was stationed somewhere without family. Hideko and I rarely went out unless we could bring the kids along. I wanted to show them things and places they'd probably never see again.

The Navy gave me the opportunity to travel to many countries and experience their cultures and foods. Whether it was eating deep-fried calamari in Cyprus or fish sauce on watermelon in Vietnam, I found that people were proud of what they had, and I respected that. It was fun learning some of the local languages, although sometimes I didn't use the correct word or said it wrong. Most people were forgiving of my attempts—at least I tried.

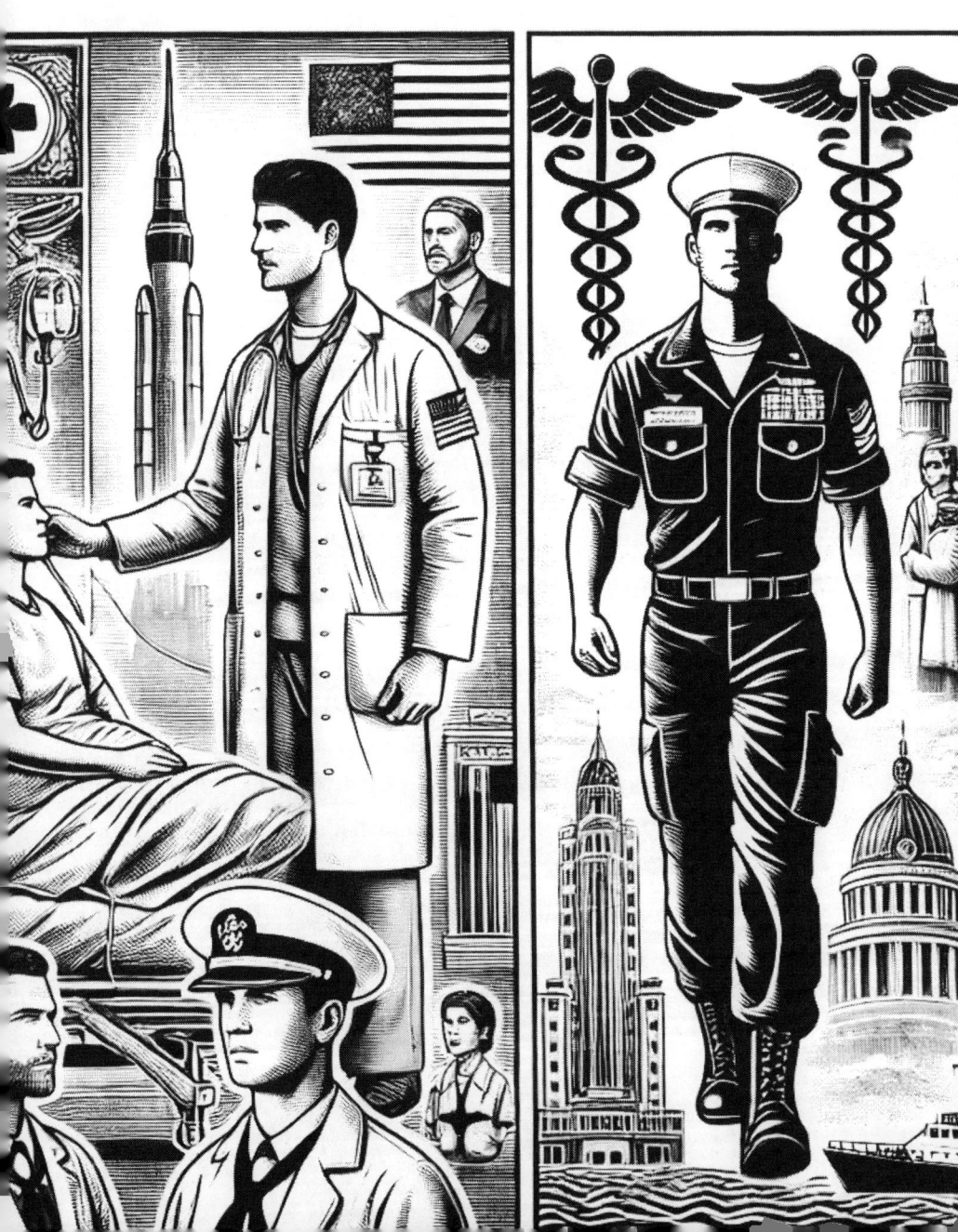

As I look back on my career as a Hospital Corpsman, I'm struck by how many opportunities the Navy provided for me to learn and grow. From working on hospital wards to later pursuing specialized training in Cardiopulmonary and Environmental Health, I was given the chance to expand my skills and challenge myself. Each time I requested further education, the Navy granted it, trusting me to prove that their investment was worthwhile. That trust fueled my determination, especially during challenging times like my unexpected leadership role at Saint Albans Naval Hospital. The responsibility was heavy, but the Letter of Commendation I received upon transfer was a rewarding affirmation of the hard work I had put in.

Before I got married, life in the Navy was a blend of hard work and camaraderie—weekends spent with friends at the Enlisted Club, or late nights at the theater and gym. Those days were marked by a sense of independence, but after marriage, my priorities shifted. My focus became sharing life's experiences with Hideko and the kids, exposing them to new cultures and places. The Navy wasn't just my career; it became a way to show my family the world. We traveled to many countries, sampling foods and soaking in local cultures. I found joy in the small things, like learning bits of language or trying unfamiliar dishes, and I admired how proud people were of their heritage. Even when I made mistakes, locals were forgiving because they appreciated the effort.

Looking back, I realize how much the Navy shaped not just my career but my perspective on life. It taught me the value of stepping outside my comfort zone and embracing what the world had to offer. Every challenge, every new country, every cultural exchange was a lesson in humility, respect, and gratitude. Those experiences made me a better person, one who strives to make the most of every opportunity and respect the differences that make each culture unique.

~ Lessons from a Navy Life ~
Turning Doubt into Drive

Two days before my high school graduation, I was in the third-period study hall when someone came in asking for help unloading graduation caps and gowns. I got volunteered for the job. After we finished unloading, there were still twenty minutes left before lunch, so we volunteers went to lunch early. That afternoon, I received a note to see the assistant principal. She gave me a dressing down and assigned me one hour of detention for skipping the last twenty minutes of class. She also told me, "You'll never amount to anything." I wasn't a bad student—I had only missed two days of school in four years—but her words stuck with me throughout my Navy career and even into my civilian jobs. I've always given 100% to any task I've been assigned. The Navy's training schools are outstanding, but many times I've had to learn through the method of "see one, do one," always under supervision.

When I reenlisted in September 1962, I had the rank, but not all the skills, of a second-class petty officer. My time at the American Dispensary in Saigon was invaluable in helping me learn the many different skills I'd need for my time with the Marines. Of course, if I hadn't reenlisted, I would never have met my wife or had two wonderful children.

During my time in the Navy, my relationship with my siblings, if there was one, faded away. I rarely wrote to either of my brothers—one in New Jersey in the Navy, the other in South Korea in the Army. Even after their service, we seldom talked or saw each other more than once every couple of years. On the other hand, my connection with my Navy family has always been close. Sure, being away from Hideko and the kids was

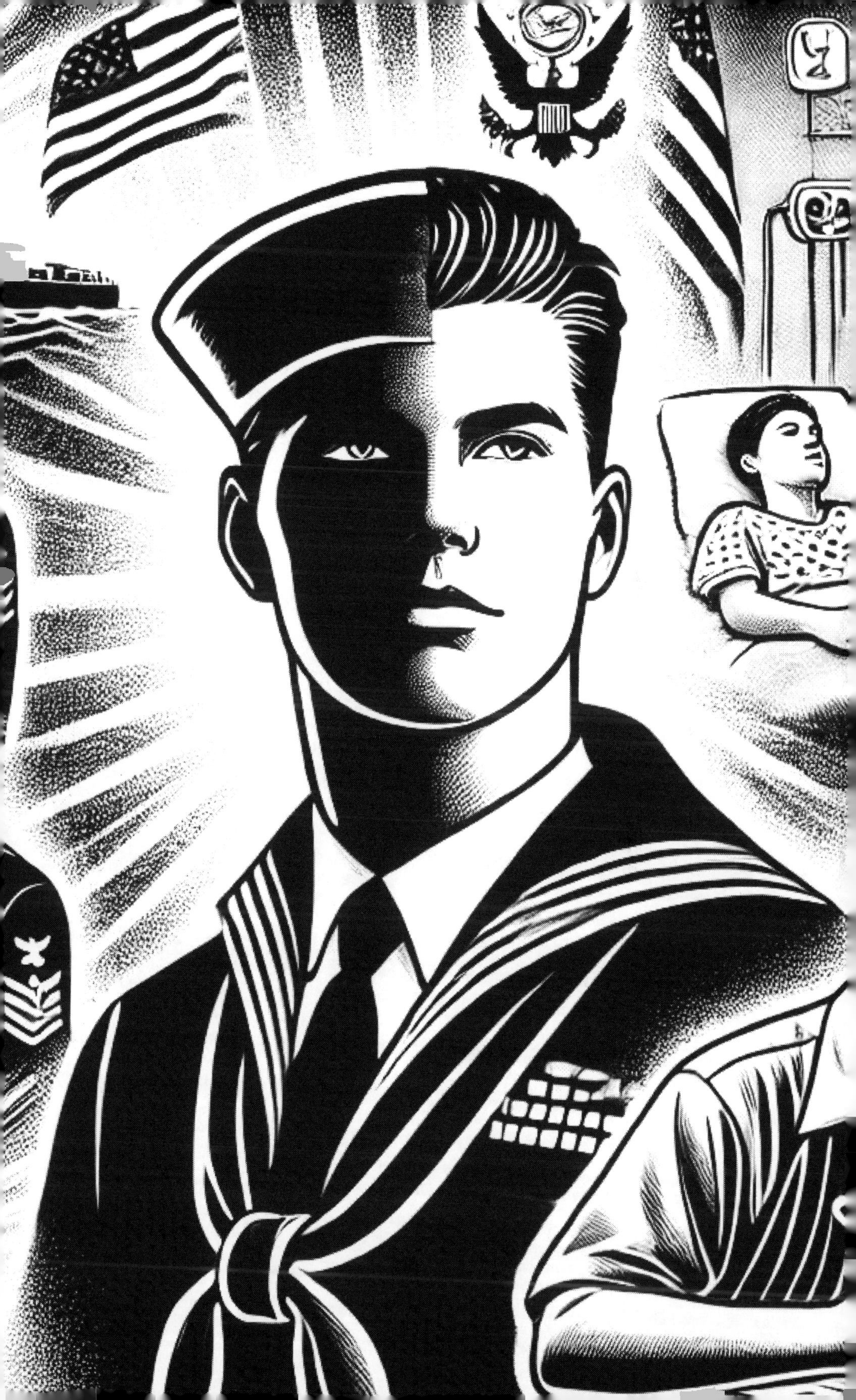

tough, but the Navy kept me so busy that I didn't dwell on the separation. Once the kids were old enough to write, they sent letters telling me what was going on in their lives. Some of those letters, I still have.

Not being promoted to Senior Chief when I was first eligible was probably my biggest disappointment in my Naval career, and it sent me into a deep depression. I wasn't proud of anything I had accomplished in my time in the Navy. Thankfully, with the help of a Navy Psychologist, I came to realize that advancing to Chief Petty Officer was a significant achievement. With his advice, I took charge of my career, and I was promoted during the next advancement cycle. I understood then that if I wanted something, I had to put in the extra effort to get it.

Both of the jobs I had after leaving the Navy seemed too easy to land. I had an interview, and I was hired. While working in Cardiopulmonary/Respiratory Therapy at Mount Carmel Hospital in Columbus, I received several job offers from other hospitals. The same happened at the Health Department, with job offers from other County Health Departments. In each case, even though switching jobs would have meant more money, I was comfortable with what I was doing, so I stayed.

Looking back on the moments that shaped my life, one of the most surprising was the assistant principal's harsh words just before my high school graduation. "You'll never amount to anything," she said. Though I wasn't a bad student, her comment lingered in my mind throughout my Navy career and even into my civilian jobs. In a way, it fueled my determination to always give 100% to whatever task was in front of me. The Navy provided exceptional training, but much of what I learned came from hands-on experience, where I had to quickly adapt and prove myself capable.

Reenlisting in 1962 was a pivotal decision, and though I didn't yet have all the skills of a second-class petty officer, my time in Saigon taught me invaluable lessons that prepared me for my future assignments with the Marines. That decision not only shaped my career but also led me to meet my wife and start our family—something I couldn't imagine my life without.

However, as my Navy family grew, my connection with my siblings faded. We were scattered across the world in different branches of service, and though we rarely spoke or saw each other, my Navy family became a constant source of support. The bonds I formed with them were strong, and even though separation from Hideko and the kids was difficult, I stayed busy enough to keep from dwelling on it. Still, the letters my children sent, full of their lives' little details, became treasures I've kept to this day.

One of the hardest moments in my Naval career was not being promoted to Senior Chief when I was first eligible. It sent me into a deep depression, making me question everything I had achieved. But with the help of a Navy psychologist, I came to see that reaching Chief Petty Officer was, in itself, a significant accomplishment. That realization gave me the drive to take control of my career, and soon enough, I was promoted. It was a turning point for me—a reminder that sometimes, you have to work even harder to achieve what you want.

After leaving the Navy, finding work seemed almost too easy, and while other offers came with promises of more money, I found comfort in the stability of the jobs I had. I realized then that success isn't just about climbing the ladder or chasing higher paychecks—it's about finding fulfillment in what you do and the people you serve along the way. Though my journey hasn't always been easy, it's been shaped by perseverance, and for that, I'm grateful.

Conclusion

Why This Story Needed to Be Told

As we come to the end of The Sailor's Compass, it's clear that this journey is not just mine, but a reflection of countless others who have navigated the unpredictable seas of life. This story needed to be told because it's more than a collection of memories; it's a testament to the power of perseverance, the strength of relationships, and the lessons learned along the way.

Each chapter of my life has been a compass, pointing me toward new experiences, guiding me through challenges, and helping me discover who I am and what truly matters. From my time in the Navy to my role as a husband, father, and friend, the decisions I made were influenced by a desire to serve, to learn, and to live with purpose. And while my path may not have always been straight, it's the twists and turns that have given it meaning.

I wanted to share this story not just to look back, but to remind others that, like a sailor navigating rough waters, we are all guided by our own compass. There will be storms, times when we question our direction, and moments of calm where everything seems to fall into place. But through it all, it's our inner compass—our values, relationships, and faith—that helps us stay the course.

For those who may be at a crossroads, unsure of where life will take them, I hope this book serves as a reminder that every step you take, every challenge you face, is part of your journey. Whether you're in the midst of a storm or enjoying a calm sea, trust your compass. It will guide you where you need to go.

This story needed to be told to honor those who have walked beside me, to remember the lessons I've learned, and to inspire those who read it to navigate their own lives with courage, integrity, and an open heart.

Because in the end, life is not just about reaching a destination—it's about the journey and the people who share it with us.

Michael H. Moore

Treasured Letters

Dad,

First comes knowledge, and with age comes wisdom. I see that in you. I didn't know growing up and traveling all over the United States that I would be so grateful. You gave us the opportunity to experience all of the different places. When talking to people who ask where did you grow up? I'm proud to tell them all the places that I have lived. I didn't know it then, but with age i now realize the opportunity we were provided. Thank you for all the sacrifices you have made in life for all of us (Mom, Chiemi, and I)

My love for 70's music started with you, and I love John Denver from that. Thank you for everything that you have done for all of us (Lauri, kids, I) from acceptance of all of us to advice, financial and physical help with this farm. I look around and see so much that you have done from the living room, heater in my room, trim, building of the apartment, pole barn, all of it and even the cow fence lol!

I look forward to and enjoy every day that I come over for lunch to see the both of you! Like yourself, you gave me a good work ethic & because of that I am the man I am today.

Just wanted to say thank you so much!

> I love you more than words can say.
> Patrick

Papa,

Every time I see someone with a Veteran's hat, shirt, jacket, or sticker on their car, I thank them for their service and it makes me think of you. Sometimes I engage in conversation, talking about you, your branch, rank, and years of service.

I am so honored, grateful, and proud that you have served.

I know that not all of the memories you have of the Navy warrants remembering, but I know that my memories of us being military are a wonderful part of what makes me, me. Seeing different places, people, and lifestyles made me more open, accepting, non-judgemental. Being raised by you in those experiences is what and why I am who I am.

So THANK YOU Papa, for choosing the military path, even though it was a gamble and not everyone was so lucky to come out alive.

THANK YOU Papa, for your honor and dedication to the US of A.

Even though we see dark times politically, we are still a GREAT COUNTRY and most importantly we have our FREEDOM. It is because of heroes like you and all of those who have served. THANK YOU, Papa, for making me so very proud to call you my Papa.

I love you so very much!

Eternally Grateful,
Eternally Blessed,
Your loving daughter, Chiemi

Og:

I am at a loss, I cannot find the words to describe my gratitude and admiration for you. Your Service to the Nation, the community, and to our family is truly inspiring and it inspires me to do more. You've never spoken this to me personally, but dad tells me of the advice you gave him, "A man's true value is his service to others." You embody service.

Family dinner is a prime example. The meals you would prepare for me and my motley crew of friends, looking back I am truly in awe And always so humble! You Let bachon take the credit but we know who cooks. You let an example in everything you do, you are a hero in every sense of the word, and I am so lucky to have you as my grandfather.

With all my love and respect,
Your grandson, Curtis

WELC
TH

with a
chapter

TO
ORLD

baby, a new
unfolds.

Sweater weather
is better together.

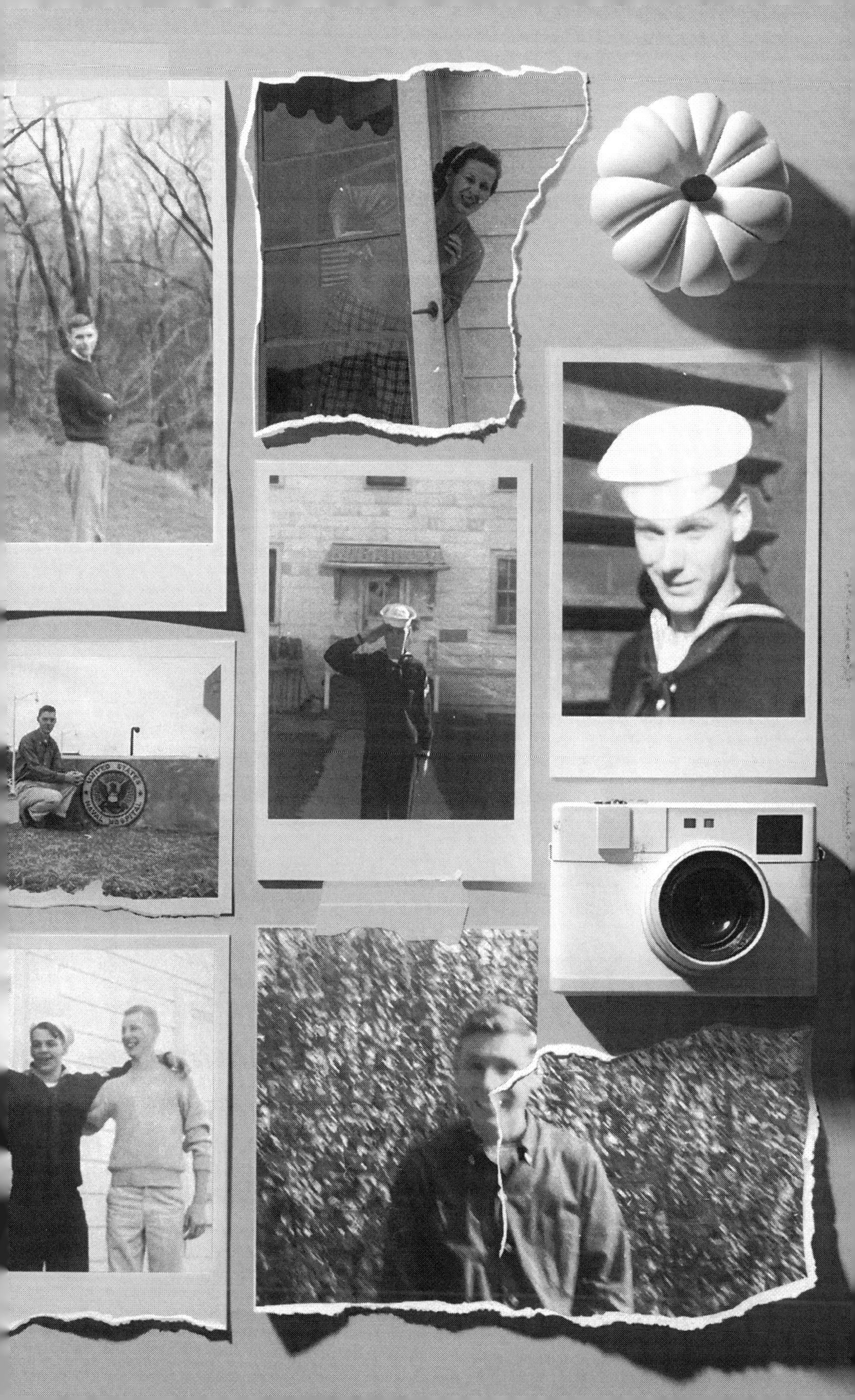
UNITED STATES

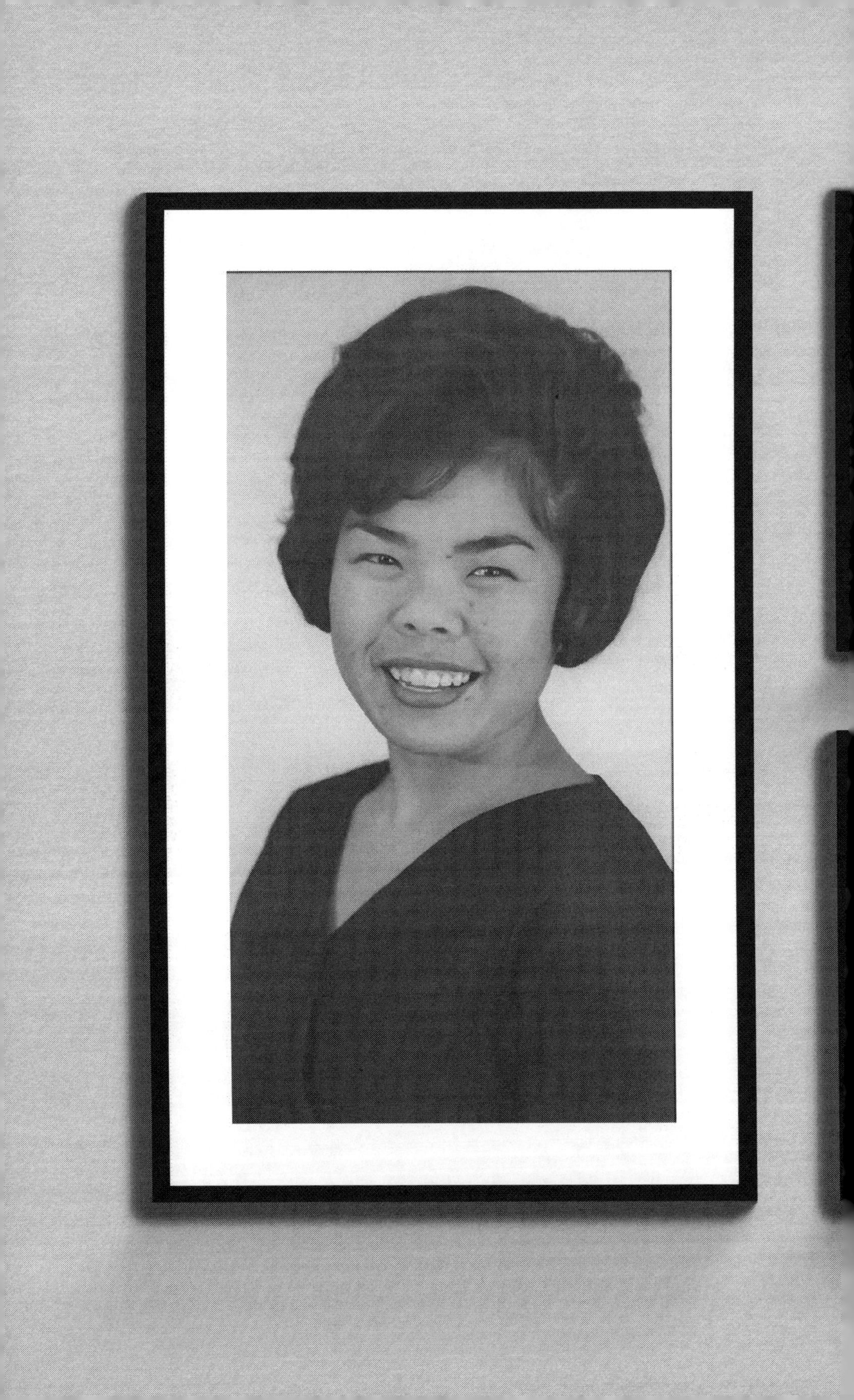

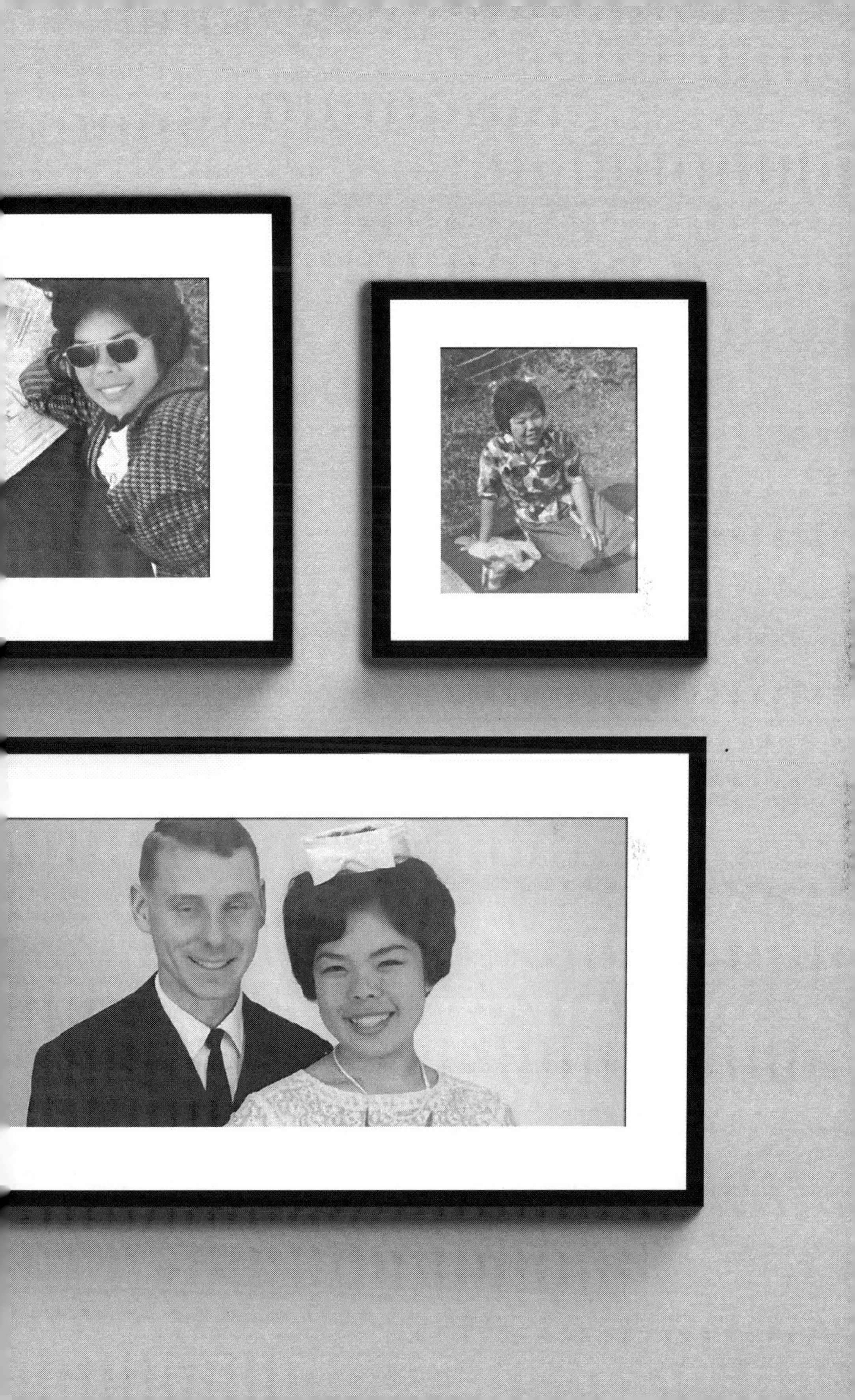

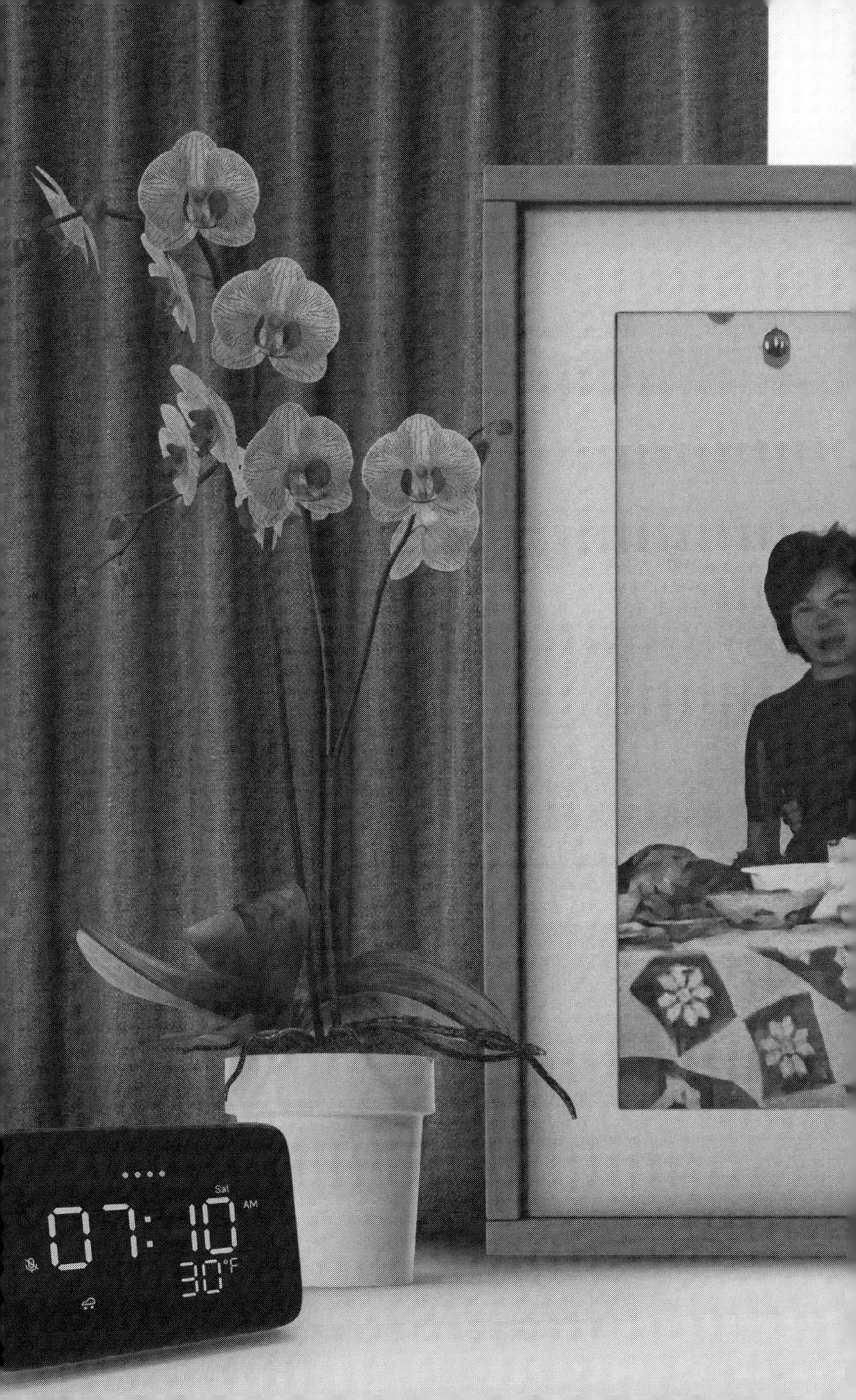
Sat
07:10
AM
30°F

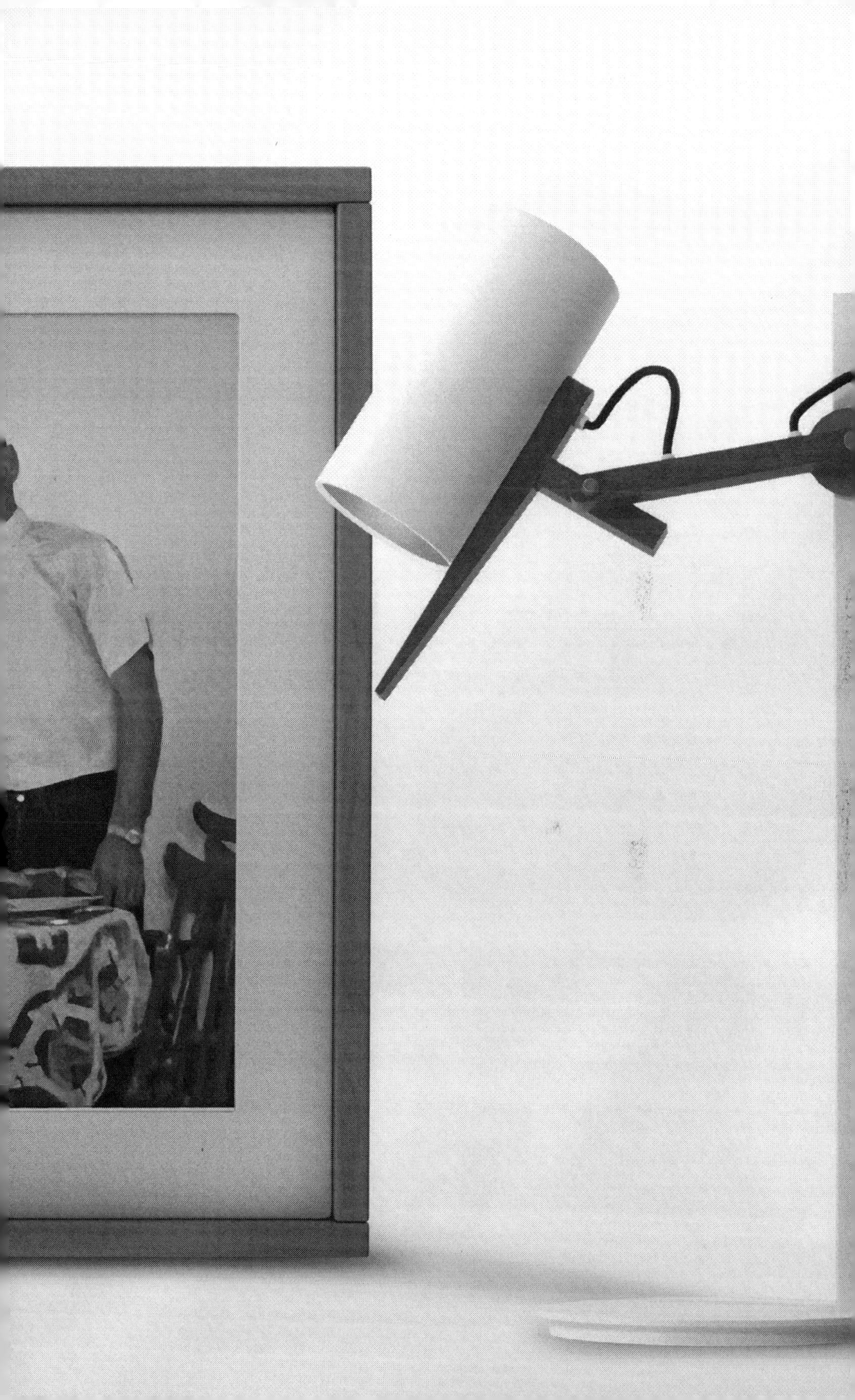

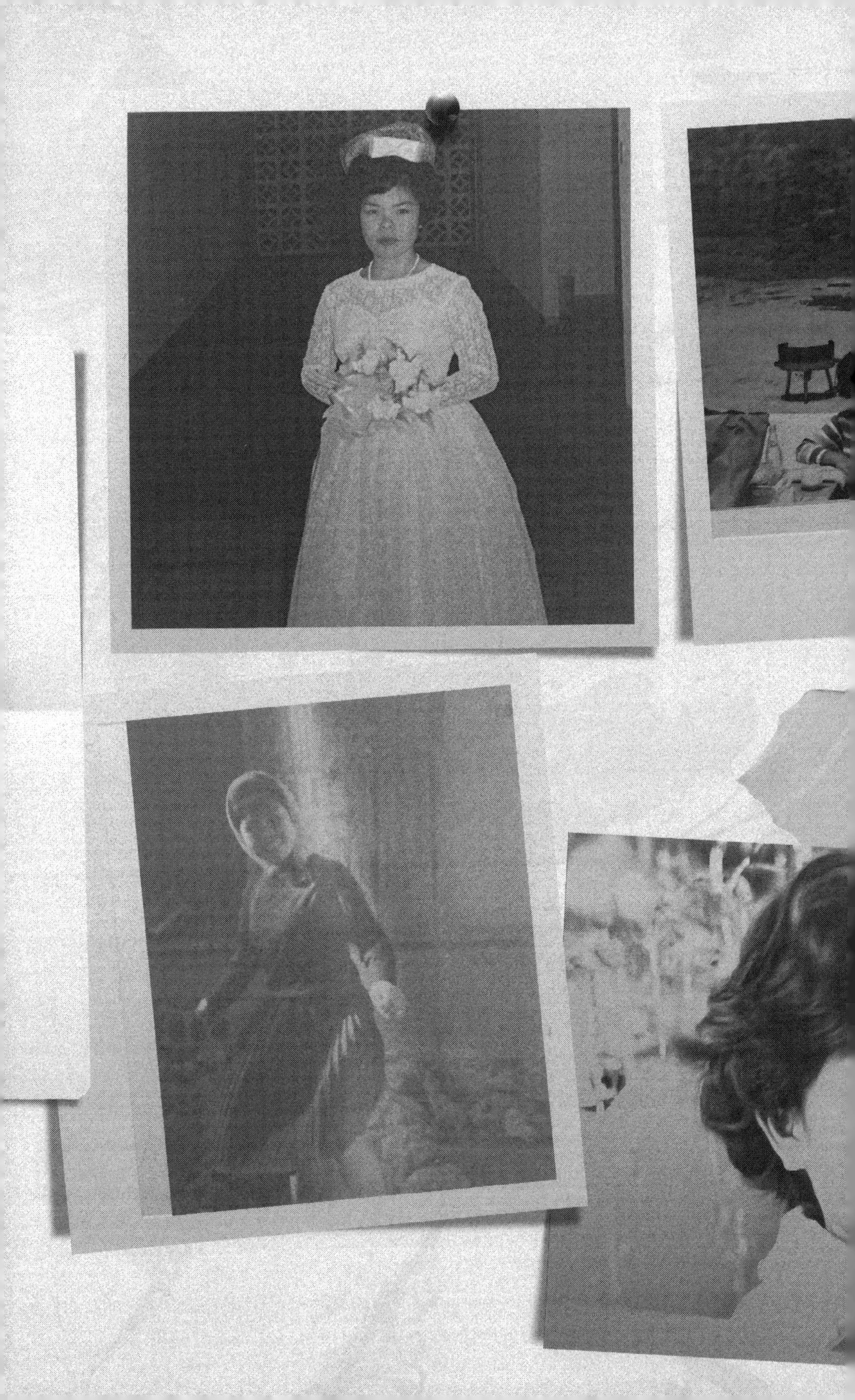

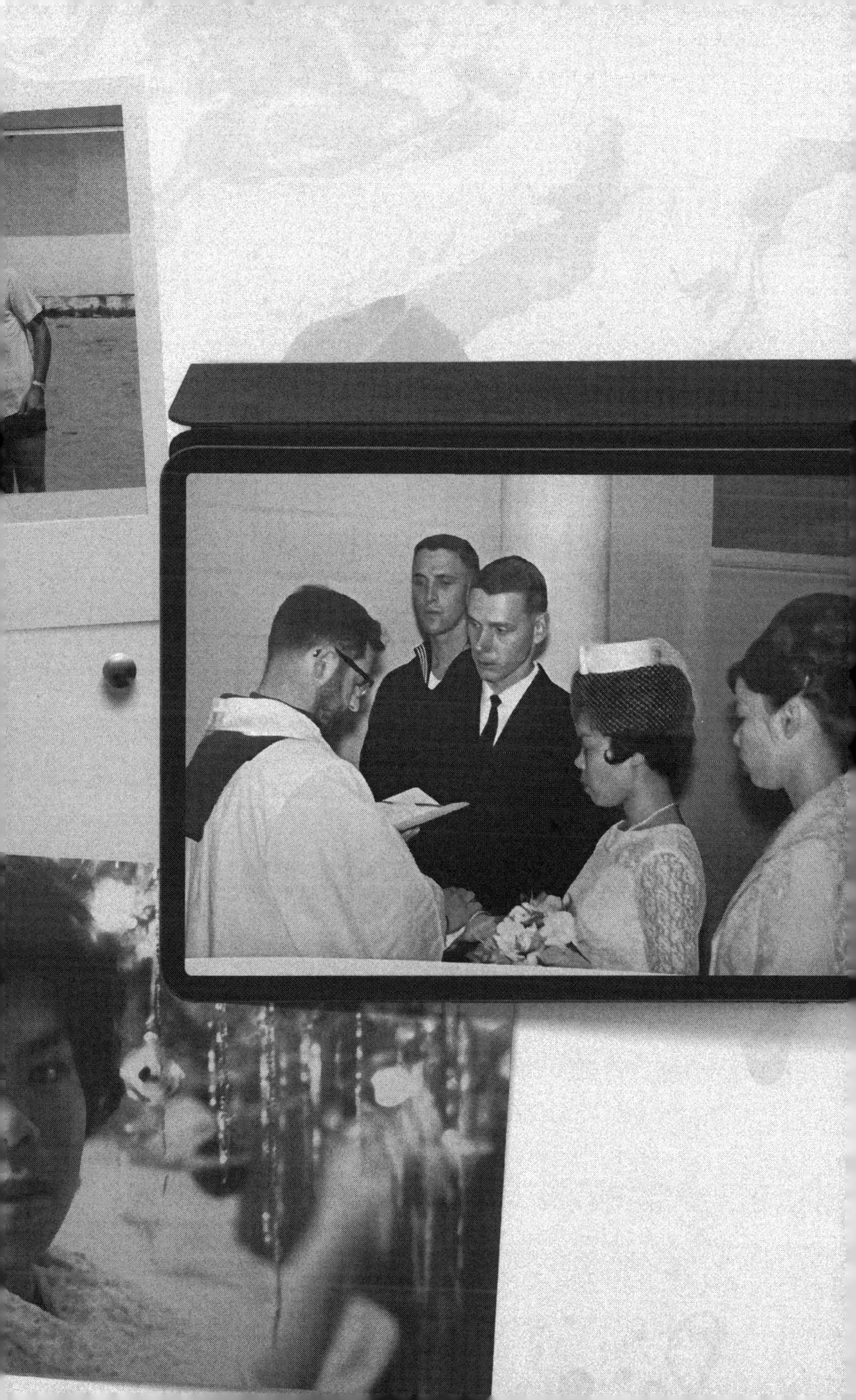

CE PORTA 400   11+   SPACE PORT

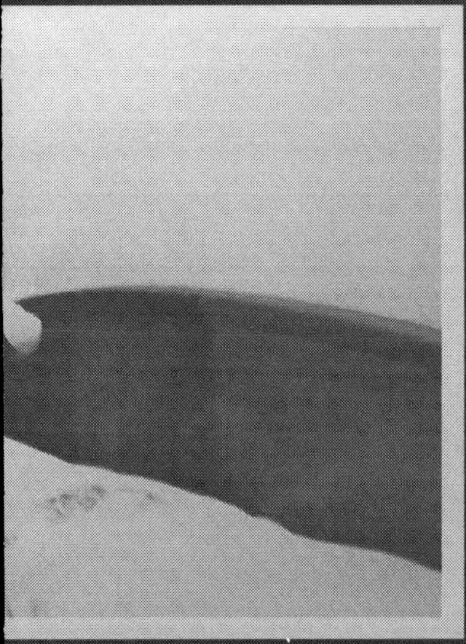

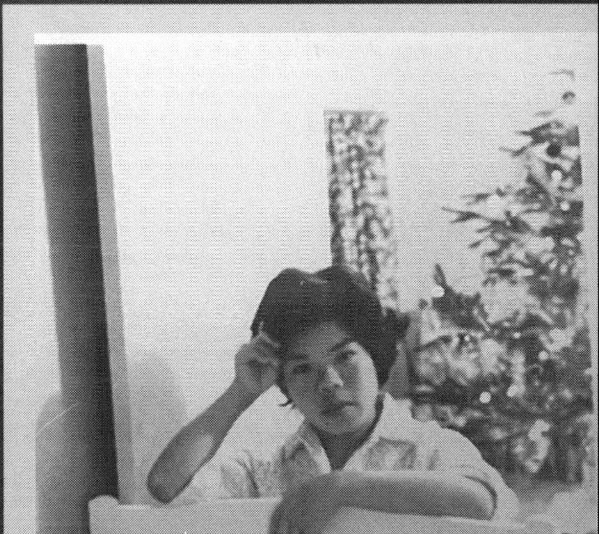

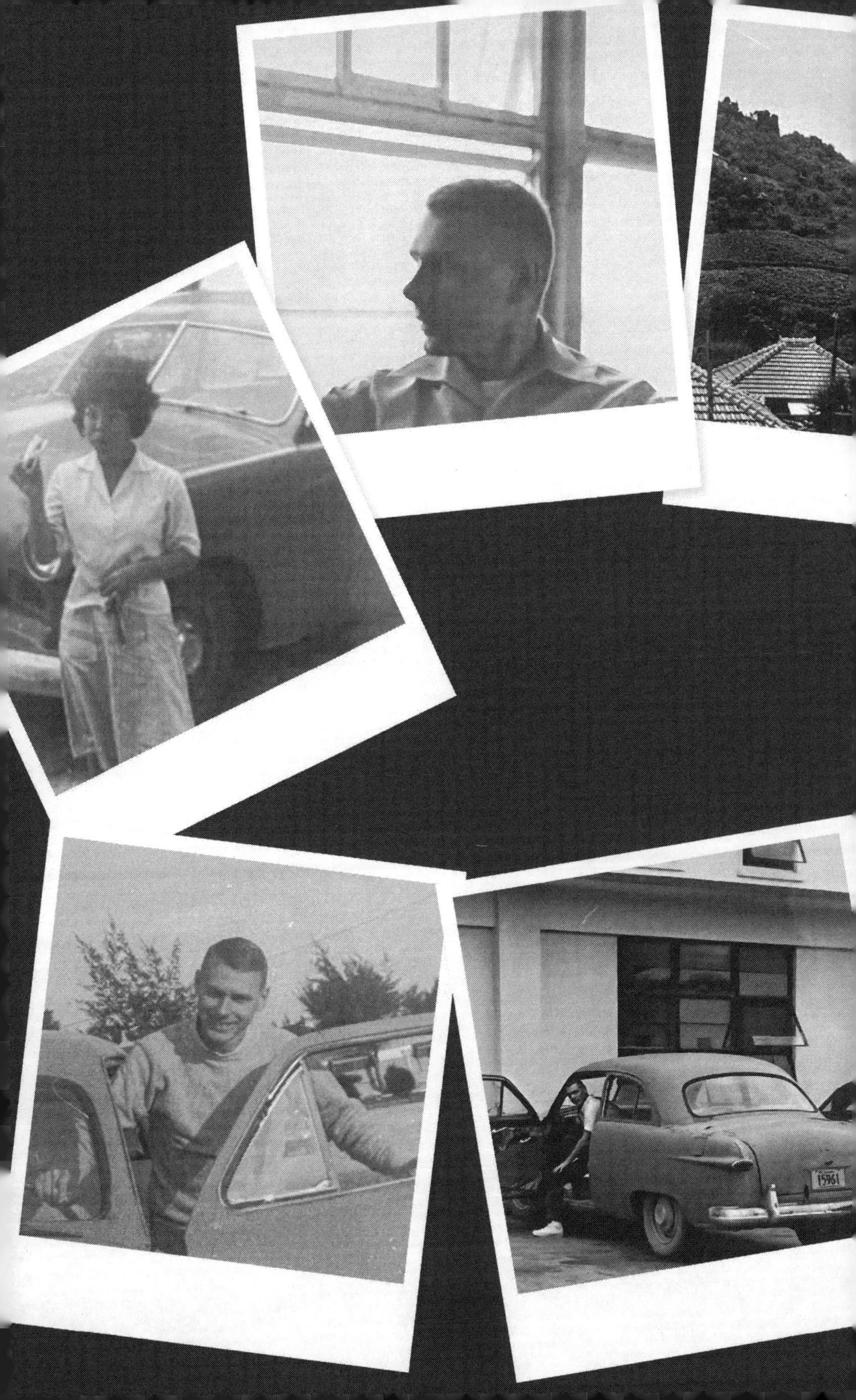
15961

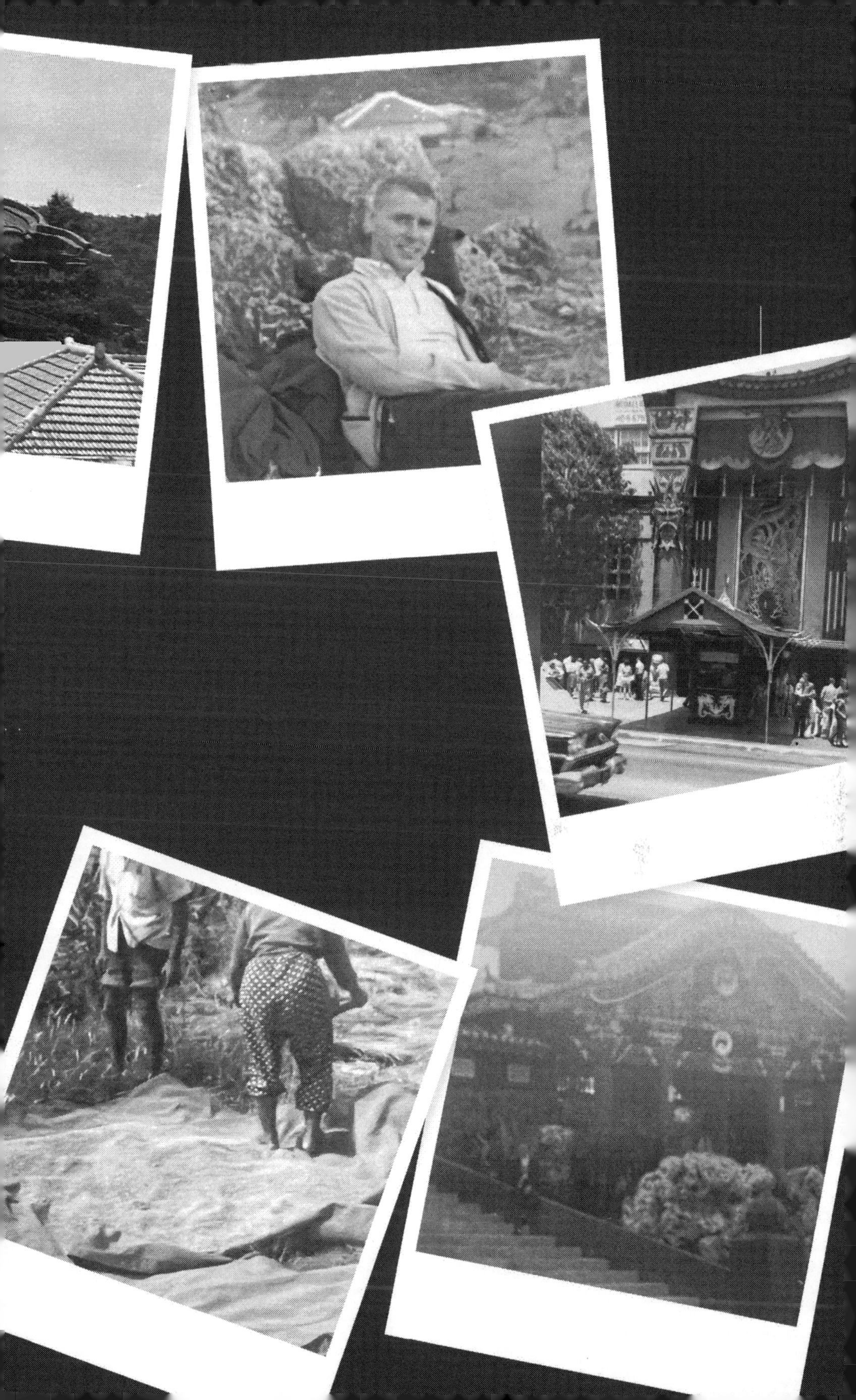

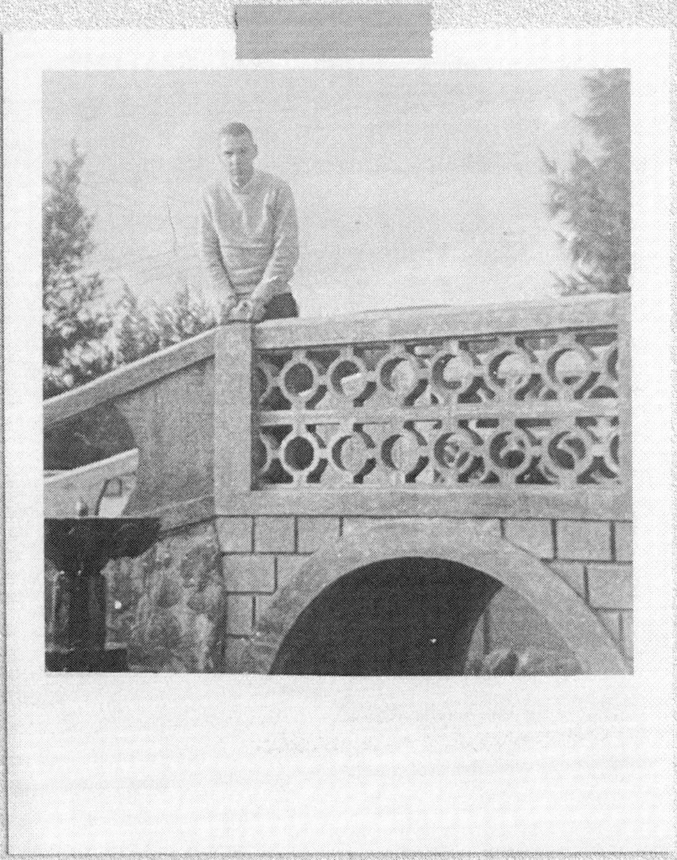

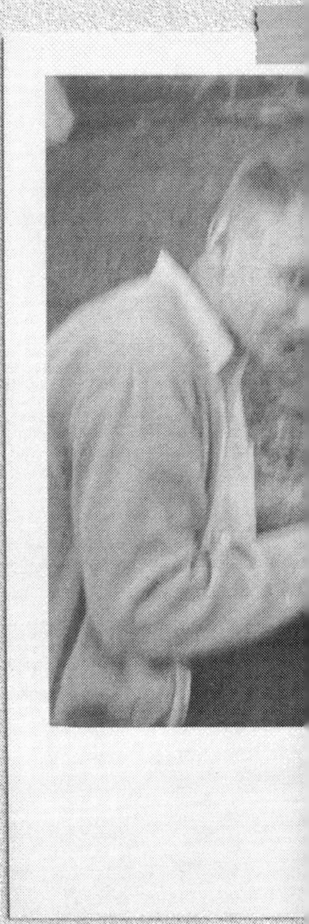

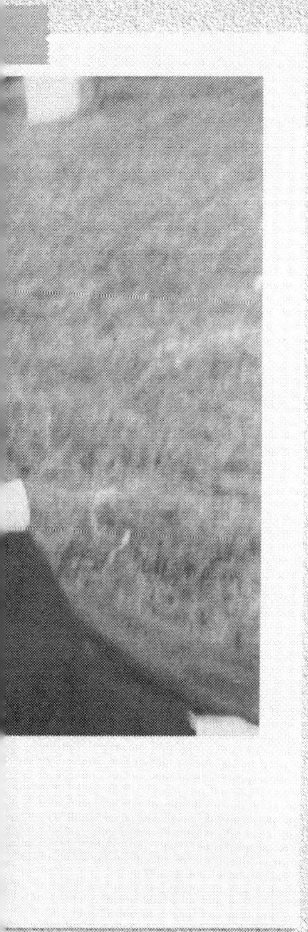

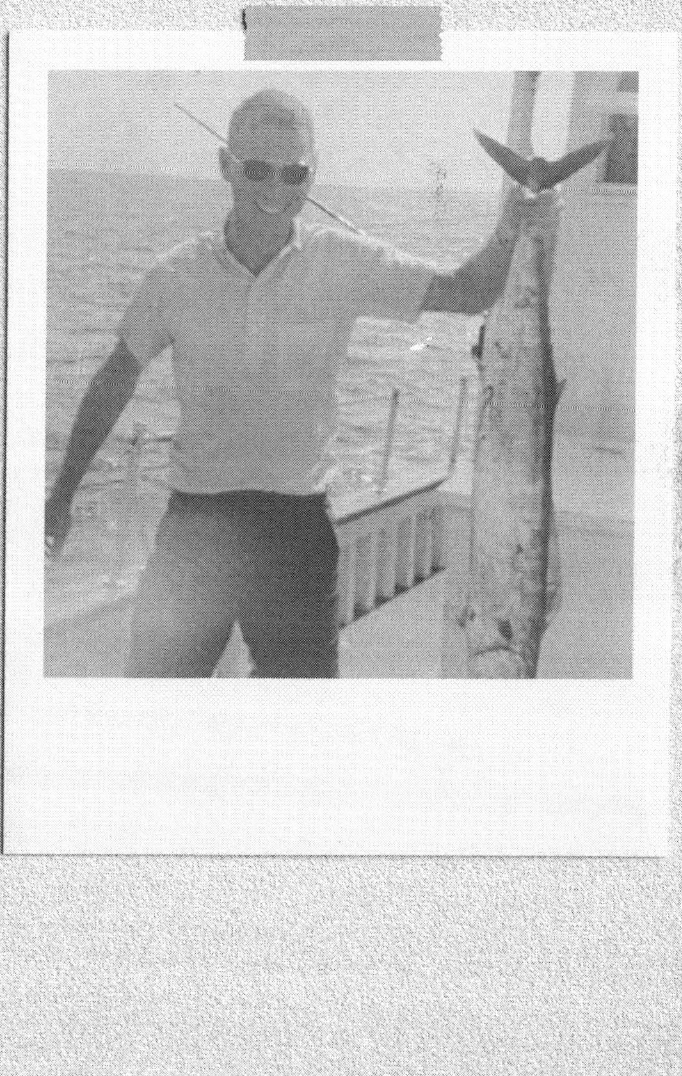

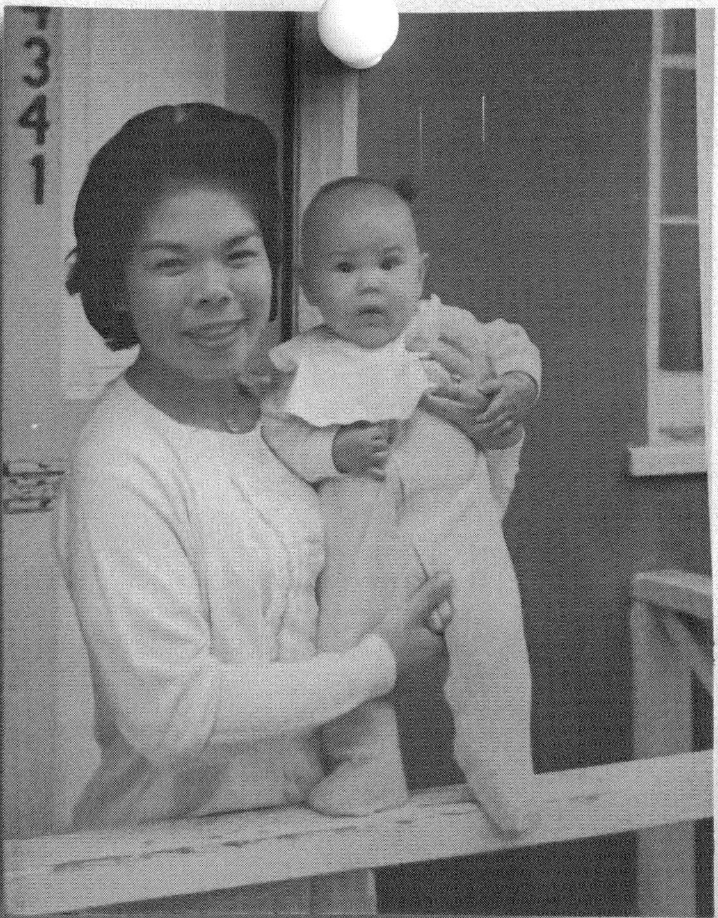
341

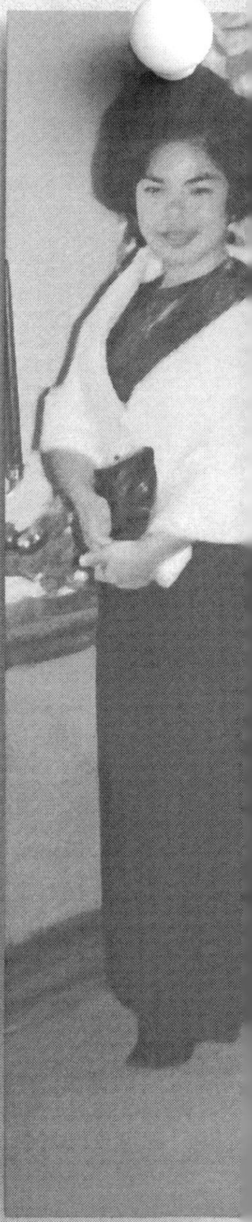

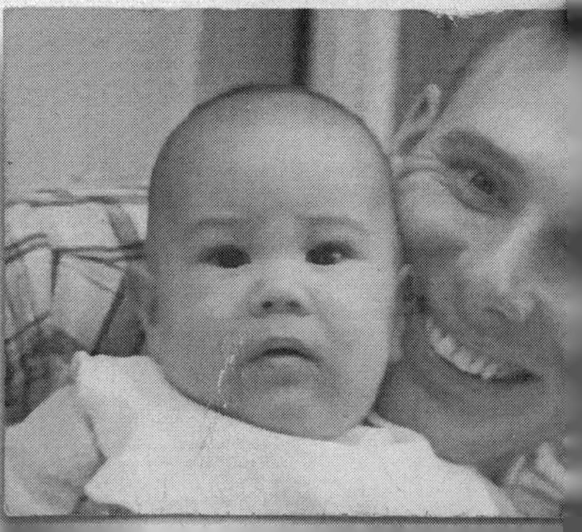

YOUR DESIGN HERE

YOUR DES

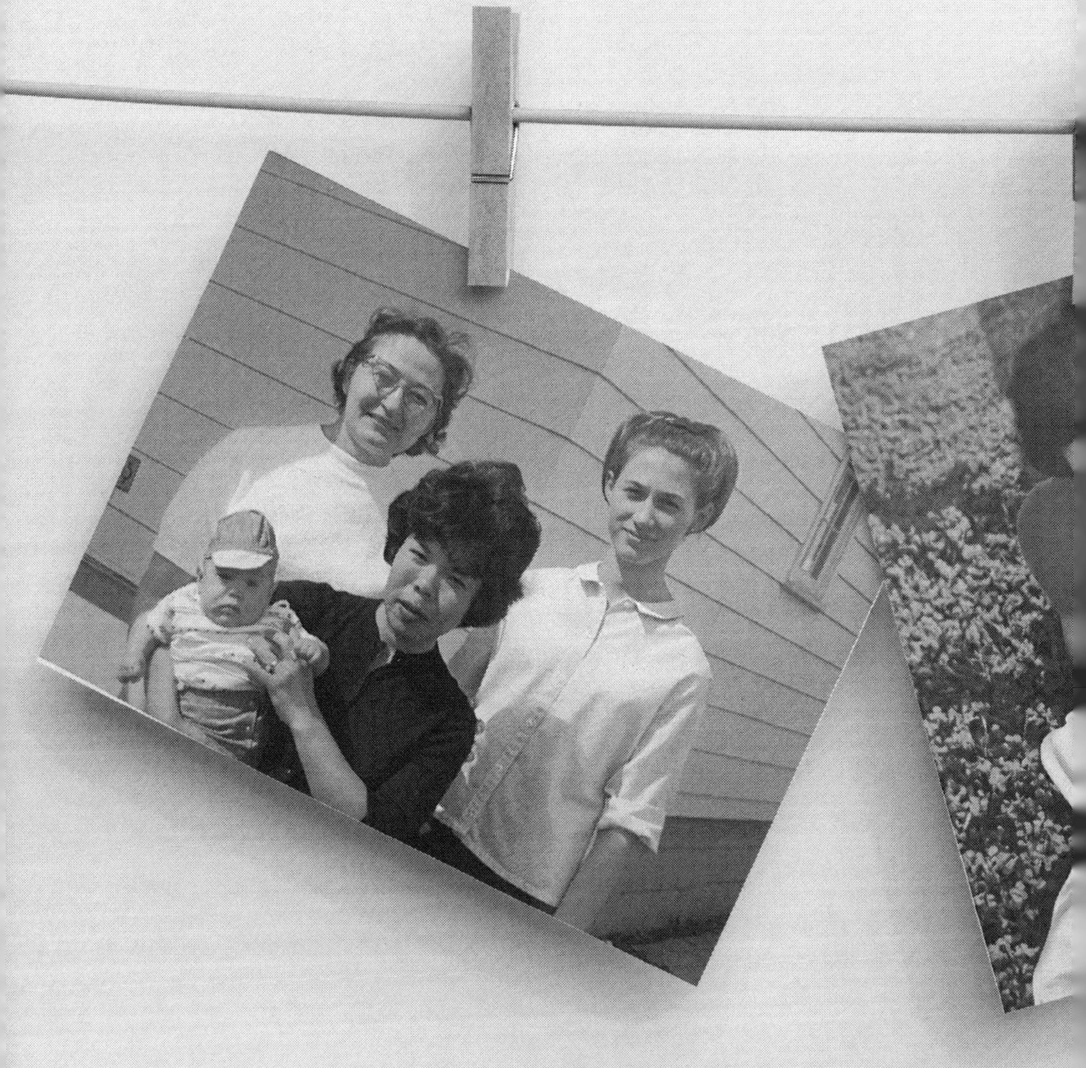

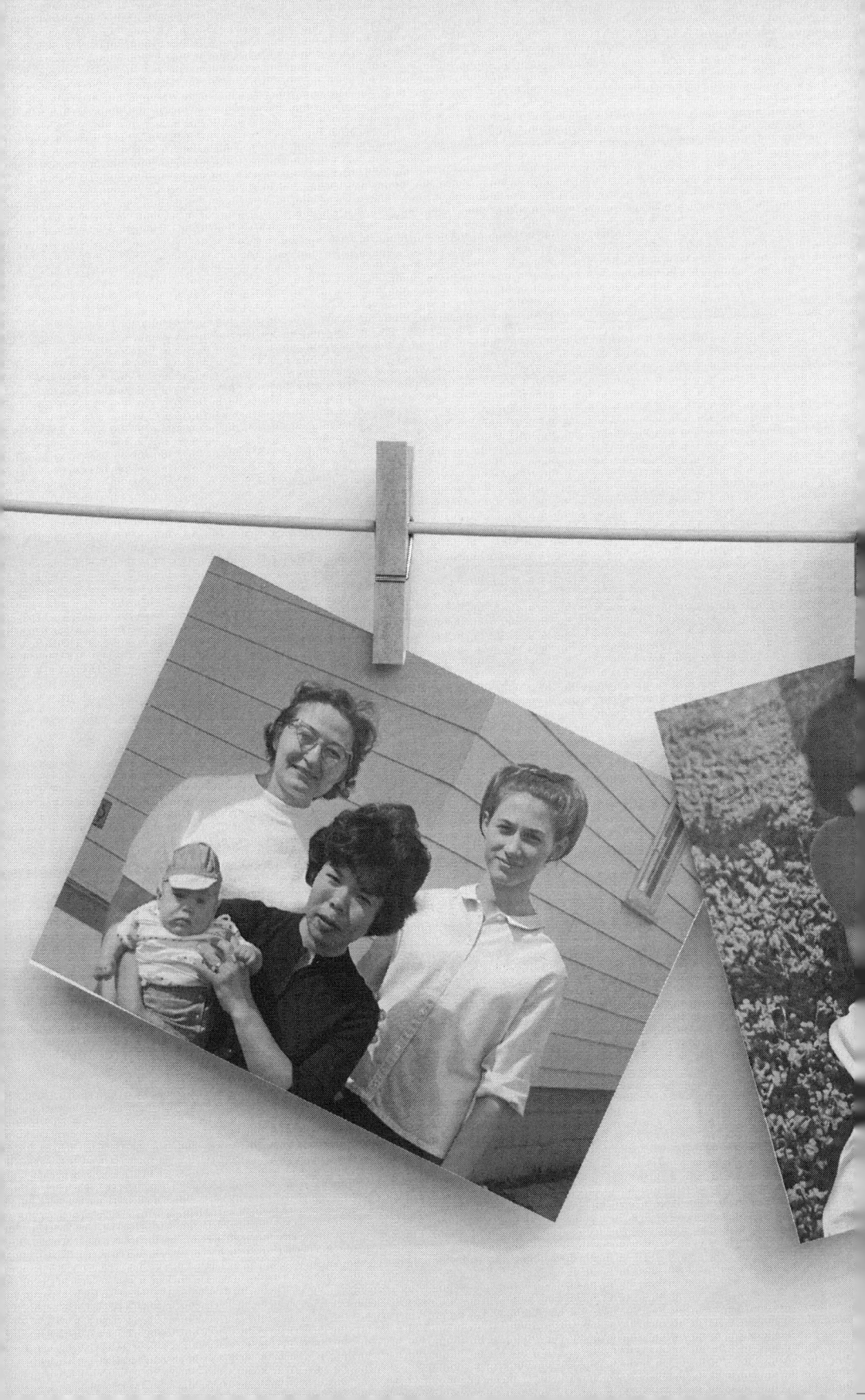

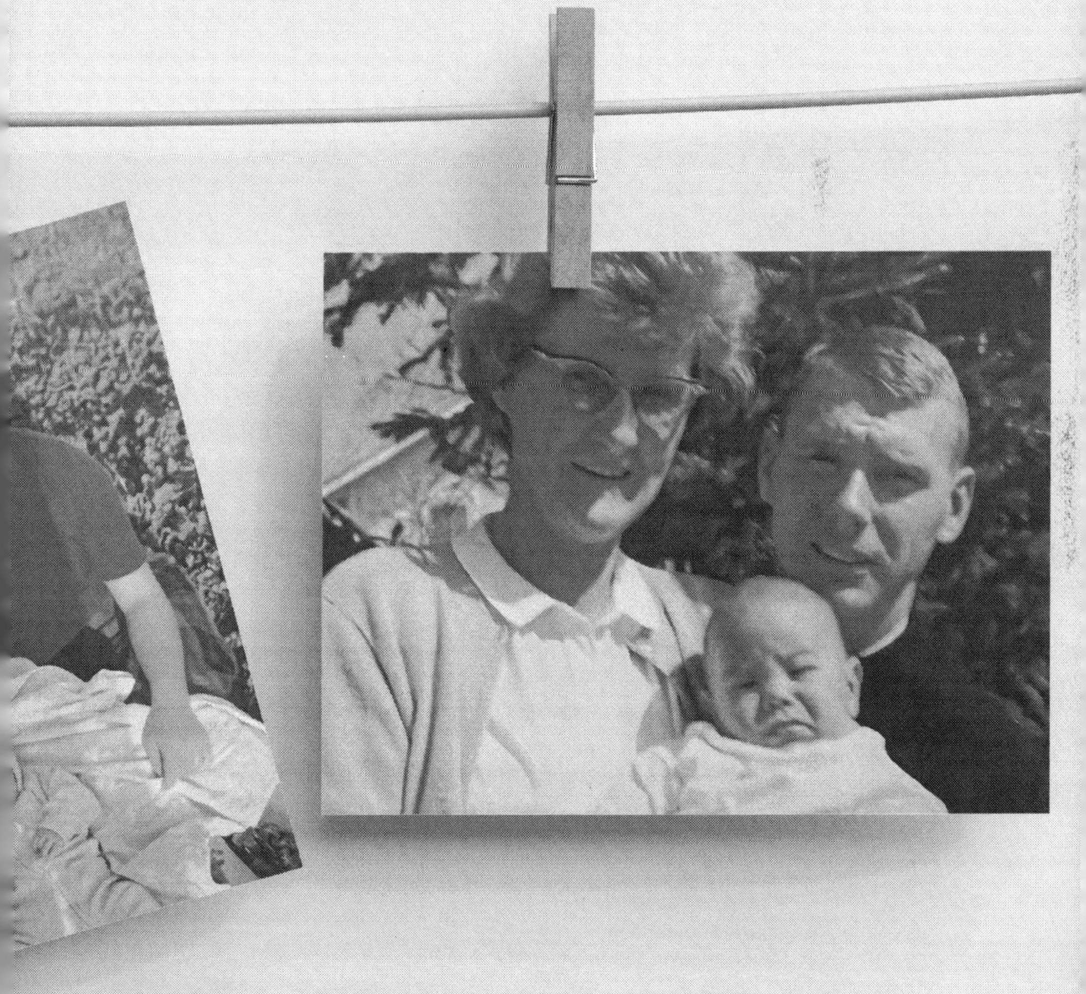

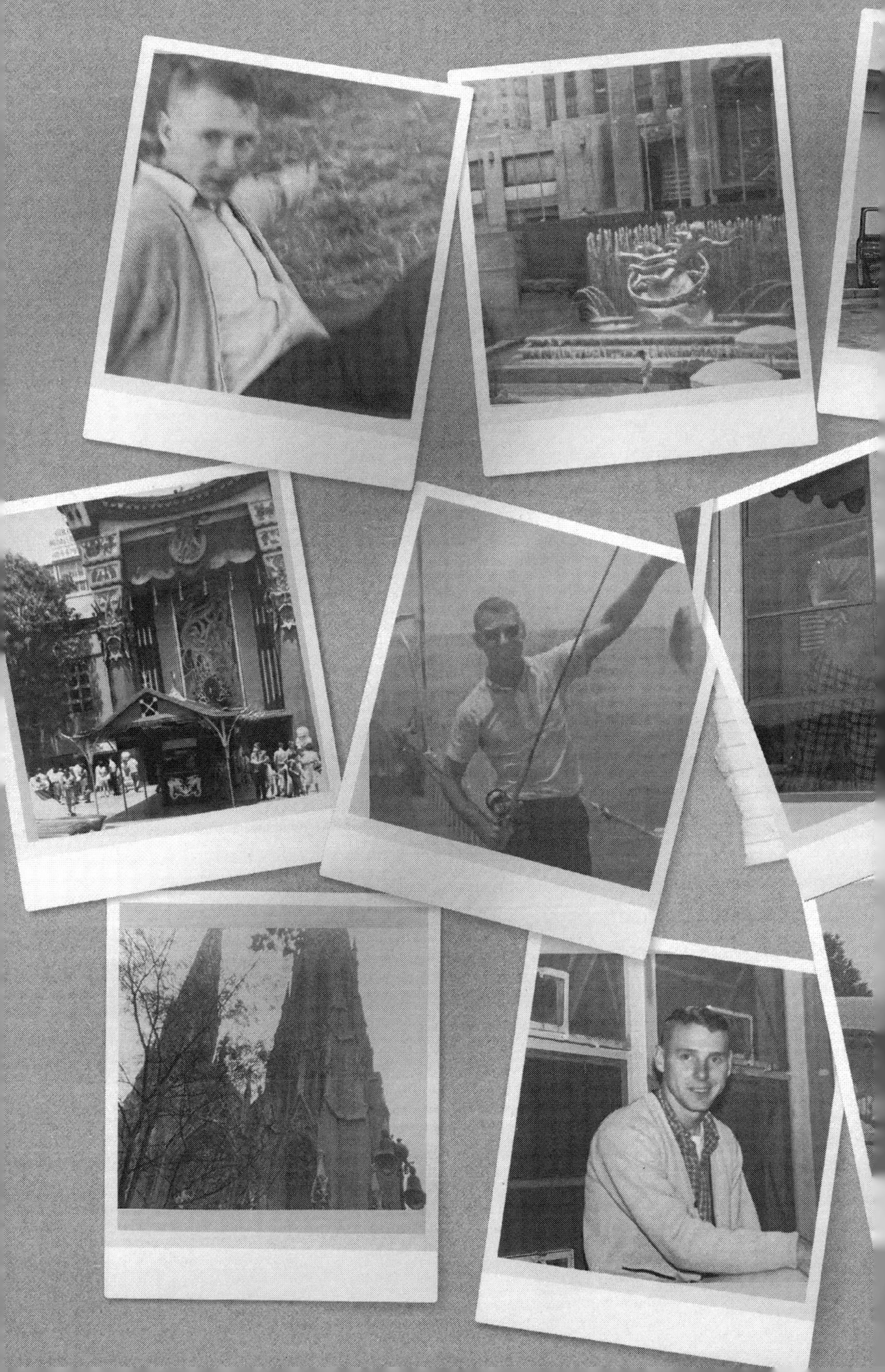

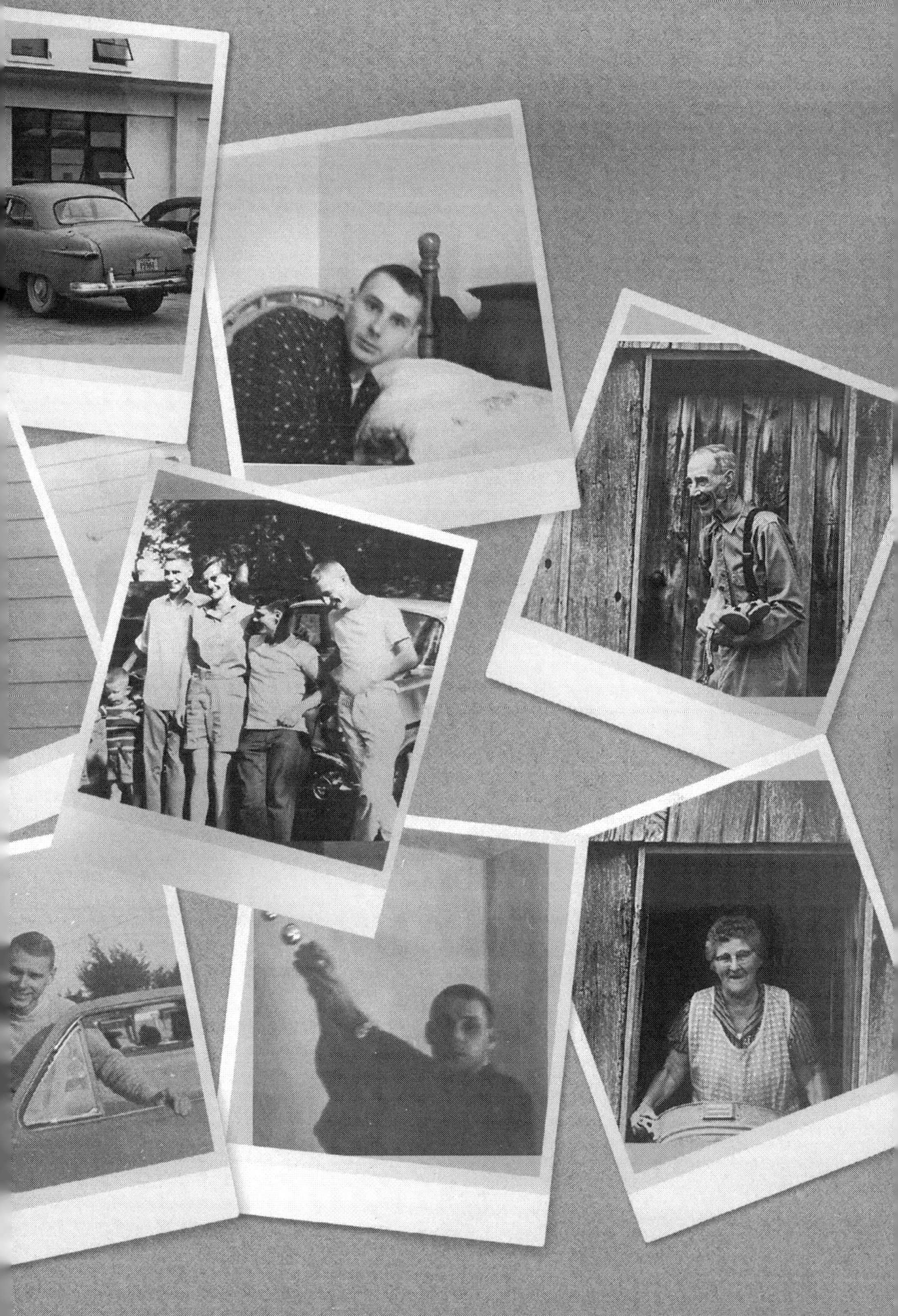

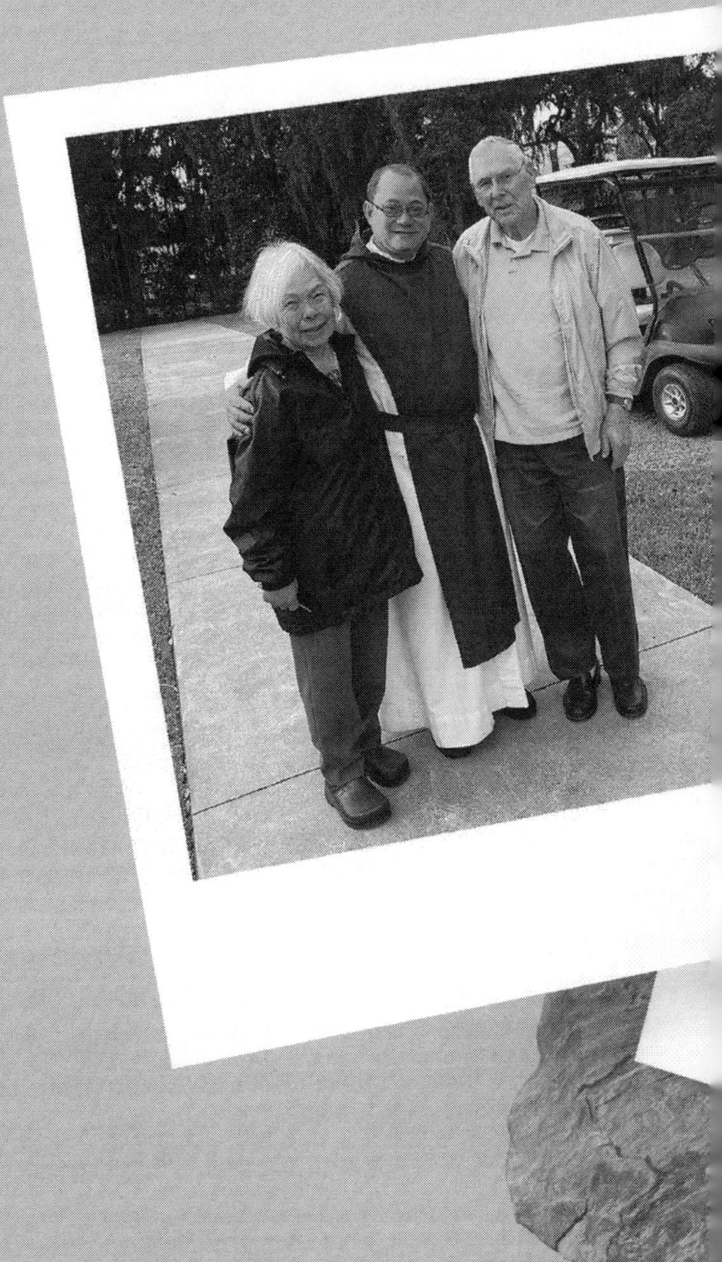

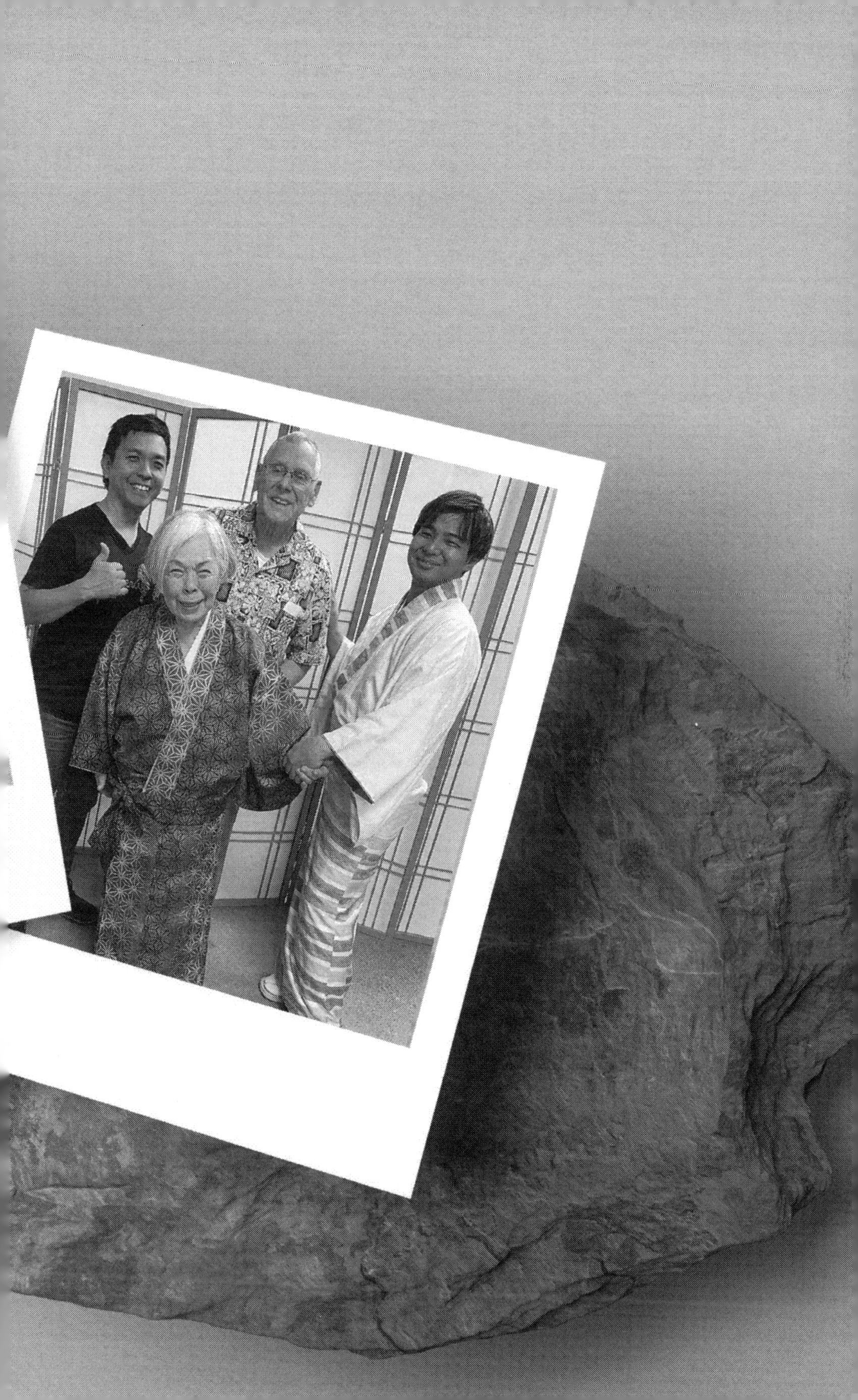

"As the years have added silver to our hair, they've also deepened our strength. For Hideko, as an Okinawan navigating life's cultural bridges, and for me, learning to honor both our worlds, the challenges shaped us. Together, we've faced the storms, embraced the calm, and found that love and faith are the compass guiding us home."

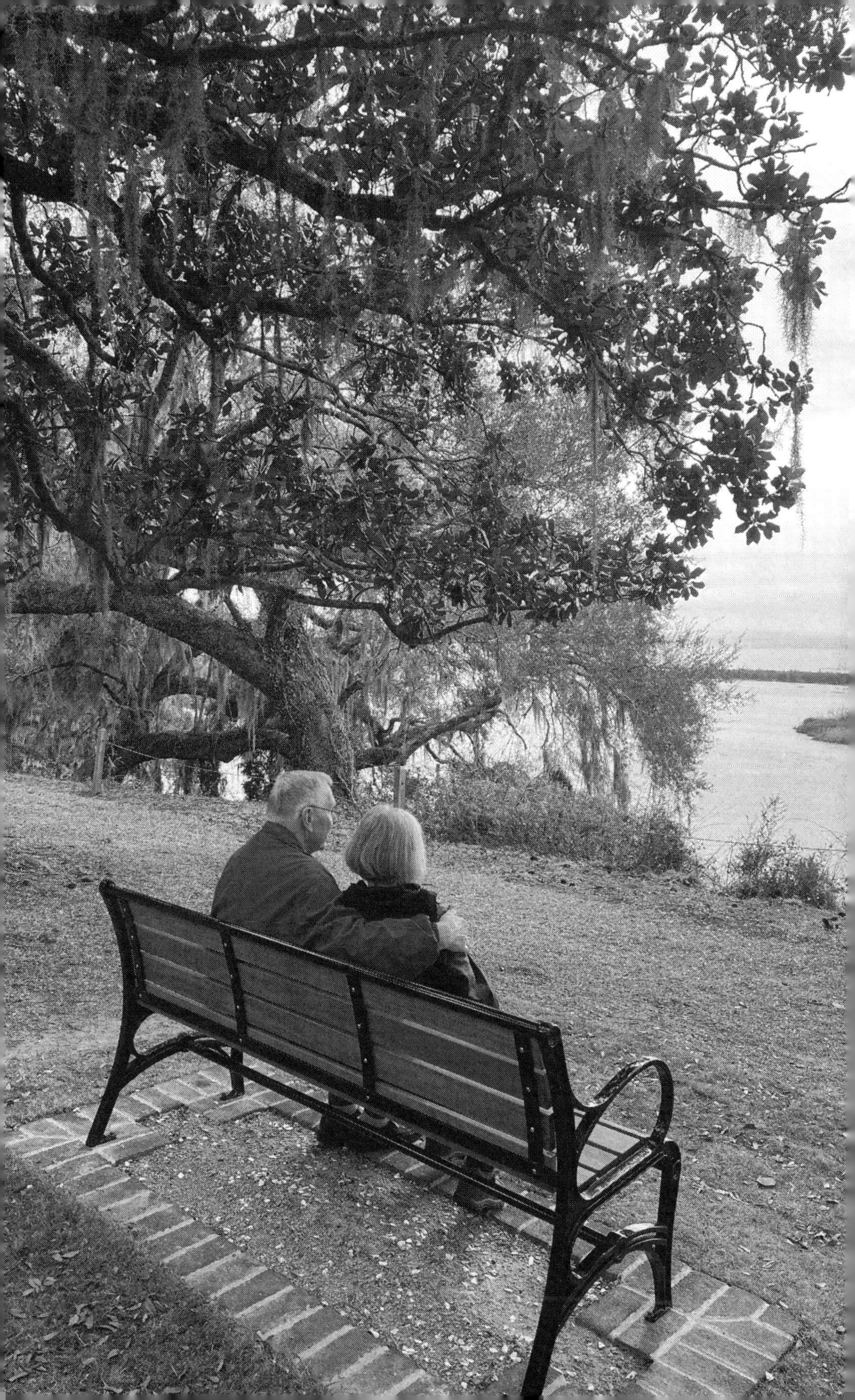

DEPARTMENT OF THE NAVY
NAVY ENVIRONMENTAL AND PREVENTIVE
MEDICINE UNIT NO. 2
NORFOLK, VIRGINIA 23511

02 December 1983

THE OFFICER IN CHARGE
TAKES PLEASURE IN PRESENTING TO

HMCS MICHAEL H. MOORE, USN

A letter of COMMENDATION
in recognition for services as set forth herein

On the occasion of your transfer to the USS MOUNT WHITNEY I would like to commend you for your superb performance and significant contributions you have made to this Unit's capability to accomplish its mission. During your tour you have served ably and competently in virtually all departments of this Unit, and have demonstrated so well the flexibility in task assignment inherent in a Preventive Medicine Technician. You served with distinction with the initial Field Sanitation Team augmenting United States Marine Corps Units of the Multinational Peacekeeping Force in Beirut, Lebanon. On promotion to the rate of Senior Chief Hospital Corpsman you assumed the Unit responsibility as Senior Enlisted Advisor. Your sensitivity to the needs and feelings of our enlisted staff indeed demonstrate your superior leadership capabilities. These are reflected in the intense respect you have engendered from civilian, enlisted and officer staff.

I would personally note my appreciation for the outstanding support you have rendered to me during your tenure. Your timely advice and encouragement have smoothed many a troubled water and have created the proper environment for problem resolution. On behalf of the staff I extend to you our best wishes for continued success and contributions to our Navy Medical Department.

W.M. PARSONS
Commander, Medical Service Corps
United States Navy
Officer in Charge

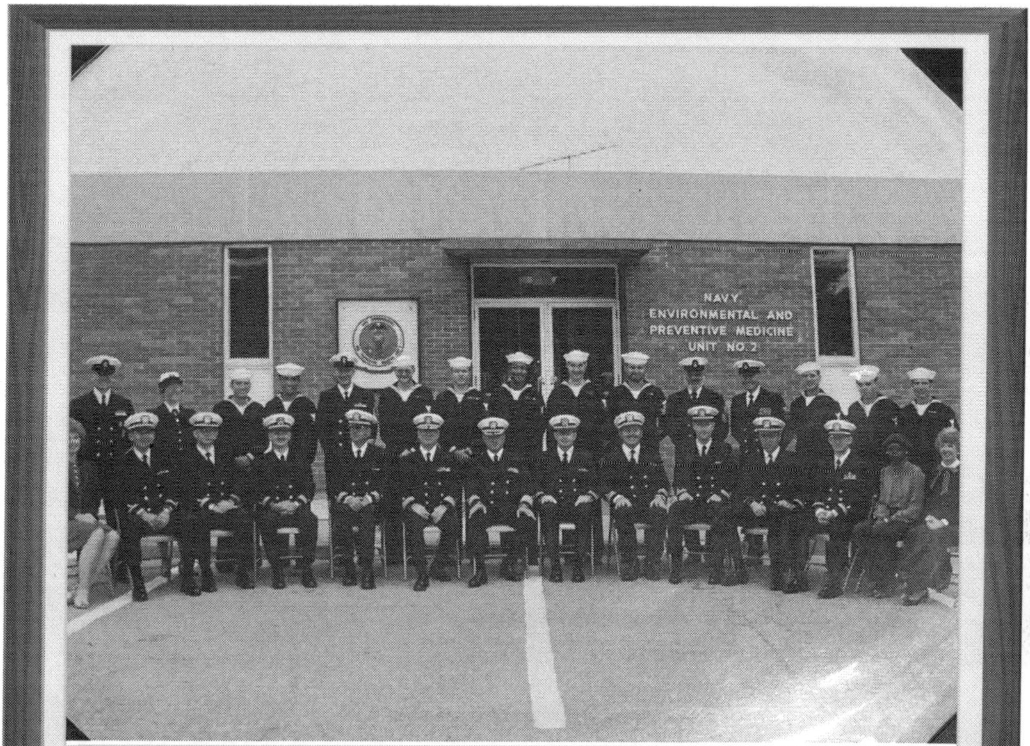
NAVY
ENVIRONMENTAL AND
PREVENTIVE MEDICINE
UNIT NO. 2

United States Marine Corps

Certificate of Commendation

THE COMMANDING GENERAL, FLEET MARINE FORCE, PACIFIC

takes pleasure in commending

CHIEF HOSPITAL CORPSMAN MICHAEL H. MOORE
UNITED STATES NAVY

for

Outstanding performance of duty while serving as Battalion Legal Chief, Battalion Medical Regulating Chief, Battalion Postal Officer, and Administrative Assistant to the Battalion Commander, First Medical Battalion, First Force Service Support Group, Camp Pendleton, California, from July 1976 through June 1978. Throughout this period, Chief Petty Officer Moore performed his various demanding duties in an exemplary and highly professional manner. He demonstrated his professional capabilities in meeting the demands of each of his assigned tasks. While serving in the capacity as Administrative Assistant to the Commanding Officer, Chief Petty Officer Moore displayed outstanding judgement, maturity, and tact in his relationships with his superiors and subordinates alike and inspired all who observed him. Chief Petty Officer Moore's exceptional professional ability, untiring determination, and selfless devotion to duty reflect great credit upon himself and were in keeping with the finest traditions of the Marine Corps and the United States Naval Service.

25 August 1978
Date

AL. E. BROWN
LIEUTENANT GENERAL, U.S. MARINE CORPS

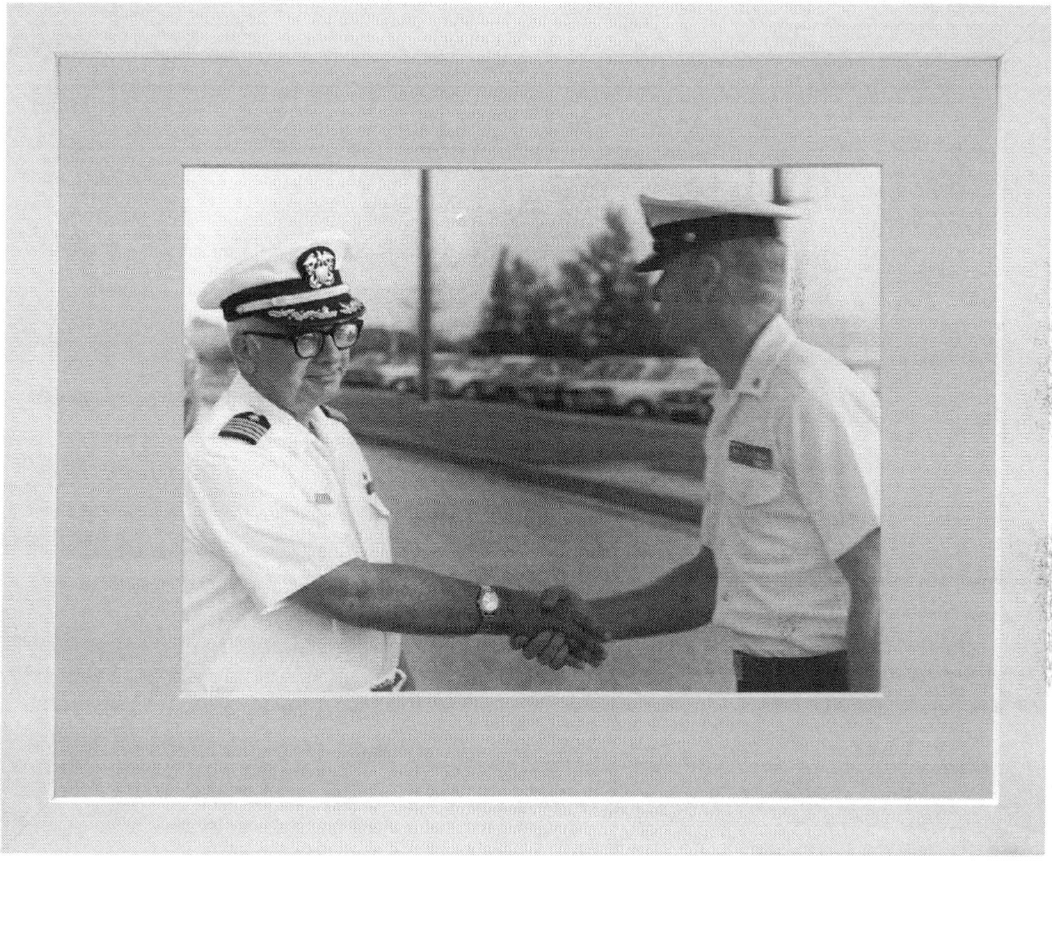

DEPARTMENT OF THE NAVY
THIS IS TO CERTIFY THAT
THE SECRETARY OF THE NAVY HAS AWARDED THE

NAVY ACHIEVEMENT MEDAL

TO

SENIOR CHIEF HOSPITAL CORPSMAN MICHAEL HAMPP MOORE, UNITED STATES NAVY

FOR

MERITORIOUS ACHIEVEMENT FROM 25 AUGUST TO 5 DECEMBER 1982

GIVEN THIS 21ST DAY OF JUL 19 83

SECRETARY OF THE NAVY

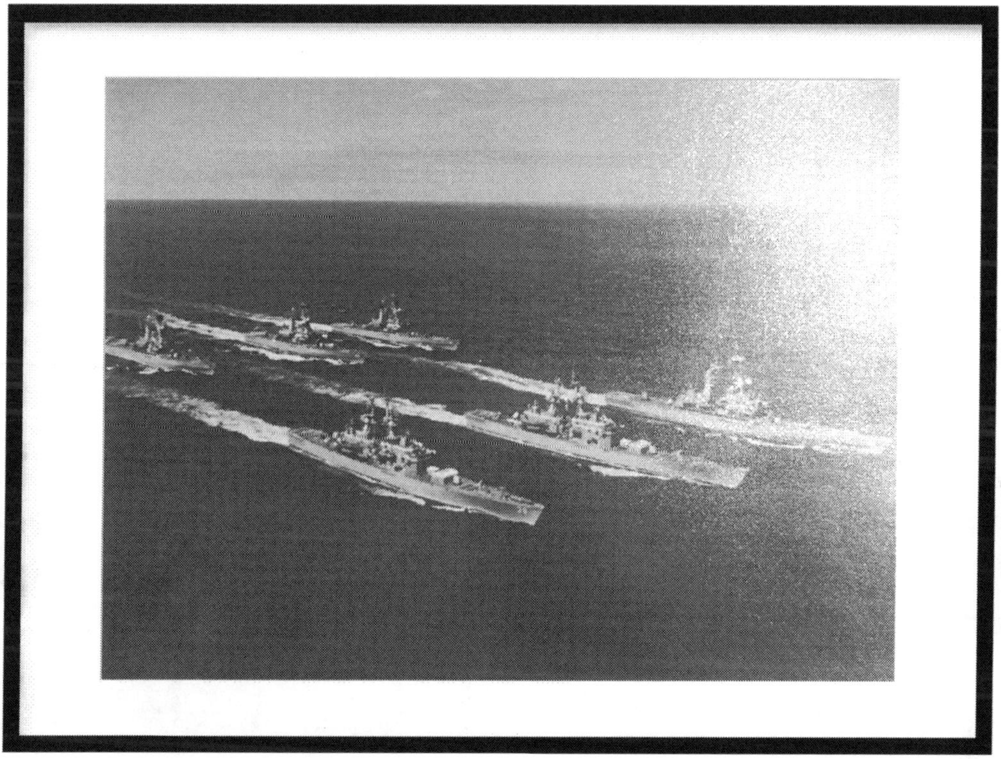

DEPARTMENT OF THE NAVY
NAVAL MEDICAL COMMAND
WASHINGTON, D.C. 20372

The Secretary of the Navy takes pleasure in presenting the
NAVY ACHIEVEMENT MEDAL to

MICHAEL HAMPP MOORE
CHIEF HOSPITAL CORPSMAN
UNITED STATES NAVY

for service as set forth in the following
CITATION:

"For exemplary leadership, achievement, and outstanding performance of duty while assigned to Marine Amphibious Unit 24, Beirut, Lebanon, as Leading Chief Petty Officer of Mobile Medical Augmentation Readiness Team Field Sanitation Unit during the periods 25 August - 10 September 1982, and 24 September - 5 December 1982. Through Chief Moore's foresight, vision, and persistence, logistical readiness for the field team was achieved prior to the initial deployment to Lebanon. His outstanding leadership qualities are reflected in the rapid assessment and establishment of disease monitoring and surveillance programs, initiation of badly needed domestic waste disposal, and facilitation of insect and rodent vector control measures. Integrating diverse personnel and equipment resources, Chief Moore applied his broad technical competence in improving living conditions, habitability, and sanitary conditions of Navy and Marine Corps forces associated with the Multinational Peacekeeping Force. His devotion to duty and willingness to respond overrode concern for his own personal safety. Chief Moore's outstanding professionalism as a Preventive Medicine Technician, and Hospital Corpsman significantly contributed to the low incidence of disease during the deployment, and are in keeping with the highest traditions of the United States Naval Service."

For the secretary,

LEWIS H. SEATON
Rear Admiral, Medical Corps
United States Navy
Commander, Naval Medical Command

The Bureau of Medicine and Surgery
of The United States Navy
Presents this

CERTIFICATE OF SPECIAL INSTRUCTION

To MICHAEL H. MOORE

a CHIEF HOSPITAL CORPSMAN in The United States Navy

who has satisfactorily completed the prescribed course of instruction for

PREVENTIVE MEDICINE TECHNICIAN

at NAVAL REGIONAL MEDICAL CENTER, OAKLAND, CALIFORNIA

and has been awarded the Navy Enlisted Classification 8432
Number

W. M. Lonergan
W. M. LONERGAN, RADM MC USN
Commanding Officer

15 FEBRUARY 1980
Date

CAREER INFORMATION AND COUNSELING SCHOOL

THIS CERTIFIES THAT

HMC MICHAEL H. MOORE

has successfully completed the prescribed course of instruction in counseling techniques and career information and has this day fully qualified for the demanding responsibilities as a

CAREER COUNSELOR

given by my hand this __16th__ day of __June 1982__

ROY R. RUSSELL, HTCM
director

AVPERS 1650/61 (REV. 2-80)

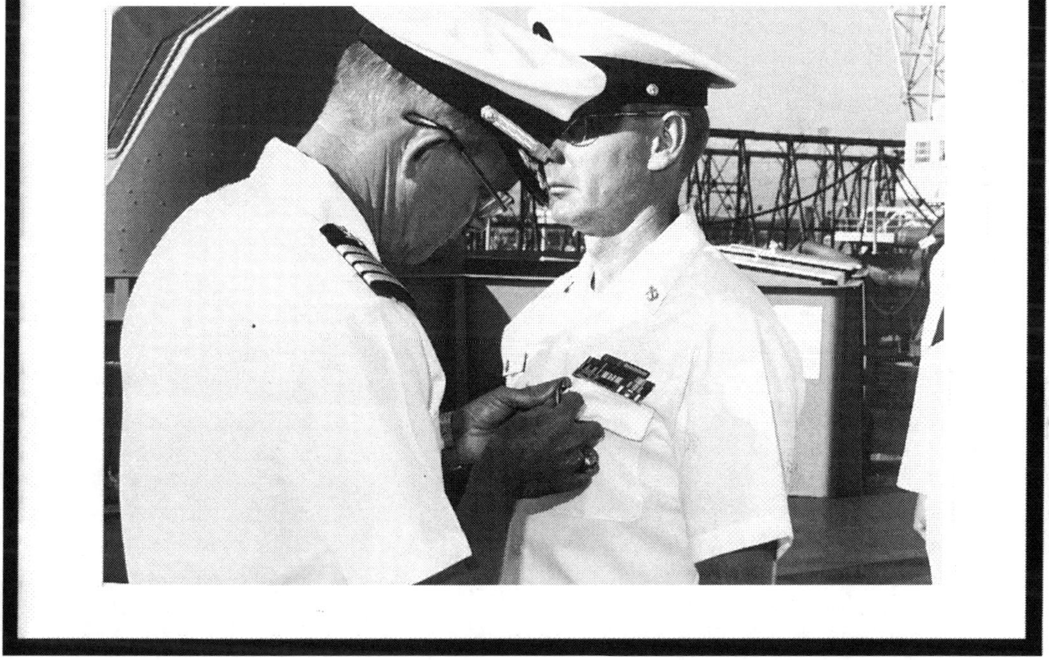

DEPARTMENT OF THE NAVY
NAVAL HOSPITAL
PORTSMOUTH, VIRGINIA 23708

IN REPLY REFER TO:
6530
712:DRL:pwp
15 NOV 1984

From: Commanding Officer, Naval Hospital, Portsmouth, VA 23708
To: Commanding Officer, USS Mount Whitney LCC-20, FPO New York, NY 09517

Subj: BLOOD DONOR AWARD

Encl: (1) One Gallon Donor Award for HMCS Michael H. Moore USN, SSN:299-34-4240

1. Enclosure (1) is forwarded for presentation.

2. Please extend my gratitude to HMCS Michael H. Moore USN for wholeheartedly supporting the Navy Blood Program. The enthusiastic effort displayed by this individual in donating so many pints of blood is indicative of his compassion for our patients and understanding of their ever-pressing blood needs. His voluntary donations deserve this recognition and an acknowledged Navy "Well Done".

W. B. ROSS
By direction

COMMENTS SECTION
(MUST NOT BE LEFT BLANK)

45. BACKGROUND DATA:
a. RATEE'S PRIMARY AND SIGNIFICANT COLLATERAL DUTIES:
Leading CPO of the Industrial Hygiene Service responsible for departmental administration, direct supervision of three technicians, use and calibration of complex monitoring equipment, and instruction/consultation of Atlantic fleet personnel in shipboard requirements for Navy occupational health programs. Collateral duties

b. SIGNIFICANT DEPLOYMENTS OF COMMAND: Rater recently deployed as a member of the MMART in support of the multinational peace keeping force in Lebanon.

c. LIST RATEE'S SPECIAL ASSIGNMENTS, SERVICE SCHOOLS ATTENDED AND OFF-DUTY EDUCATIONAL ACHIEVEMENTS:
During the reporting period HMC MOORE completed academic requirements and was granted an Associate of Science degree. He was assigned to and finished Command Career Counselor School with receipt of an additional NEC 9588. Ratee attended Leadership Management Education Training School at the Naval Amphibious Base, Little Creek,-from 21 June - 2 July 1982. He also participated in training exercises for the MMART

46. EVALUATION COMMENTS: (Use to further describe ratee's performance and qualifications. If ratee is in rating or billet which provides services to shipmates and/or dependents, comment MUST be made on his ability to provide courteous, responsive and efficient service and must be reflected in items 13, 15, and 22. Use also to amplify certain marks in blocks 27, 29, 33, and 34 thru 41.)

This extremely competent and intelligent CPO continues to perform his duties in a most superior manner. Exceptionally quick to learn and grasp pertinent details, this versatile ratee can adapt to most any situation, and produce outstanding results. Requiring an absolute minimum of supervision, HMC MOORE's work is always thorough, complete, well thoughout, and has no loose ends. He excels in his administrative duties, and in his preparation of official survey reports. His ability to conduct independent underway evaluations with instrumentation has proven invaluable. Complimentary feedback from line commands has been received concerning ratee's expertise and cooperativeness during shipboard surveys. Very tactful and diplomatic, he interrelates equally well with superiors and subordinates, and secures a high degree of respect and loyalty. His excellent leadership qualities have been demonstrated by his capacity to efficiently direct and control subordinates, yet to inspire their trust and a desire to perform. His selection as MMART LCPO and Command Career Counselor were based on his competency in evaluating problems, delegating responsibilities, and consistently achieving quality results. As an instructor, HMC MOORE is unsurpassed. Written class critiques obtained from students attending this Unit's

I have read and understand USN Regs, 1973, Art. 1110. I DO/DO NOT desire to make a statement.

DATE _____

47. JUSTIFICATION COMMENTS: (Use only to document any TOP/BOTTOM 10/5/1% marks in the Evaluation Section, blocks 13 thru 25.)

45 (a) Continued
include: Managing Editor of "HEALTHSCOPE", Watch Bill Coordinator, LCPO - Mobile Medical Augmentation Readiness Team (MMART), member - Enlisted Performance/Quality Control Review Board, alternate member - MG-31 Nuclear Disaster Response Team, and chairman, 1981-82 Combined Federal Campaign.

45 (c) Continued
conducted at Camp LeJuene, North Carolina, from 8-12 March 1982. Ratee completed the Navy correspondence course, Low Temperature Sanitation and Cold Weather Medicine.

I HAVE SIGHTED THIS REPORT _____
(Ratee's Signature)

CHECK BLOCK AND CONTINUE ON REVERSE IF MORE SPACE REQUIRED [X]

NAVPERS 1616/8 (REV. 2-78)   S/N 0106-LF-016-1641

REPORT BUPERS 1616-1

Know all men by these presents that
HMCS Michael H. Moore
having attained significant military experience in Surface Ships and having successfully completed the established personnel qualification standards and having demonstrated the requisite professional skills and knowledge while serving in
USS Mount Whitney LCC-20
has qualified as an
Enlisted Surface Warfare Specialist
and is authorized to wear the Enlisted Surface Warfare Specialist Breast Insignia

In witness whereof this certificate has been signed and a seal affixed hereunto on this the 25 day of April , 1986

NAVY ENVIRONMENTAL AND PREVENTIVE MEDICINE UNIT NO. 2

NORFOLK, VIRGINIA 23511

1 December 1981

THE OFFICER IN CHARGE
TAKES PLEASURE IN PRESENTING TO

HMC MICHAEL H. MOORE, USN

*A Letter of Commendation
in recognition for services as set forth herein*

For the second straight year, you have been the motivating force in the successfulness of this Unit's participation in the Combined Federal Campaign.

As Unit Campaign Leader for the 1981-1982 Combined Federal Campaign, you were successful in achieving 175% of the assigned Unit goal.

I wish to commend you for your dedicated efforts in achieving these outstanding results.

HARRY J. CANDELA

Copy to:
PERSUPPDET NAVSTA

NAVY ENVIRONMENTAL AND PREVENTIVE MEDICINE
UNIT NO. 2
NORFOLK, VIRGINIA 23511

```
                                        Code 11:JGB/jc
                                        1650
                                        10 July 1981
```

From: Officer in Charge, Navy Environmental and Preventive Medicine Unit No. 2, Norfolk, VA 23511

To: HMC Michael H. MOORE, 299-34-4240

Subj: Letter of Appreciation

1. It is with pleasure that I convey to you my sincere appreciation for your efforts as the Unit Campaign Leader for 1980-1981 Combined Federal Campaign.

2. Your enthusiasm, initiative and resourcefulness were the motivating forces leading to a highly successful campaign and resulting in achieving 121% of the assigned goal for the Unit.

3. With all due respect to your outstanding work in this regard, I extend to you the traditional Navy "Well Done."

                            HARRY J. CANDELA

Copy to:
PERSUPPDET NAVSTA

CERTIFICATE OF PERMANENT APPOINTMENT

To all who shall see these presents, greeting:

Know Ye, that reposing special trust and confidence in the patriotism, valor, fidelity and abilities of

MICHAEL HAMPP MOORE

I do hereby appoint you a Permanent

SENIOR CHIEF HOSPITAL CORPSMAN

in the

UNITED STATES NAVY

to rank as such from the *sixteenth* day of *March*, nineteen hundred and *eighty-four*.

TO THE APPOINTEE

Your appointment carries with it the obligation that you exercise additional authority and willingly accept greater responsibility. Your every action must be governed by a strong sense of personal moral responsibility and leadership. You will observe and follow such orders as may be given by superiors acting according to the rules, articles and provisions of United States Navy Regulations, General Orders, Uniform Code of Military Justice, and supporting orders and directives.

Given under my hand at USS MOUNT WHITNEY (LCC 20) this *sixteenth* day of *March* in the year of our Lord nineteen hundred and *eighty-four*.

R. C. JOHNSON, JR
Captain, U.S. Navy
COMMANDING OFFICER

NAVPERS 1430/32 (10-74) S/N 0106-LF-014-3160

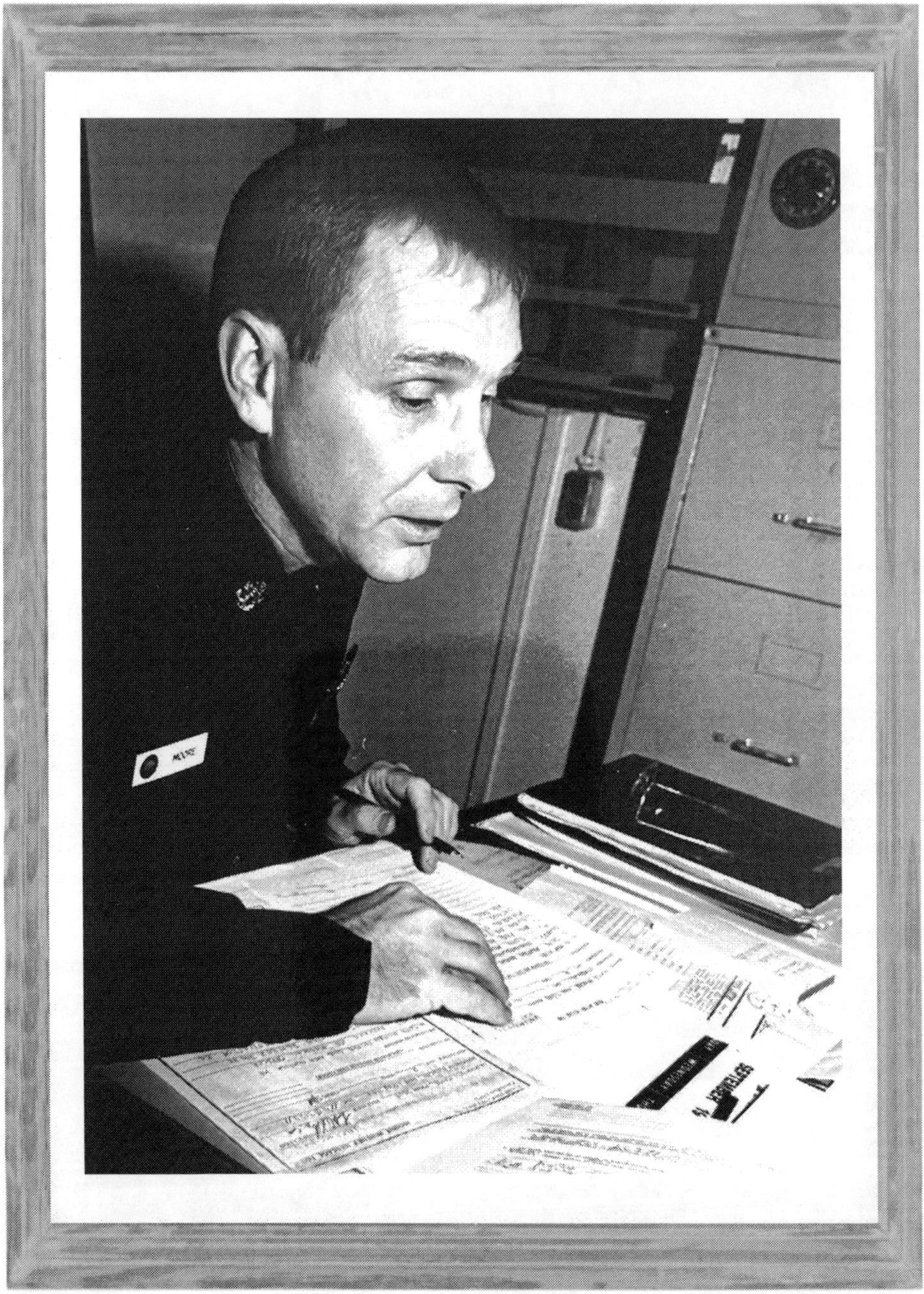

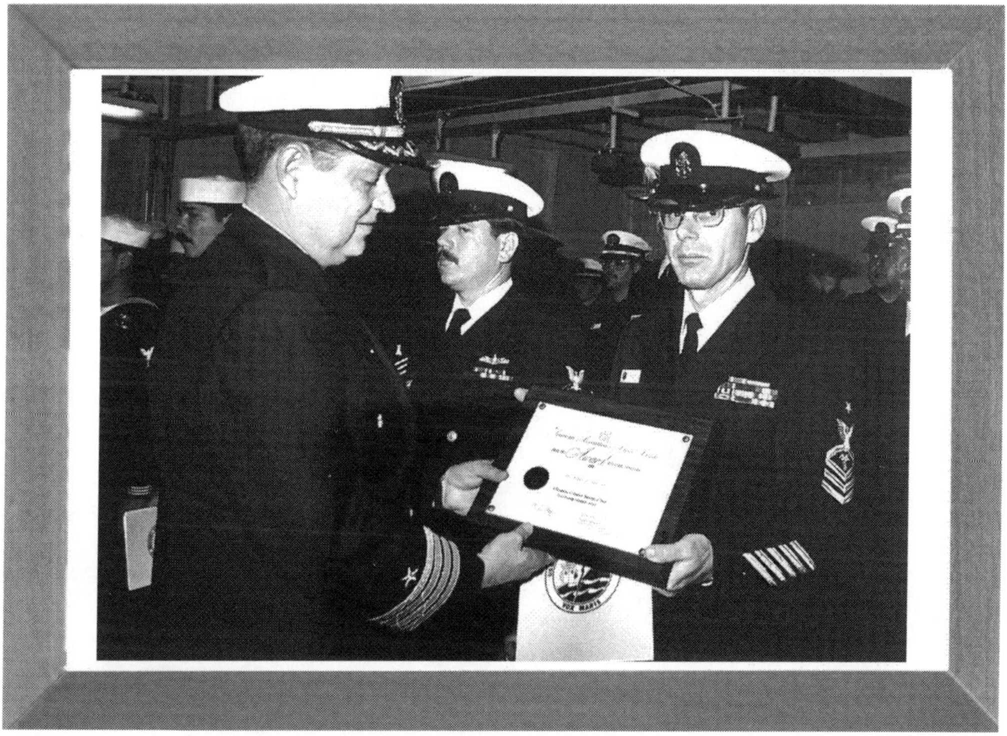

NAVMEDCOM-00C:SWB:rp
25 April 1983

DEPARTMENT OF THE NAVY
NAVAL MEDICAL COMMAND
WASHINGTON, D.C. 20372

MASTER CHIEF PETTY OFFICER OF THE FORCE

HMC Michael Hampp Moore, USN
Navy Environmental and Preventive
  Medicine Unit No 2
Norfolk, Virginia 23511

Dear Chief Petty Officer Moore:

It is a pleasure to extend my personal congratulations and those of the Naval Medical Department on the occasion of your selection for advancement to Senior Chief Hospital Corpsman.

Throughout your naval service, you have earned the respect of both your seniors and contempories and have distinguished yourself as a highly skilled Chief Petty Officer through your technical expertise and professional competency. Your advancement is not only a fine tribute to your ability as a health care member but also shows that you possess the potential for managerial positions. Your perseverance in attaining this goal and your interest in self-improvement through diligent study are commendable.

As you accept the challenges of your new paygrade, you will also assume greater responsibilities as a leader and counselor. In your new duties, you will be expected to motivate and guide personnel to improve their performance as members of the health care team. I am confident that you will be successful in accomplishing these new tasks.

My best wishes go to you for continued success throughout your Navy career.

Sincerely,

STEPHEN W. BROWN
United States Navy
Force Master Chief

NAVY ENVIRONMENTAL AND PREVENTIVE MEDICINE UNIT NO. 2
NORFOLK, VIRGINIA 23511

00:HJC:crd
5060

From: Officer in Charge
To: HMC Michael H. MOORE, USN, 299-34-4240/8408

Subj: Letter of Commendation

1. During the period of 25 August 1982 through 10 September 1982, you were assigned as a member to the Field Sanitation Augmentation Unit Number One, which deployed to Lebanon to provide preventive medicine services to the U.S. Forces of the Multinational Force.

2. While deployed, you performed your demanding duties with clearly superior, demonstrative results which contributed significantly to the successful conclusion of the unique operation. Working smoothly and efficiently with the Marines ashore, you provided continous inspection of field sanitation programs, ensured sanitary preparation and stowage of food and water ashore, and devised sound methods of waste disposal.

3. The results of your efforts while deployed, attest to the efficiency and professional competence of your abilities; thus keeping with the highest traditions of the Medical Department and United States Navy.

H. J. CANDELA

Know all men by these presents that

HMCS Michael H. Moore

having attained significant military experience in Surface Ships and having successfully completed the established personnel qualification standards and having demonstrated the requisite professional skills and knowledge while serving in

USS Mount Whitney LCC-20

has qualified as an

Enlisted Surface Warfare Specialist

and is authorized to wear the Enlisted Surface Warfare Specialist Breast Insignia

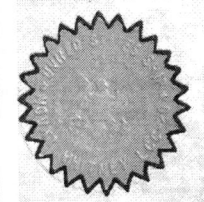

In witness whereof this certificate has been signed and a seal affixed hereunto on this the 25 day of April , 1986

COMMENTS SECTION
(MUST NOT BE LEFT BLANK)

45. BACKGROUND DATA:

a. RATEE'S PRIMARY AND SIGNIFICANT COLLATERAL DUTIES:
Leading CPO of the Industrial Hygiene Service responsible for departmental administration, direct supervision of three technicians, use and calibration of monitoring equipment, and instruction/consultation of Atlantic fleet personnel in complex shipboard requirements for Navy occupational health programs. Collateral duties

b. SIGNIFICANT DEPLOYMENTS OF COMMAND: Rater recently deployed as a member of the MMART in support of the multinational peace keeping force in Lebanon.

c. LIST RATEE'S SPECIAL ASSIGNMENTS, SERVICE SCHOOLS ATTENDED AND OFF-DUTY EDUCATIONAL ACHIEVEMENTS:
During the reporting period HMC MOORE completed academic requirements and was granted an Associate of Science degree. He was assigned to and finished Command Career Counselor School with receipt of an additional NEC 9588. Ratee attended Leadership Management Education Training School at the Naval Amphibious Base, Little Creek,-from 21 June - 2 July 1982. He also participated in training exercises for the MMART

46. EVALUATION COMMENTS: (Use to further describe ratee's performance and qualifications. If ratee is in rating or billet which provides services to shipmates and/or dependents, comment MUST be made on his ability to provide courteous, responsive and efficient service and must be reflected in items 13, 15, and 22. Use also to amplify certain marks in blocks 27, 29, 33, and 34 thru 41.)

This extremely competent and intelligent CPO continues to perform his duties in a most superior manner. Exceptionally quick to learn and grasp pertinent details, this versatile ratee can adapt to most any situation, and produce outstanding results. Requiring an absolute minimum of supervision, HMC MOORE's work is always thorough, complete, well thoughout, and has no loose ends. He excels in his administrative duties, and in his preparation of official survey reports. His ability to conduct independent underway evaluations with instrumentation has proven invaluable. Complimentary feedback from line commands has been received concerning ratee's expertise and cooperativeness during shipboard surveys. Very tactful and diplomatic, he interrelates equally well with superiors and subordinates, and secures a high degree of respect and loyalty. His excellent leadership qualities have been demonstrated by his capacity to efficiently direct and control subordinates, yet to inspire their trust and a desire to perform. His selection as MMART LCPO and Command Career Counselor were based on his competency in evaluating problems, delegating responsibilities, and consistently achieving quality results. As an instructor, HMC MOORE is unsurpassed. Written class critiques obtained from students attending this Unit's

I have read and understand USN Regs, 1973, Art. 1110. I DO/DO NOT desire to make a statement.

DATE _____

°47. JUSTIFICATION COMMENTS: (Use only to document any TOP/BOTTOM 10/5/1% marks in the Evaluation Section, blocks 13 thru 25.)

45 (a) Continued
include: Managing Editor of "HEALTHSCOPE", Watch Bill Coordinator, LCPO - Mobile Medical Augmentation Readiness Team (MMART), member - Enlisted Performance/Quality Control Review Board, alternate member - MG-31 Nuclear Disaster Response Team, and chairman, 1981-82 Combined Federal Campaign.

45 (c) Continued
conducted at Camp LeJuene, North Carolina, from 8-12 March 1982. Ratee completed the Navy correspondence course, Low Temperature Sanitation and Cold Weather Medicine.

I HAVE SIGHTED THIS REPORT _____ (Ratee's Signature)

CHECK BLOCK AND CONTINUE ON REVERSE IF MORE SPACE REQUIRED [X]

NAVPERS 1616/8 (REV 2-78) S/N 0106-LF-016-1641

ORIGINAL-BUPERS (PERS-38)

REPORT BUPERS 1616-1

NAVAL HOSPITAL
ST. ALBANS, NEW YORK

Made in the USA
Columbia, SC
22 February 2025

cac0067b-524a-4130-91dd-5364fd874995R01